THE BOOK OF
Tequila

To Mayo,

Enjoy reading the book
and learning about

Tequila

Bob Emmons

Texas

Mexico

González

Tequila Arandas
Puerto Vallarta   Guadalajara   Pénjamo
Ciudad Guzmán

Mexico City

THE BOOK OF
Tequila

A COMPLETE GUIDE

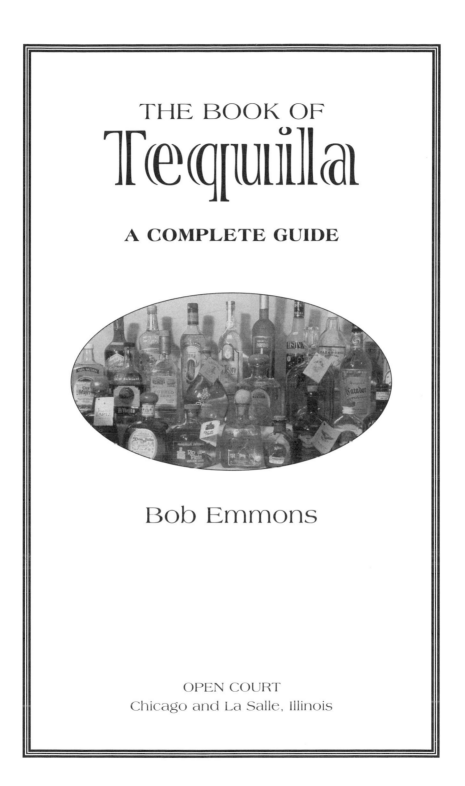

Bob Emmons

OPEN COURT
Chicago and La Salle, Illinois

Open Court Publishing Company is a division of Carus Publishing Company.

First printing April 1997
Second printing October 1997

Printed and bound in the United States of America.

Library of Congress Cataloging-in-Publication Data
Emmons, Bob, 1940–
    The book of tequila : a complete guide / Bob Emmons.
      p.   cm.
    Includes bibliographical references and index.
    ISBN 0-8126-9351-5 (cloth : alk. paper). — ISBN 0-8126-9352-3 (pbk. : alk. paper)
    1. Tequila   I. Title.
TP607.T46E46   1997
663'.5—dc21   97-1270
                                            CIP

Contents

Preface

Tequila, the spirit of Mexico! We all think we know what tequila is. It's the liquor that goes into a margarita. Or it's that stuff where you lick the salt, bite the lime, and shoot the tequila. Or, wait a minute, is it bite the lime first? I can never remember.

The correct answer is: lick the salt, sip the tequila, bite the lime. But there are other ways to drink tequila. In fact, there's a whole world of tequila lore which has been unavailable to the ordinary person until the publication of this book. And in addition to what we don't know, there's plenty we 'know that ain't so'. Misconceptions and unfounded legends abound, yet as with so many areas of life, the facts are often just as fascinating as the myths.

The biggest and most serious misconception about tequila is that we all know what it tastes like. Most people outside Mexico, who think they've tasted top-quality tequila, haven't. Everyone is familiar with the $20-a-bottle tequila that you buy to mix up a batch of frozen margaritas—probably with a pre-mix where you just add the tequila to the bucket and put it in the freezer overnight. But when the curious drinker, attracted by that mysterious, intriguing flavor, decides to try tequila neat, or drink it the authentic way, the way the movies have shown Mexicans doing it—licking the salt and biting the lime—it often seems disappointing.

There's a reason for that. If you have never been to Mexico, or have never made an informed search in your local liquor stores, the odds are that you have never tasted a really fine tequila. There are in fact two broad types of tequila available, and generally speaking, the finest tequilas belong to the more expensive, less easily available type.

Let me explain. Tequila is a very unusual distilled beverage. It has a history and a character all its own. It is not made from a fruit, a grain, or a root, but from the swollen stem of the *agave*, a Mexican flowering plant (technically a succulent, *not* a cactus). The unique tang of tequila, that elusive tequila magic, comes from the *agave* plant. The very best tequilas are made from *agave* and nothing but *agave*. The tequila you probably pick up from your liquor store, or drink in the margaritas served to you in most bars outside Mexico, is made only partly from *agave*. Other plant products—usually cane sugar derivatives or corn syrup—are mixed with the *agave* juice before fermentation. The resulting drink is a cheaper type of drink the Mexicans call *mixto*, and it is *mixto* which occupies most of the shelf space for 'tequila' in liquor stores outside Mexico.

This book explains how both types of tequila are made, the differences between them, and the differences between tequila and other Mexican beverages—especially 'the one with the worm', a related but very different liquor called *mezcal*.

This book is a comprehensive guide to all aspects of tequila. Years ago, I became fascinated by tequila and determined to find out as much as I could about it. I would have been delighted to get my hands on a book like this, but as far as I have been able to determine, no book remotely like this has ever appeared before. It offers a compilation of information about tequila which has never been attempted before. I am conscious of my failings both as writer and tequila expert, and no doubt this book has its share of shortcomings, but I can claim without the slightest hesitation that no work on tequila remotely approaching *The Book of Tequila* in comprehensiveness, accuracy, and thoroughness has ever appeared, at any time or in any language.

I have put thousands of hours into getting the real low-down on tequila, and the result is this book. I have talked with the field hands who harvest the *agave* plant, with the distillery workers and owners, with the firms that import tequila to the United States, with restaurateurs, chefs, bartenders, and connoisseurs in both Mexico and the United States.

Readers will come to *The Book of Tequila* with different interests. You can read it straight through, you can pick out just the chapters that particularly interest you, or you can dip into it as a work of reference. I would strongly recommend, however, that you do not skip Chapter 1.

Chapter 1 explains the basic facts about tequila: why tequila is different, misconceptions about tequila, the various kinds of tequila (two basic types and seven broad categories), and a brief discussion of other Mexican beverages, such as *mezcal* and *pulque*.

Chapter 2 explains how tequila is made, starting with the harvesting of the *agave*, and proceeding through cooking and milling, fermentation and distillation, to aging, blending, and bottling.

Chapter 3 gives an account of the history of tequila, along with a brief look at the wonderful country with which tequila is so intimately associated.

Chapter 4 provides an overview of the locations of all the distilleries.

Chapter 5 is long: it lists *all* the companies that manufacture tequila, with a description of each of them. Wherever feasible, I provide the history, equipment, production methods, output and export statistics, and philosophies of each distillery, together with a personal account of some of the distillery's peculiarities.

Chapter 6 explores the importing and distribution system which brings the tequila to its customers in Mexico and the United States.

Chapter 7 presents tasting notes on many of the 100 percent *agave* tequilas, both those available in the U.S. and those currently available only in Mexico.

Chapter 8 gives advice on how to hold a tequila tasting party.

Chapter 9 explains some basic facts about the most famous of tequila cocktails, the margarita.

Chapter 10 is a selection of recipes using tequila, both for mixed drinks and for food.

Chapter 11 describes how I learned about tequila, especially from my earliest visits to Jalisco.

Chapter 12 briefly sets forth my views on the future of tequila and alcoholic beverages in general.

The *appendixes* at the end of this volume provide concise information on some detailed aspects of tequila.

You will get the most out of *The Book of Tequila* if you read it through. But let's suppose that you have just acquired this book and you have a bottle of tequila you want to check out. Look up the brand name or 'label' in Appendix A, which lists over 300 tequila labels, including all the good ones. This will tell you the number of the distillery company, in the order in which these companies are listed in Chapter 5, so you can quickly turn to the descriptive entry for that distillery company in Chapter 5. Having read that entry, you can turn to the tasting notes in Chapter 7, where the distilling companies appear in the same numerical order. Having read my tasting note on your label, you may then possibly find more background on that label or distillery in Chapter 4 or Chapter 6. In Appendix C you can find the address and phone number of the distilling company, and in Appendix D you may find the address and phone number of your label's U.S. distributor.

Acknowledgments

I am grateful for the valuable assistance rendered by the following: Sr. Ramon González Figueroa, Director General, Consejo Regulador del Tequila; Sr. G. Miguel Cedeño G., Destiladora González González; Sr. Eduardo González Garcia, Tequila Tres Magueyes; Sr. Marco Antonio Cedano Nuñez, Plant Manager, Tequila Tres Magueyes; Sr. Hendrik Nollen, Marketing Manager, Tequilas del Señor; Sra. Louise M. Walsh, International Manager, Tequila Herradura; Sr. Martin Grassl, Destileria Porfidio; Sr. Heriberto Gomez González, Agroindustrias Guadalajara; Martin Crowley, St. Maarten Spirits; Mr. Scott Kemper, Kemper Advertising; don Raul Romero, Tequila Tres Magueyes; Sr. Rodolfo Vasquez, my driver in Jalisco; Mrs. Evelyn Mizak, who devoted many hours of her time to proofreading; Mr. Darrel Corti, Corti Brothers, Grocers, an expert in wines, spirits, and languages; Dr. Roger Boulton, Professor of Enology, University of California, Davis; Dr. Vernon L. Singleton, Professor Emeritus of Viticulture and Enology, University of California, Davis. Last, but most certainly not least, Robert Denton and his partner Marilyn Smith, of Robert Denton and Company, whose help in gathering and compiling the necessary information for the book and guidance in the direction of the industry have been invaluable.

These are but a few of those who have contributed to the completion of this book, and my thanks go out to all those who have helped in a host of ways.

1

What Makes
It Tequila

Tequila is a unique alcoholic beverage. It has its own haunting individual flavor, quite different from the other main groups of distilled spirits such as the brandies, the whiskeys, or the rums. Brandy is made from grapes or, with proper qualification, from other fruits, whiskey is made from grains, and rum from sugarcane or other sugar-producing plants. Tequila, however, is a product of the plant known as the blue *agave*.

According to Mexican law and international agreement, any product labelled 'tequila' can be made only in Mexico—just as scotch can be made only in Scotland and bourbon only in the United States. Furthermore, the Mexican government restricts the possible tequila production areas, in the same way that the French government rules that brandies called 'cognac,' 'armagnac,' and 'calvados' can be produced only in specific small areas of France. As a general rule, liquor producers strongly favor such government restrictions, because they make it more difficult for other drinks, possibly cheaper and inferior, to compete with those that bear the much-prized label.

Tequila must be produced—from growing the *agave* to distilling the tequila—within certain designated areas, primarily within

1

the state of Jalisco, where the great majority of tequila is produced, but also including certain designated villages within four other states: Guanajuato, Michoacán, Nayarit, and Tamaulipas.

Since there is now such a boom in the demand for tequila, plans for opening new distilleries are emerging all the time. But at the time of writing, there are only two distilleries actually producing tequila outside the state of Jalisco: one of them (in the village of González, Tamaulipas) has been operating for over 15 years, while the other (in the village of Pénjamo, Guanajuato) opened in June of 1996.

The Blue *Agave*

Tequila starts with the celebrated blue *agave* (pronounced 'ah-gah-vay'). The blue *agave—Agave tequilana Weber, blue variety,* to give it its full scientific name—is just one of hundreds of different species of *agave* plants, most of which grow in Mexico, and many of which have industrial uses. In fact, many different varieties of *agave*

plants play a significant role in the Mexican economy. Some *agave* plants are used for making different kinds of alcoholic drinks, some are used as food (for humans or livestock), and most significantly, some are used to provide tough fibers used in making ropes and construction materials. Sisal hemp, henequen, and cantala are important fibers, each derived from a different *agave* plant. There are also minor industrial uses such as cosmetics and medicinal salves, and several kinds of *agave* are in demand for purely decorative or horticultural purposes.

There are actually three words in common use as names for the *agave* plant: *maguey, mezcal,* and *agave.* The first word to be used, *maguey,* comes from the Náhuatl word *mahayuel,* referring to the god of this plant. The second was adapted from the Náhuatl word *mexcalmetl,* loosely translatable as 'agave species.' The name *agave* is Greek in origin, derived from

An agave
field in the
Highlands of
Jalisco

a word meaning 'noble,' and became applied to the plant in furtherance of scientific classification.

The three names have now settled down into distinct usages. *Agave* is the scientific name, always used by botanists. It is also the international name: the English for *agave* is 'agave', but I have italicized the word throughout this book to remind readers of its pronunciation. The word *maguey* (pronounced 'mah-gay') is most commonly used in Mexico to refer to the plant in the ground, and the word *mezcal* now mainly refers to some of the various distilled drinks made from the *agave* plant.

There may be as many as 30 regional versions of different alcoholic beverages made from various species of *agave*. Besides tequila, a few of the other types are *pulque* (the only non-distilled version), *mezcal, bacanora, comiteca, raicilla* (pronounced 'rice-ee-ya'), *sotol,* and *mezcal de olla.* Of all the agave-derived drinks only tequila and *mezcal* are currently available outside Mexico, and some of the other drinks are so obscure that they are known only to people who thoroughly familiarize themselves with the local culture in some corner of the country. I will describe *mezcal* and say a little about some of the other *agave*-derived drinks at the end of this chapter.

3

To the non-botanist, the non-gardener, or the non-tequila enthusiast, all *agaves* look very similar. The exact number of varieties of the *agave* plant is difficult to determine because the plant hybridizes very easily, and the only way to determine the exact classification is to allow it to reach maturity and set seed. Over 200 different types of *agave* have been scientifically classified, but botanists estimate there could be as many as 500 varieties in existence, with the exact number yet to be determined.

The *agave* is classified as a succulent—definitely not a cactus. The genus *Agave* belongs to the *agave* family of the flowering plant order *Liliales*. In the United States, the most familiar *agave* is the 'century' plant, well known to gardeners.

The *agave* plant grows in the form of a rosette of long swordlike leaves with thorns on the tips and along the edges. An *agave* can be large: the blue variety may reach a height of from five to eight feet and a diameter of from eight to twelve feet.

The length of time needed for the various types of this plant to reach maturity varies somewhat, but for the blue *agave,* it will normally take from eight to twelve years. The blue *agave* was classified in 1902 by the botanist Weber, though by that time it and other varieties had long been used for making beverages. 'Blue' (*azul* in Spanish) refers to the color of the stems and leaves, a pale, silvery green-blue, not the blossoms, which are in fact pale yellow to yellowish white. In the wild, the blossoms give way to seed pods, black with a hard exterior, approximately one inch long and half an inch wide. When moistened, the pod casing will split into three parts, releasing small, light gray seeds.

But no one engaged in producing tequila ever sees the blossoms or seed pods of *agave* plants, because these plants are not permitted to reach sexual maturity. Before they can flower, the flower stalk is cut. This injury changes the growth of the plant, causing the central stem to become swollen. This swollen, juicy stem is the part used for making tequila. It is sometimes called a *piña*, because it resembles a pineapple, and sometimes a *cabeza,* meaning 'head.'

Under natural conditions, the plant reproduces both asexually and sexually. The asexual method is by sending out suckers or 'rhizomes'—horizontal underground stems which develop their own roots and eventually become distinct new plants. When it grows wild, the plant reproduces by this asexual technique in its fourth to sixth years; a further four to six years after that, it puts forth a spike from the center of the rosette, which flowers, blooms and produces seed in the form of berries. Having produced seed, the plant dies.

Under cultivation for tequila production, the 'daughter' *agave* plants produced by the rhizomes are separated from the 'mother' plant by severing the connecting fibers. This happens when the mother plant is between four and six years old. When they are about one year old, the separated daughter plants are then moved to a nursery area. The mother plant continues its growth cycle for a further four to eight years, and is then harvested. When the daughters are about two years old, after a year in the nursery area, they are then moved to their final growing site, where they become new mother plants.

Each mother can produce many different daughter plants. In the wild it can also reproduce by a third method, producing asexual flowers on the stalk, called 'bulbuls,' which drop to the ground, take root and produce a new plant. With three alternative reproduction methods, the *agave* is fertile and prolific.

The *campesino* (farmer) watches the growing plant for the growth of the flower spike. This spike is then cut off, forcing the growth which would have gone into the long spike back into the heart of the plant, swelling the central stem which thus becomes the *piña*. When the plant is ready for the *piña* to be harvested, the plant seems to shrink slightly, and rust-colored splotches form on the lower leaves close to the central mass.

To harvest the *piña*, the *jimador* (harvest worker) cuts the plant loose from its roots, then removes the spiky leaves from the *piña*, with a special razor-sharp tool called a *coa*. With all the leaves cut away, there remains the *piña*, a large blue-and-white, egg-shaped object between 35 and 75 kilograms in weight. Except for the color, this object looks remarkably like a giant pineapple, but the resemblance is superficial: the *piña* is not a fruit.

While many types of alcoholic beverages use agricultural products that require a year or less from planting to cropping, the long cycle of maturity for the *agave* can cause risky fluctuations in supply. Since it takes from eight to twelve years for the *agave* to become ready for harvest, tequila producers, even more than most drinks producers, are very sensitive to long-term trends in demand.

The same problem of long-term forecasting is important with other drinks. Scotch or bourbon has to be aged for some years in oak barrels. Wine and brandy are affected by the peculiarities of grape-growing. After planting a vine, it takes five or six years before the vines begin to bear grapes. If tree fruit is used (as in plum or cherry brandies), the period from growth to fruit-bearing may be ten years or more. However, the forecasting problem is particularly acute in the tequila industry. Once vines or trees are mature and bearing at full capacity, they will continue to produce fruit every year for 25 to 50 years. By contrast, when each *agave* is harvested, after eight to twelve years of growth, *it is then totally consumed in the production process*. Thus, the current supply of new *agave* juice for making tequila is almost entirely fixed by what was planted eight to twelve years ago. Furthermore, unlike grains or fruits, the blue *agave* has no alternative uses if it is not employed to make tequila.

A jimador *harvesting* piñas *by chopping away the leaves*

6

If, during times of high demand for *agave*, the *campesino* responds mechanically by planting more *agave*, it may turn out, eight to twelve years later, that the market is flat and prices have gone down. So *agave* planting, even more than most farming, is a risky business. There has been a trend for some tequila companies to buy or lease land for growing *agave*, instead of relying on the crops of numerous *campesinos*. This trend could possibly arise from the companies' desire to insure themselves against fluctuations in *agave* prices. Some years ago, attempts were made to store frozen *agave* juice, but these trials were not successful. Continual refrigeration proved too costly, and there was some loss of flavor.

The Kinds of Tequila

There are two basic types of tequila, and these two are further subdivided, so that there are actually seven kinds. Let's begin by looking at the two fundamental categories: 100 percent *agave* and 'mixed' tequila or *mixto*. Some connoisseurs will snootily tell you that only 100 percent *agave* tequila is *really* tequila. They do have a point, but *mixto* is commonly described as tequila, is legally permitted to be called tequila, and makes up the great majority of 'tequila' consumed outside Mexico. A bottle of *mixto* will not say '*mixto*' on the label, but if it doesn't say '100 percent *agave*,' you can be absolutely sure it is in fact *mixto*. Mexican law permits unaged *mixto* tequila to be exported in bulk and bottled outside Mexico, whereas all 100 percent *agave* tequilas and all aged tequilas must be bottled within Mexico.

As you would expect, '100 percent *agave*' tequila is distilled entirely from the fermented juice of the *agave* plant. *Mixto* is distilled from a mixture of *agave* juice and other sugars. For some years the legally-imposed minimum ratio for *mixto* was 51 percent *agave* to 49 percent other sugars, though there were always variations within the legal limit, with some *mixtos* even claiming to be 99 percent *agave*. In 1995 the legal minimum was raised to 60 percent *agave* and 40 percent other sugars, which we would expect to mean, other things being equal, that most tequila consumed in the U.S. would be slightly better in flavor while costing somewhat more. In fact, U.S. tequila prices have not risen perceptibly. (There are persistent rumors, which I have so far been unable to definitely confirm or refute, that U.S. bottlers have been reducing the percentage of *agave* by adding grain alcohol to bring the proportion of *agave* back down to 51 percent.) Further increases in the legal minimum ratio are quite likely in the future.

Non-*agave* sugars are normally mixed with water until they are six to ten percent sugar solution, and are then added to the *agave* juice just prior to the start of fermentation. Different distilleries use different ratios, but none will normally be fermented at more than ten percent. The juice of the *agave* will usually come from the cooking and milling process at between ten and twenty-five percent sugar, and will be diluted with water until it is about the same percentage as the other sugars. *Agave* and non-*agave* sugars are then mixed together just before yeast is added and fermentation commences. Water is also added in the production of 100 percent *agave* tequila, because fermentation works better with a lower concentration of sugar.

The distinction between 100 percent *agave* tequila and *mixto* bears obvious comparison with other cases of superior and inferior versions of a beverage, the best-known being the single-malt scotches and the blended scotches. Most scotch consumed is blended—a mixture of several single malts plus from 70 to 90 percent grain alcohol. The grain alcohol has little character or subtlety: all the interesting features of a particular blend come from the specific single malts included in it, or from their proportion in relation to the grain alcohol. Like 100 percent *agave* tequila in relation to *mixto,* single-malt scotch is usually more expensive than a blend.

However, there are differences. Most importantly, blends are made after the single malts which go into them have been distilled and aged, whereas the addition of the non-*agave* sugars in *mixto* tequila occurs right at the beginning of the process of fermentation. It follows that, whereas many single malts may be blended with grain alcohol to produce a blended scotch, this is not usual in the case of *mixto* tequila.

When we speak of 'blends' of scotch or bourbon, we are, of course, referring to the mixing of spirits *from different distilleries*, with the addition of grain alcohol. All distilleries 'blend' in the sense that they carefully combine different barrels with different taste and nose characteristics, to achieve a desirable balance, and to maintain some consistency from year to year. Tequila distilleries are no exception.

The range of different flavors with single-malt scotches is immense. The difference in flavor between Lagavulin and Cragganmore, for instance, is so vast that it is difficult to believe they are both members of the same species of beverage. These differences arise partly because of the lengthy aging process in the barrel. The differences among 100 percent *agave* tequilas, while substantial and striking, are less extreme. Whereas tasting one single-malt scotch will not enable you to know whether you like other single-malt scotches, tasting one 100 percent *agave* tequila of good quality will probably give you a good idea of whether you will like others.

These differences have an important practical consequence for the discriminating imbiber. Among serious scotch drinkers, blends are usually judged good enough for mixing, and it would be considered a waste to add anything but water to a single malt: the distinctiveness of the single malt would largely be lost, or might even be an irritating distraction, in a mixed drink. With tequila, however, the superiority of the 100 percent *agave* comes through even when mixed in a cocktail. Not only have most Americans never tasted a really fine tequila—believe it or not, most Americans have no idea what a good margarita tastes like!

Originally, all tequilas were 100 percent *agave*. *Mixto* production began in the 1930s because of an increase in demand for tequila, while there was a limited harvest of *agave*. Because of the long time period needed for the *agave* to reach maturity, steep increases in demand for tequila may be met either by steep increases in price or by the addition of non-*agave* sugars. Since the 1930s, the tequila industry has had plenty of time, of course, to adjust the output of *agave* to increasing demand. To some extent, this has been accomplished by varying the ratio of *agave*

9

Harvested agave cabezas *at the distillery*

to non-*agave* sugars. Chiefly, though, the continued production of *mixto* reflects the fact that there is a large and growing demand, especially in the U.S., for something which is recognizably tequila, is comparatively inexpensive, and need not possess the very finest quality of flavor. And this demand exists because tequila has been increasingly exported to countries where people don't have a tequila-drinking tradition, and have no well-established standards of tequila quality.

This may now be changing. Most bars or lounges outside Mexico offer only *mixto* tequila, and even if they carry 100 percent *agave*, they will probably use *mixto* to make cocktails. But a few discriminating taverns and restaurants now make a point of using only premium 100 percent *agave* tequila, even for popular cocktails such as the margarita or the 'brave bull.'

It is possible that tequila may evolve as bourbon has evolved: at one time consumption of bourbon blends dwarfed consumption of 'straight' bourbon (the counterpart of 'single malts'). But now the overwhelming majority of bourbons are 'straight,' and bourbon blends are vanishing. Seeking a way to distinguish the best bourbons and capture the growing market for superior prod-

10

ucts, bourbon producers have promoted the 'single barrel' approach, picking out a few specially favored barrels within a distillery's output.

Tequila will probably follow a similar trend, with the gradual elimination or marginalization of *mixto,* and then the growing awareness of fine distinctions among the best 100 percent *agave* tequilas. This should be easier for tequila because, to some extent, such an awareness already exists within Mexico itself: it does not have to be newly created. In the U.S., however, the process of enlightening the consumers is being temporarily retarded by the sales pitches of the *mixto* importers and bottlers.

In addition to the two basic types of tequila, there are four classifications based on what happens to the tequila after distillation. Combining these four classifications with each of the two types would give eight varieties of tequila, but in practice one of the classifications is virtually never combined with one of the types, so there are actually seven varieties.

The four types of tequila are:

1. *blanco* or *plata* ('white' or 'silver')
2. *reposado* ('rested')
3. *añejo* ('aged')
4. *joven abocado* ('young and smoothed'; often called 'gold')

The seven varieties of tequila are:

1. 100 percent *agave—blanco*
3. 100 percent *agave—reposado*
5. 100 percent *agave—añejo*
2. *mixto—blanco*
4. *mixto—reposado*
6. *mixto—añejo*
7. *mixto—joven abocado*

White or *blanco* tequila is a clear liquid which, in the bottle, usually looks much like water. It may be bottled immediately after distillation or allowed to rest in stainless steel tanks for a period of time no longer than 60 days, while awaiting bottling. It may be 100 percent *agave* or *mixto.*

Reposado must be placed in wooden storage tanks or barrels for a period of not less than two months. Usually, *reposado* is stored in larger tanks from 10,000 to 30,000 liters, but some is aged in barrels. Reposado may also be *cien por ciento de agave* or *mixto.*

Añejo tequila must be aged in wooden barrels no larger than 600 liters, for a period of time no less than one year. Like *blanco* or *reposado, añejo* may be 100 percent *agave* or *mixto.*

Gold or *joven abocado* tequila is unaged, but treated with additives to achieve some of the same effects as aging. Legally, it has the same requirements as the white, but the addition of coloring and flavoring is allowed to maintain continuity of taste and color. The additive is predominantly caramel (burnt sugar). The primary difference between white and gold *mixto* tequilas is this burnt sugar coloration, the use of which varies with the individual manufacturer. *Joven abocado* is virtually always *mixto,* and this treatment can succeed in mellowing or disguising the harshness of a *mixto.*

Color and flavor additives are widely used in tequila production, both *mixto* and 100 percent *agave,* but they are employed much more sparingly with 100 percent *agave.* Caramel is primarily used to round off the rough edges of a *mixto.* It is unlikely that anyone would want to produce 100 percent *agave joven abocado,* as a *joven abocado* is mainly a treatment for overcoming the flavor problems inherent in a *mixto.*

As a broad generalization, the better the tequila, the less it can be enhanced by additives. However, various additives are widely employed in making all kinds of tequila, though not in all brands of the higher-quality tequilas. Coconut is currently in vogue, to give the tequila a little more complexity, especially in the nose. When coconut is added in very small quantities to make a slight adjustment to a fine tequila, it is doubtful whether even the most accomplished taster can be sure, just by taste and nose, of the coconut additive's presence.

The aging times for *reposado* and *añejo* vary, but most of the finer 100 percent *agave reposados* will have been in the wood for

Traditional pot stills for converting mosto *into* tequila blanco

three to nine months prior to bottling, and the better 100 percent *agave añejos* spend from 18 months to three years in the barrel. One hundred percent *agave añejos* are very seldom kept in the wood for more than four years, since the *agave* flavor which makes the spirit distinctive can be overpowered by too much exposure to the natural agents in the wood.

Which Kind of Tequila is Best?

Of the seven kinds of tequila, which is best? Beyond dispute, it has to be one of the three 100 percent *agave* types—*blanco, reposado,* or *añejo.* Although the best *mixto* is far better than the worst 100 percent *agave,* 100 percent *agave* is, as a rule, superior to *mixto.* No *mixto* can hope to match the highest-quality 100 percent *agave* tequilas.

It is widely reported by tequila drinkers that it is much more difficult to get a hangover with a 100 percent *agave* than with a

13

mixto. This may sound like a contemporary legend, but it is the testimony of many people of experience and good judgment, and, for what it's worth, I can personally corroborate it. Perhaps someone will one day find backing for an ingenious roundabout explanation, such as the taste of 100 percent *agave* being so much more subtle that you are more inclined to sip it slowly. However, there are chemical differences between the two kinds of tequila, and it is surely possible that these may influence the imbiber's bodily reaction to the alcoholic content.

Blanco, reposado, and *añejo*—all three have their serious and respected advocates. Obviously, *some* people must believe that *añejo* is better than *reposado,* and *reposado* better than *blanco,* since for any given brand, *añejo* is significantly more expensive than *reposado,* and *reposado* more expensive than *blanco.*

All the same, I maintain that the very best tequila is the *blanco.* It has the truest nose and the truest taste. If you drink tequila only rarely, you may prefer an *añejo* or a *reposado,* because you will find these drinks less shocking. They may remind you somewhat of other drinks, such as bourbon or brandy. And if the tequila that comes off the still is not the very best, aging may soften some of the discordant notes. But people who drink tequila steadily over time, with fastidious attention to quality, usually come to prefer the *blanco.* This is because a *blanco* gives you in its purest form what is distinctive to *tequila,* by contrast with drinks of European origin, that elusive, poignant sensory quality which comes only from the blue *agave.* In my opinion, a 100 percent *agave blanco* has the fullest and most distinctive aroma, the freshest taste, and the strongest *agave* flavor.

The *reposado* is the favorite of the ordinary Mexican tequila consumer. *Reposado* accounts for 63 percent of tequila sales in Mexico. *Reposado* is also less disconcerting to the occasional tequila drinker. It is a little smoother than *blanco,* while still retaining some of the *blanco*'s freshness. The best *reposados* are indisputably fine tequilas. However, if a tequila is of middling quality or worse, the *reposado* may be a distinct improvement on the *blanco.*

Though some tequila drinkers swear by the *añejo,* it departs most from the distinctive *agave* nose and flavor. The *añejo* displays the greatest effects of aging in the wood, with a darker color, a smoother flavor, and in some cases a richer flavor. Though aging may often improve a *mixto*, it is more hazardous in the case of a 100 percent *agave*. Some of the delicate nuances of the 100 percent *agave* can easily be overwhelmed by the oak, or by the sweet vanilla tones that derive from new charred wood. I doubt if much of the subtle virtues of a 100 percent *agave* tequila could survive being left in the wood for more than three or four years. Very often, however, those new to serious tequila drinking will find a good *añejo* the best introduction. And, despite anything I may say, some will persist in preferring it even after lengthy trials. *Chacun à son goût.*

The Market for Tequila

In 1996, the total output of tequila, 100 percent *agave* and *mixto* combined, was over 98 million liters, of which almost 80 percent was *mixto*. However, the vast majority of the 100 percent *agave* tequila was consumed in Mexico. Less than a tenth of the 100 percent *agave* tequila was exported, whereas over two-thirds of the *mixto* was exported. This, of course, is contrary to the usual rule, observed throughout history and in many industries today, that the highest quality, more expensive goods in any particular category are more likely to be exported.

If we rank nations by their *consumption* of tequila, the U.S. easily heads the list, with Mexico second, and Germany a distant third. The European Community as a whole still consumes less tequila than Mexico, though that may change in the near future. Mexico's tequila exports to Europe have suffered from competition from various bogus tequilas, the most prominent being the 'Dos Pistolas' label produced in the Canary Islands. As many as 30 other brands have been imported into Europe from Brazil, South Africa, Thailand, and other countries. Most of these brands are not distilled from fermented *agave* juice, but are distillates of non-*agave* products with a little tequila flavoring added later. In 1996 an agreement was reached between Mexico and fifteen European governments, in which each country agreed to respect and

15

enforce the denomination of origin for products from all of the other countries. The marketing of non-Mexican products as 'tequila' has now effectively been stopped in Europe.

Production of 100 percent *agave* tequila increased 20 percent in 1995, and although most of this increase was consumed in Mexico, knowledgeable people who watch the industry agree that a major growth in international demand for *cien por ciento de agave* is about to occur.

Despite the fact that over nine-tenths of all 100 percent *agave* tequila is consumed in Mexico, almost 70 percent of the tequila consumed in Mexico is *mixto*. It may seem surprising that the switch from *mixto* to 100 percent *agave* is occurring more dramatically in Mexico than in the United States, but Mexico is a developing country with millions of people receiving very low incomes. It is also the country where many people perceive that *mixto* is cheaper than 100 percent *agave* but not so satisfying. Outside Mexico, most tequila drinkers are not even aware of the distinction between *mixto* and 100 percent *agave*. So it is not really so remarkable that, as the Mexican economy develops and Mexican incomes rise, Mexican people switch to 100 percent *agave* more quickly than people north of the border. Although the Mexican economy has suffered a serious setback in the past few years, the long-term growth of an affluent Mexican middle class is not in any doubt.

At the time of writing, there are 46 company names which have been issued NOMs by the Mexican government, the registration number for the manufacture of tequila. Two of these are subsets of other companies. The licensing arrangement is that a license is needed to make *mixto*, and a further license, with additional inspection and quality controls, to make 100 percent *agave*. There is currently only one company (see Chapter 5) licensed to make *mixto* without being licensed to make 100 percent *agave*. Eighteen months ago, there were 35 companies altogether, and eight of them were not licensed to make 100 percent *agave*. These figures illustrate the rapid repositioning in the tequila industry, with new distilleries opening and a new awareness that the future lies with the superior quality products. There are several companies which choose to make only 100 percent *agave* tequila, and their number can be expected to grow rapidly.

By Mexican law, all aged or 100 percent *agave* tequilas must be bottled in Mexico. Unaged *mixto,* whether *blanco* or *joven abocado,* may be transported in bulk and usually is. About 90 percent of all tequila exported travels in bulk. The most common method of bulk transportation is in tanker trucks called *pipas,* each of which holds about 25,000 liters of tequila. These trucks take the tequila from the distillery into the United States, usually crossing into Texas, since most of the bottling plants are in the Eastern half of the U.S. Heublein, the importer of Jose Cuervo tequila, has its bottling plant in Hartford, Connecticut, and Domecq Imports, the importer of Sauza and a subsidiary of the liquor conglomerate Allied Domecq, have their bottling plant in Bardstown, Kentucky.

The tequila is either collected from the distillery by U.S. trucks, or it is conveyed in Mexican trucks to the border, where it is transferred to U.S. trucks. The tequila travels at a strength of 55 percent alcohol; it is then transferred to large tanks at the bottler, and diluted, usually with distilled water, before being bottled at

A few of the serious tequilas now available, if you're prepared to look

the strength of 80 proof (40 percent alcohol) required by BATF regulations.

The Mexican government imposes various restrictions on these bulk shipments. If the tequila is *joven abocado*, the addition of caramel must be done in Mexico. The importer is not permitted to resell bulk tequila to other bottlers, but should label the bottles to identify both the manufacturer and the importer. The Mexican government also encourages bottlers to include on the label the NOM or distillery registration number.

The new boutique tequilas introduced within the last ten years are making steady gains in sales, and public awareness is improving, even though the importers do not normally use the mass media for marketing.

An agreement between the United States government and the major liquor companies has for the last 40 years 'voluntarily' proscribed the advertising of distilled spirits on radio and television, though the beer and wine companies suffer through no such restrictions (The Seagram liquor company has just begun test marketing television and radio advertising for their products, in certain restricted areas). Without making use of the primary avenues of advertising, it is difficult to inform the public about these new products. The only advertising available to importers of tequila is the print media (newspapers or magazines) or outdoor advertising (billboards).

Mezcal and other *Agave*-derived Drinks

If you start talking about tequila with a group of non-Mexican friends, it is almost certain that within a few minutes, one of them will confidently state: 1. that tequila is made from cactus-juice, and 2. that tequila sometimes has a worm in the bottle. Usually the first question is: 'Tell me about the worm.' This illustrates just how much ignorance prevails about tequila, for tequila is not made from cactus-juice and tequila never has a worm in the bottle. The drink that sometimes has a worm in the bottle is *mezcal*, which is also made from *agave* (not cactus), though from different species of *agave* than the blue *agave* used to make tequila.

The first *agave* drink was *pulque* (pronounced 'pull-kay'). As far as we can tell, this was invented around the year 200 C.E., and the method of manufacture has changed little. Three different varieties of *agave* (but not the blue *agave*) are considered appropriate for making *pulque*. A cut is made in the stalk of a living *agave* plant, and a cavity is scraped out in the center of the plant. This cavity fills up with sap, which is removed from the plant by the *pulquero* (*pulque* brewer) twice a day, netting about two liters each time. The sap is a sweet, nutritious liquid called *aguamiel* or 'honey water.' After the collection of sap has begun, the plant gradually produces less sap, and usually lives for only about six months before dying.

After the *aguamiel* is gathered, it is transported to *tinacales* (fermentation sheds) where it ferments for about a week. *Pulque* spoils rapidly, usually within a few days, and cannot be canned or distilled. Fermentation causes a long chain polymer, similar to a plastic, to form in the *pulque,* giving it an albuminous character like egg white. This effectively prevents distillation. When *agave* plants are used for distilled products like tequila, the plant is first cooked, which chemically changes the plant, so that, after milling and fermentation, the long-chain polymer does not form.

Before the Spanish arrived in 1519, the only alcoholic drink available in Mexico was *pulque*. The Spanish introduced distillation, probably in the 1520s. All of the different forms of distilled spirits made from *agave* plants were originally called '*agave* wine' or '*mezcal* wine.' Tequila did not emerge as a separate drink until the late 1800s. According to one account, which may perhaps be accurate, the separation of tequila from other drinks was effected by Don Cenobio Sauza in about 1873, when he decided that the best species of *agave* for this type of *agave* wine was the variety now known as *Agave tequilana Weber, variedad azul.* The other manufacturers in and around the village of Tequila followed Sauza's lead. Tequila gradually became recognized as a product distinct from other versions of *mezcal* wine.

The many *agave*-derived drinks other than tequila and *mezcal* underwent a similar kind of evolution, but without achieving the prominence of tequila, and without legal recognition. Technically, it is not strictly wrong, though it is old-fashioned, to say that

19

tequila is a form of *mezcal*, but it is a definite mistake to say that *mezcal* is a form of tequila.

Some brands of *mezcal* have a worm inside the bottle. The worm lives inside the *agave* plant, and is the larva of a moth. Today the worms are grown commercially for this purpose, and introduced by hand into the bottles. Two types of worm (the larvae of two different kinds of moth) may be used in *mezcal*, the most common being a white worm called *blanco*, and occasionally a red worm called *rojo*. The different colored worms live in different areas of the plant, with the red worm living in the root mass and the white worm living in the leaves. One type of *mezcal* that may be found in the United States is sold under the brand name 'Dos Gusanos' (two worms) and contains one worm of each color.

The most common type of *mezcal* available in the U.S. is Monte Alban, named after the ancient city of the Zapotec Indians in the state of Oaxaca ('O-ah-hah-kah'), in south central Mexico. While *mezcal* is made in many parts of Mexico, the area which is most recognized for the production of *mezcal* is Oaxaca. In Oaxaca, you will sometimes find a small cotton bag tied around the neck of a bottle of *mezcal*. Inside the bag is a powder that is normally made up of crushed dried worms, salt and *chile*. When you pour a glass of *mezcal*, you can sprinkle a pinch of this powder on top of the liquid and then shoot or sip it. It adds a certain warmth, depending upon the type of *chile* that is mixed with the worms.

There are other differences between the spirits tequila and *mezcal*, mainly in the varieties of *agave* used in their manufacture and the methods used to prepare them. The main difference affecting the taste of the two products is that the *agave* used to make tequila is cooked inside ovens or autoclaves employing steam, while the *agave* used to make *mezcal* is cooked in underground ovens employing wood charcoal fires, resulting in a characteristic smoky taste being imparted to the *mezcal*.

Mezcal is also made from a number of different varieties of *agave*, eight varieties being approved for this purpose, but the main one being 'espadin' *(Agave angustifolia Haw)*, which is used in about 80 percent of the *mezcal* currently produced. Traditionally, *mezcal* was distilled only once whereas tequila normally undergoes two distillations. But nowadays, *mezcal* is also distilled twice. (*Mezcal de olla* has the first distillation performed in a clay pot).

There are many stories of how the worm came to be introduced into the bottles of *mezcal*. There are claims that the worm, having lived inside the *agave* and thus being an actual part of the plant, inherits the magical properties of the plant. Since the ancient peoples of Mexico considered the plant to be a 'gift of the gods,' it was also believed to be a source of divine assistance.

The practice of swallowing the worm when the last glass of *mezcal* was poured from the bottle derives from some of this belief, with the hopes that the worm will pass along the magic and bring good fortune to the person lucky enough to swallow it. It is also great fun to introduce the new drinker of *mezcal* to this mystique and to enjoy the looks of uncertainty or apprehension from the uninitiated. The worm is actually quite harmless and is a source of protein, with some vitamins and minerals.

One story of how the worm was originally introduced to the bottle is as follows. In the old days, there were no scientific aids, such as hydrometers, to determine the alcohol content of the finished product. This could invite problems with customers and even cause the *mezcal* to spoil if the alcohol content was too low. By placing a worm in the bottle of *mezcal*, it could be determined whether the beverage was safe to drink. If the worm pickled and was preserved, the *mezcal* was good. If the worm decayed, throw it away and re-distill the *mezcal*.

It is sometimes claimed that the worm absorbs impurities from the *mezcal* and thereby improves the flavor, but this is dubious. The introduction of the worm into the bottle is a traditional practice which seems to work well as a promotional device. Everyone seems to have heard at least one version of why the worm is in the bottle, how it should be consumed, and what it does to the *mezcal*—but despite the success of such stories, most people still confuse *mezcal* with tequila. The best *mezcals* do not include a worm.

Mezcal de olla is a variant of *mezcal* which has the first distillation carried out in a clay pot (*olla*). This pot is usually between

100 and 500 liters, and has a cover fitted over the top. With the top removed, the *olla* is filled with fermented must, and a fire is lit under the pot. The top is replaced, and as the must gives up its alcohol in the form of vapor, this is drawn off through a coiled tube.

Pulque is the original *agave* beverage, made today in much the same way as it was 1,500 years ago. The only *agave*-derived drink not to be distilled, it is widely available in rural Mexico, but it does not can or bottle well, so it is unlikely to be exported.

Bacanora is an *agave* distillate made in Sonora, in the north, from a small variety of *agave* about 18 inches high at maturity.

Raicilla is something of a bootleg liquor made in central Jalisco and some other areas, from a small variety of *agave* called *lechuguilla*. It has a sour flavor and strikes most people, including me, as unpleasant at first. Some say that a taste for it can be acquired, but I think it would be hard work.

Sotol and *comiteca* are two other regional variants of *agave* distillates, neither of which I have yet been able to sample.

How Tequila
Is Made

It's a beautiful day in Tequila Country, a day of comparatively equable temperature because you're at an elevation of around 7,500 feet. Early in the morning, at 6:00 A.M., the temperature is around sixty degrees Fahrenheit. You know it will get up to around eighty later in the day. You are ready to go to work.

You are a *jimador*, a harvester of *agave*. These *agaves* were planted years ago. Your work is the second movement in the symphony of tequila production. You have finished sharpening your *coa*, the specialized tool that you use to cut the *agave;* the round disc of steel is now as sharp as a razor and wrapped in rags, both to keep the edge from getting dulled and to keep anyone from getting hurt. You lay the four-foot handle over your shoulder as you wait for the truck to come and take you to the fields.

Here comes the truck. It stops to pick you up. You hand up your *coa* and lunch box to the other men in the truck, amid greetings and the same old jokes. You climb aboard the truck and join the other men and boys in your crew of *jimadores* and assistants. Your own assistant, the son of your older sister, is already on the truck, but he is still half asleep.

You are teaching him all the things a *jimador* must know: the signs and ways of the *agave*, when to cut the spike, how there is a slight shrinkage in size when the plant is ready for harvest, how the color changes on the leaves and around the base, the signs of disease which can make the plant unusable for tequila, how to use your foot to push and roll the plant while you use the *coa* to remove the *pencas* (the long, spiny leaves), the proper angles to strike from when cutting, how close to the *cabeza* to cut. Too short and you lose some of the weight of the *piña;* too long, and the plant becomes difficult to handle. All the things that you must know about the *agave*, the 'gift from the heavens,' to become a good *jimador*.

He is a good boy, your nephew, just out of school at fifteen and eager to learn this most mysterious of arts, the ways of the land and the *agave*, the mystique of tequila. He has been waiting all of his life, for your family has always, it seems, been involved in growing or harvesting the *agave*, or making the tequila. His father works inside the *fábrica* as a stillman. You teach him the techniques of harvesting; later, when a new position opens inside the plant, he may get to learn something about subsequent stages of tequila production.

The razor-sharp coa, *specialized tool for harvesting the* agave

You are the eighth of nine children, and your own children are still too young to begin working. You hope that they can get the education to keep them from the fields, but it is hard to raise the money for education; first, everyone has to eat.

Three of your brothers have gone to *Los Estados Unidos del Norte* to find work. They send some money home to help raise their own families and assist your parents, but it is still hard to make ends meet.

The truck pulls up to the gate of the field that has been selected for harvest today, a standard-sized field of about 200 hectares or 500 acres. It holds about half a million *agave* plants in various stages of growth. The field has been planted for about seven years, so some of the plants are ready while others are not.

Strange how the *agave* ripens. Two plants that were placed in the ground on the same day might differ in harvest times by four years. Oh well, such is the way of the land.

A few months before you came along to harvest the *agave* plant, its central flower spike was cut, forcing the plant's growth into the center and causing the great, swollen *piña* to form. Just before it is ready for harvesting, the height of the plant actually shrinks a bit, and rusty brown spots appear on the bases of the leaves. If the plant is left too long, these spots will expand and merge, and then turn black. The *agave* is then unusable.

In the Highlands, the land that grows the *agave* is *tierra rojo* (red earth); in the valleys, *tierra negro* (black earth). The *rojo* seems to grow the *agave* a little larger and sweeter, but perhaps you think this because you are from the Highlands, where the earth is red. You know that the *jimadores* from the valleys also claim that their *agave* is the best.

You have often observed fields being deep-ploughed in preparation for new *agave* plants, and seen the new plants laid out in

The jimador *pushes the* agave *with his foot, while cutting the* pencas.

25

straight lines. More work for you, six or seven years down the road.

The truck drives down the narrow dirt track to the area where the owner of the land has decided that most of the *agave* is ready for harvest. The truck pulls by the harvesting area, and the crew unloads and moves down the rows between the plants, looking for the best place to start. The decision is made, and each *jimador* picks a row and begins working. First there's a downward stroke, to clear a space for the foot to go, then you push the plant to bring the root mass into view.

Bending far over, you cut the plant free from the roots and roll it up on its side. Once the plant is rolled, the leaves are sliced evenly from the base to the top with smooth strokes. The heavy blade of the *coa* slices cleanly with each stroke, removing the *pencas*, until only the *cabeza* or *piña* is left. As you move on to the next plant, your nephew and one of the other assistants move the harvested *agave* back to the truck to be loaded.

It's funny how you can never tell exactly how big the *piña* will be before you remove the leaves. Yes, you can tell the difference between very small and very large *agave*s, but plants that appear close in size before harvest may vary as much as twenty kilos afterwards. Most of the plants from the valleys are 35 to 75 kilos in size, but here in the Highlands, they grow larger. The normal size is between 50 and 90 kilos, but 100 kilos is not very uncommon. During your 20 years in the fields, you have seen some monster plants that would harvest at 200 kilos, but such are rare.

After about four hours' work, your team of *jimadores* and assistants has filled the truck. It takes three to five minutes to harvest each plant, depending upon the spacing of the other plants, the proximity of the harvestable plants, and obstructions such as weeds. When the truck is full, with about 250 harvested *piñas*, or twenty metric tons, it leaves for the *fábrica*.

You and your crew continue cutting until there are enough *piñas* to fill the truck again, and then it's time for a short break. Time for lunch, and rest, and a little gossip about local events. When the truck returns, you will help with the loading and be told where the next cutting will be. Sometimes you may stay in the same field for days, but it is more usual to move every day or so.

The jimador *makes a cut separating the* agave *from the root mass.*

After the truck has been loaded for the second time, you can go home for the rest of the day. The *fábrica* can cook no more than 40 tons per day, and the truck holds 20, so two truckloads per day is as much as the *fábrica* can handle. But you decide to go help in the plant, and give your nephew a chance to see his father.

The truck takes the *piñas* to the distillery, where they are off-loaded into a large pile. Two men in the reception area pick up their axes and begin cutting the *piñas* into halves and quarters. This is the hardest job in the factory, for they must also pack the *agave* into the *hornos* (ovens), and unload them when the *agave* is cooked. Some companies now use autoclaves, but your company believes that the old ways are best, so they continue to use ovens.

The autoclaves are giant, stainless steel pressure cookers. They may be faster in the cooking process, but somehow the tequila seems to suffer. Whether it's the waxy residue, called bitter honey, washed from the outside of the plant when the steam is injected into the autoclave, or possibly a failure to properly hydrolize the starches inside the *agave* and totally convert them into the flavorful sugars, something about speeding up the process doesn't seem to allow the full flavor of the *agave* to be imparted to the tequila.

An *horno* normally takes three days to properly cook the *agave*. Thirty-six hours cooking and 36 cooling, though some companies use 48 cooking and 24 cooling. This process fully converts all of the starch into sugar. It just doesn't seem possible that an autoclave that cooks the *agave* in only six hours can be doing as good a job as the ovens.

When all is said and done, the proof of the tequila is how it tastes. Much of the tequila made with autoclaves is *mixto,* and is exported to other countries. You are proud of your company for making only *cien por ciento de agave* tequila, and while some is exported, the majority is sold here in Mexico and is well received.

You're not sure whether the methods used to crush the *agave* still need to be traditional. The company you work for now uses a mechanical crusher-juicer, but your cousin works at another company that still uses the *tahona,* and he fiercely insists that the old ways are best.

At the distillery where your harvest is taken, the yeasts employed in fermenting the juice are the same strains that have been used in the factory for 50 years. They are kept alive and growing in the fermentation tanks, and checked by the laboratories each week to ensure that there is no contamination. Each new batch of *agave* juice is fermented by the same methods and the same yeasts. You know that many of the larger companies in Tequila use commercial yeasts, but this also appears to affect the taste of the tequila. It seems that everything has an effect on the taste of the tequila, including the precise growing conditions—climate, elevation, and quality of soil—where the *agave* is grown.

You once harvested a monster *agave* that weighed over 200 kilos. After the first cut, you found that it was sitting on a nest of fire ants. Not an amusing experience, though the other men talked and laughed about it for days. Your antics while trying to get the fire ants off your body must have looked funny, but you had painful welts for days. Both the talk and the pain ended about the same time, thank goodness. You were very tired of both.

But what a *cabeza!* It was enormous, the largest that you had ever seen. It took four men to load it on the truck. The nest of ants must have had something to do with the *agave* growing to that size. Even ants can affect the size of the plant and, maybe, the taste of the tequila.

Your company separates the *agave* fiber from the juice prior to fermentation, because it is easier to handle just the juice. You can move the juice through pipes and hoses. The company that your cousin works for leaves the fiber in the juice during fermentation and even the first distillation. Their tequila is wonderful, but everything must be done by hand. From carrying the juice and fiber to the fermentation tanks, to the loading of the still, it is all done by workers with buckets. And it is messy. It is not easy cleaning out the still after each distillation run. At your company's distillery, handling liquid juice, they just open a drainage valve and flush the tank with water.

Which way is best? The never-ending question. What changes can be made for reasons of expediency or sanitation without affecting the final taste of the tequila? All of the traditional ways have been changed at one time or another, and the most drastic was the addition of other sugars to stretch out the *agave*, when there was little *agave* available for harvesting. Less expensive to make, but by using cane sugar, the mixture seems to be half 'rum', and it doesn't taste the same as the tequila that uses only the juice of the *agave*. How could it? It isn't the same.

The cabeza, *with all the leaves removed, looks like a gigantic pineapple.*

29

You understand why it was started, to meet the demands of the market. But now those methods continue only because it is less expensive to make tequila when you cut corners. You have heard of some of the biggest companies in Tequila, whose only concern seems to be to make money. Nothing wrong with making money. Everybody needs money to live. But it should be possible to make money by making good tequila. You have heard that some companies, having tried the new ways, have begun to return to the old.

You go on through the factory with your nephew and stop for a while to visit with his father, your sister's husband. He is a good man, and one of the best still-masters in the business.

The smell of *agave* is stronger around the stills, but it permeates the atmosphere everywhere inside the *fábrica*. From the aroma around the large fermentation tanks where the juice ferments into *mosto*, to the final run through the stills to convert the *ordinario* to tequila, you can smell the *agave*.

Hector, your brother-in-law, says that he is so used to the smell that he doesn't notice it any more. But he can tell the percentage of alcohol in the *ordinario* simply by looking at it. Something about the viscosity of the clear liquid and the way it flows from the pipe into the holding tank, before the second distillation which turns it into tequila.

Then to the *bodegas*, where the tequila is being aged for transformation into *reposado* or *añejo*. After the walk around the distillery, showing the boy how things happen inside the plant, the day is over. Time to go home for the evening meal.

There we leave our *jimador* to his well-earned relaxation, while we pursue the *agave* through its metamorphosis into tequila.

Cooking and Milling

The methods and tools used to harvest the *agave* are unique, because the *agave* is unique. Though entirely different in growth pattern and appearance, it is a little like tuberous plants such as sweet potato or yam, especially after it is cooked. The starches inside the *piña* are converted into sugar compounds that taste much like candied yams.

Agave cabezas, *in front of the ovens into which they will be loaded*

The physical changes within the *agave,* involving the chemical conversion of starch to sugar, are caused by prolonged exposure to moderate heat. This breaks the long chain molecules of starch into shorter sugar molecules. The cooking process used to convert the starches inside the *agave* into fermentable sugars is different from the processes used in the manufacture of other spirits, in which natural enzymes such as amylase or diastase convert the starches inside grains into sugars.

After the *piñas* are brought into the factory, they are cut up and placed in cooking vessels: ovens or autoclaves. When ovens are used, live steam is forced around the inside walls of the ovens, gradually raising the temperature to 135–145° Fahrenheit (57–63° Celsius) over a 36-hour to 48-hour time period. After the desired temperature is reached, the steam is turned off, and the *agave* continues cooking through residual heat. The ovens are allowed to cool for another 24 to 36 hours. While the *agave* is cooking, a sweet liquid is exuded from the plant mass, flows from a special

31

The crushing and juicing line at Centinela

vent at the bottom of the oven, and is collected for later addition to the wort. This liquid is called cooking-honey and can be as much as 20 percent sugar. It is diluted with water and placed in with the other juice prior to fermentation.

The dark brown cooked *agave* is then removed from the cooking vessels and moved to the crushing-juicing equipment, by hand in the smaller and more traditional distilleries, or by conveyor belt in the large mass-production plants.

Distilleries which abandon traditional methods for the sake of cutting costs use autoclaves instead of ovens. The autoclave is a big pressure cooker—essentially, it is a gigantic version of the familiar receptacle used in hospitals to sterilize medical instruments.

When autoclaves are employed, the steam is injected directly into the container, and the interior temperature may be raised much more quickly than in the ovens. High pressure permits far higher temperatures, so that the total time spent cooking and cooling is 18 hours or less—sometimes it is reduced to as little as eight hours.

High temperatures can cause the destruction of some of the enzymes and flavoring compounds, and may result in elimination of some congeners. (Congeners are substances present in tiny quantities in distilled spirits; they affect the aroma, taste, and

32

color of the spirit, and some may have medicinal effects. They may also affect the body's absorption rate of alcohol.) An additional problem in using autoclaves is that the steam injection washes a natural wax, called bitter-honey, from the outside of the *agave*. This water-wax liquid can impart a bitter taste to the tequila, so the first portion of the juices has to be discarded. The use of autoclaves reduces the quality of the tequila, and should be reserved for *mixto*.

The autoclaves used to cook *agave* can be made up to any size, but most are from ten to twelve feet in diameter and at least twenty feet long. The shortest cooking time of which I have been informed was four hours; in that case, the autoclave was erected vertically, the *agave* was shredded before being loaded into the top of the autoclave, and was unloaded from the bottom, directly onto the conveyor belts leading to the juicing equipment.

The traditional method, going back over 200 years, of separating the fibrous pulp of the *agave* from the juice, is the great stone wheel, called a *tahona* (pronounced 'ta-ona'). In the old days, in some areas only ten years ago, the wheels were very large and were pulled by oxen or horses. In some cases the wheels were up to eight feet in diameter, from two to three feet thick, and weighed as much as ten tons.

The *tahona* was placed in a circular pit lined with cobblestones, with a pivot pole in the center. Another pole ran from the pivot pole, through a hole in the center of the stone wheel, and was harnessed to the animals used to turn the stone. The pit was filled with the cooked *agave*, and the animals pulled the stone wheel around the circular pit, crushing the fibrous material and

Crushing agave *the old-fashioned way, with a* tahona

expelling the juice. After the *agave* was fully crushed, the juice would be lying on top of the mat of fiber and could be picked up with buckets and placed in the fermentation tanks.

Some companies employ these traditional techniques, and some are returning to them, but currently most use the grinder-juicer machines, involving large crushers similar to those used in juicing sugar cane.

Fermentation

After being separated from the fiber, the juice is placed in fermentation tanks with water, and yeast is added.

Companies that make only 100 percent *agave* tequila usually have a natural yeast culture which they have developed over the years. Many of the companies that make *mixto* use commercial yeast products similar to brewer's yeast. The yeasts selected have a definite effect upon the taste of the finished product. One of the tequila companies has isolated 15 different strains of natural yeasts and determined that each affects the final taste of the tequila in a different manner.

One company, Tapatio, takes the fiber from the pit and re-introduces it into the juice before beginning fermentation. This is done because Tapatio believes that leaving the fiber and the juice together as long as possible enhances the *agave* flavor and aroma of the finished product. Tapatio also leaves the fiber in the fermented must through the first distillation, so that the must is introduced into the still by hand, and the *bagasse* (leftover fiber) is cleaned from the still in the same way. Not until the *ordinario* is ready for the second distillation can the liquid be moved by any method other than manually, with buckets. The methods used by this company are the most labor-intensive of any of which I am aware, but the final taste of the tequila proves that it is worth it.

If the distillery is making *mixto*, the non-*agave* sugar is added after the juice has been placed in the tanks, just before yeast is added. Commonly, the non-*agave* sugars are added in liquid form, in carefully measured amounts, to the freshly pressed *agave* juice.

Bagazo, *left-over fiber after crushing and juicing*

Most often used is granulated cane sugar that has been dissolved in warm water. Next is *piloncillo*, dried sugarcane juice (brown sugar), formed into large cones and packaged in paper bags. Sometimes these two products are used in conjunction with each other. Then there is a commercially prepared liquid sugarcane product called *Glucosa,* and finally there is plain old corn syrup. Any of these will be introduced at a concentration of six to ten percent sugar in the liquid.

Natural fermentation usually takes from seven to ten days, but for *mixto* tequilas many companies use yeast nutrients called 'accelerators.' These are nitrogen compounds such as ammonium phosphate which encourage growth of the yeasts and improve conversion of the sugars to alcohol and carbon dioxide gas. This allows the companies to cut down the fermentation time from days to hours. If all of the shortcuts that can be used are utilized in making tequila, the process, which normally takes from ten to twelve days, can be cut to one or two days, but the quality of the tequila may suffer accordingly.

During fermentation, the juice boils and bubbles, and a foamy crust of bubbles and particulate matter forms on the surface of the juice, now called 'fermented must' or *mosto*. In some instances, the process can become quite violent, causing the tanks to vibrate from the force of the chemical conversion. A reaction this dramatic is usual only when accelerators are used, so that the release of carbon dioxide is very rapid. Generations ago, animal dung or other sources of urea were used as yeast nutrients. Sounds unpleasant, but the distillation process does not allow any solid material into the final spirit, and the heat of fermentation kills any infectious bacteria.

Distillation

After all of the sugar has been converted to alcohol, the reaction ceases and the fermented must is then emptied into a holding tank to await the first distillation. The recommended method of distillation is the pot, or alembic still, and two distillations are the recommended norm. A pot still is just a giant pot with a long-necked cover welded on and a coil of steam-carrying pipe around the bottom of the pot.

The must is piped into the still and heated to somewhere between 190° and 205° Farenheit by live steam injection through a spiral pipe at the base of the unit. The precise temperature needed to vaporize the alcohol may vary according to the percentage of alcohol contained in the fermented must. Since the vaporization point of alcohol is 172.5° Farenheit, this allows the alcohol vapor to be separated from the other components in the must, and rising because of the heat, to be drawn off through the long neck into a cooling condenser called a 'worm.'

The worm is surrounded by a jacket full of cold water, which causes the alcohol vapor to condense. The liquid alcohol, now called *ordinario,* then runs down a pipe into a holding tank. The first and last portions of the distillation run will be discarded or placed into the next run, since they may contain high levels of unwanted aldehydes and congeners.

The second run, which turns the *ordinario* into tequila, will usually be made through a second still, though some very small companies have only one still. See, for example, Distillery #14 in

Part of the line of 14 pot stills at Herradura

Chapter 5, the distillery which produces the tequila 'Los Valientes.' It has only one still of about 750 liters and both runs have to go through that unit.

Pot stills were originally all made of copper, and the most authentic are made that way today, but many are now made of stainless steel. There is, however, another type of distillation unit. It has been called by many names, from 'Coffey' (the name of the inventor), to 'patent' (pronounced 'pay-tent'), to 'continuous action' still, but the most recognized name today is 'column still.' This distillation unit processes large amounts of fermented must in a short time.

The column still looks like a large vertical pipe, with many attachments to the exterior. The fermented must is introduced into the central portion of the column, and live steam is injected into the bottom of the pipe. As the steam passes through the fermented must, the alcohol is heated to vaporization point and rises into the upper portion of the column, where there are plates that are kept progressively cooler causing the various components of the distillate to condense selectively. The resulting liquids are drawn off through a collector and pipe arrangement.

While tequila normally requires two distillations in a pot still, many companies using a column still make only one distillation run, feeling that once the proper concentration of alcohol is reached, that is good enough. Since this is a continuous action unit, the discarding of the heads or tails of the distillation is handled in a slightly different manner, with the separated components which contain the unwanted volatile flavors being discarded and the other products being re-combined into tequila. If improperly operated, this may result in a lessening of the quality of the tequila. There are no legal requirements that either type of distillation unit be utilized, but the use of pot stills is preferred when making 100 percent *agave* tequila.

Aging and Blending

When the tequila leaves the still after the final run, it is as clear as water, or very close to that. It's similar to what whiskey makers in Kentucky and Tennessee call 'White Dog'. This first stage of tequila is called *blanco* or *plata*. From *blanco*, all other kinds of tequila are made. As we saw in Chapter 1, it is controversial whether a really good *blanco* is improved by aging, though a poor or mediocre *blanco* may lose some of its rough edges.

The product often described in the U.S. as 'gold' or *oro* is usually called *joven abocado* in Mexico. The only difference between 'gold' tequila and *blanco* is the addition of coloring and perhaps a small amount of some sweetening agent. Possibly the only thing added would be caramel, which both colors and sweetens. The best-quality tequilas would never be made into *joven abocados*.

The *blanco* may also be put into wooden containers for aging. The legal categories for aged tequilas are *reposado* and *añejo*. Although *reposado* means 'rested' and *añejo* means 'aged,' these are both really categories of aging, the *reposado* being aged for a shorter time. Furthermore, *añejos* may vary considerably in their length of aging.

Tequila described as *reposado* must be aged in wood for a minimum of two months. This aging is usually carried out in large wooden tanks, each holding from ten thousand to thirty thousand liters. Some *reposado* tequilas are aged in 180-liter barrels, but most is in the large tanks. The Mexican government inspects these tanks and places paper seals on the bungs to ascertain that the time limit is met. After the minimum time, the tanks or barrels may be opened and the tequila bottled, but it is more usual for the tequila to be left in the wood for a longer period, usually from four to eight months.

Anything under a year in the wood is called a *reposado*, because the *añejo* must legally be kept in barrels of 600 liters or less for at least a year. The barrels are usually 180–200 liters and most were previously used by the whiskey companies of Kentucky and Tennessee, though some companies are experimenting with new oak barrels. Many companies are still using barrels that may be fifty years old or older. Some barrels were purchased by the founders of the companies and have sentimental value to their descendants.

The tequila that is aged in used barrels doesn't change as much as that aged in newer barrels. The method used by the cooper in preparing barrels for aging whiskey involves charring the insides of the barrels. This action caramelizes and releases the sugars present in the wood, modifies the tannins and releases some of the other flavoring agents in the oak. Many of these wood fractions are absorbed by the whiskey that is first placed inside the barrels, but many are left to smooth and color the tequila.

Other wines and spirits do not use charred barrels, though some may use a method called 'toasting'. Most employ the wood in its natural state, and allow the interaction between these two elements to bring the wine or spirit to maturity. Tequila is more delicate than most other spirits however, so the preferred method of aging in barrels is to utilize barrels that have been previously used. The previous use of these barrels has drawn off a large part of the extractable flavoring and coloring agents present in the wood, and reduces the impact of the wood on the tequila.

This is the stage at which all spirits gain their coloration, either by the addition of artificial coloring or by aging in oak barrels. All distilled spirits are clear when they come from the still, and the transformation into brown spirits is caused by the inter-

A bodega *with* barricas *(barrels); the ones standing on end are empty.*

action between the spirit and the wood or the addition of other forms of coloring.

The effect on the tequila is determined in part by the age and use of the barrels. If the barrels have been used continuously for a long period of time, the extractives that change the spirit are slowly depleted. The natural extractives will all be pulled from the wood by successive generations of tequila that have been stored in the barrel, and the rate of change in the spirit will diminish.

This problem, if it is perceived as such, can be rectified by the addition of new staves or barrel ends that have been charred, but this process requires that the barrel be disassembled and reconstructed. The purchase of new used barrels is easier and less expensive, but sometimes the barrels become scarce, and reconstruction is the only way to maintain the proper balance of sugars in the wood.

After aging, the tequila is prepared for bottling. For both *reposado* and *añejo* tequilas, blending between various age groups is common, but any age statements, on the label or elsewhere, must legally be determined by the age of the youngest component. At this point, caramel is sometimes added, mainly to ensure continuity and stability in the color of the spirit. Flavorings are also used by some manufacturers, with the current favorite being coconut.

The blender is the person responsible for the continuing aroma, taste and appearance of the *reposado* and *añejo* tequilas. The blenders use all of their senses in the practice of this art. Their aim and intention is to keep the spirit the same in appearance, aroma, and flavor from year to year. Their noses are crucial, for while the appearance may be adjusted with coloring additives and the taste may be modified with flavor additives, the aroma is more difficult.

The sense of smell is arguably the most accurate and intense judge of quality that we humans possess, being able to detect as few as five parts per billion of certain fragrances. It has been shown that smell is the controlling factor in our sense of taste, and as such, is the most useful sense in the blending of all types of spirits.

The blender takes different tequilas from his stock of the distillery output and mixes them in such a manner as to ensure that the tequila stays the same in all respects on a year-to-year basis. The aim is that you will not be able to tell the difference between one bottle and another bottle of a certain brand and type of tequila, even if they were made ten years apart. This is not always feasible, since growing conditions vary greatly from season to season, but the effort is made to come as close as possible.

The final stage at the distillery is the bottling or shipment of the product. All aged or 100 percent *agave* tequilas must be bottled inside Mexico, and most companies have a small bottling and packaging facility. These types of tequila are bottled and packed in cardboard boxes for shipment by truck to the Mexican distributors or to the various exporting companies. For *mixto*, the most common method of shipment is in tanker trucks, which are filled with tequila at the distillery. These trucks each carry around 6,500 gallons (or 25,000 liters) of *blanco* or gold tequila to the rectifiers and bottlers in the United States or elsewhere.

Of the 315 or so labels registered with the Mexican government, approximately 150 are imported into the U.S., but there are

How Tequila Is Made

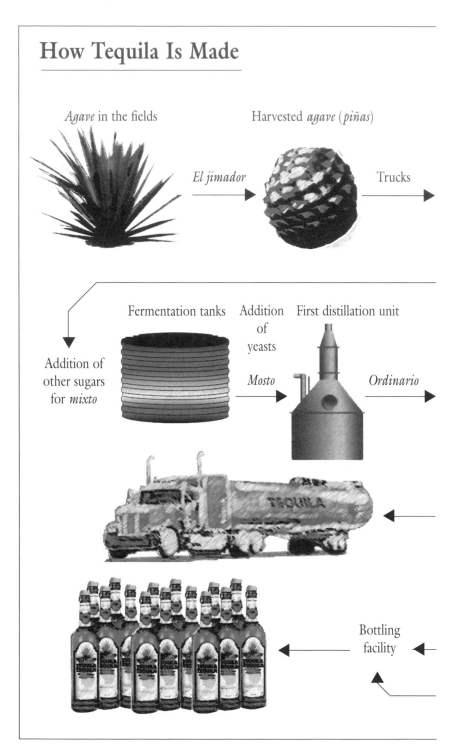

Agave in the fields

Harvested agave (piñas)

El jimador

Trucks

Fermentation tanks

Addition of yeasts

First distillation unit

Addition of other sugars for mixto

Mosto

Ordinario

Bottling facility

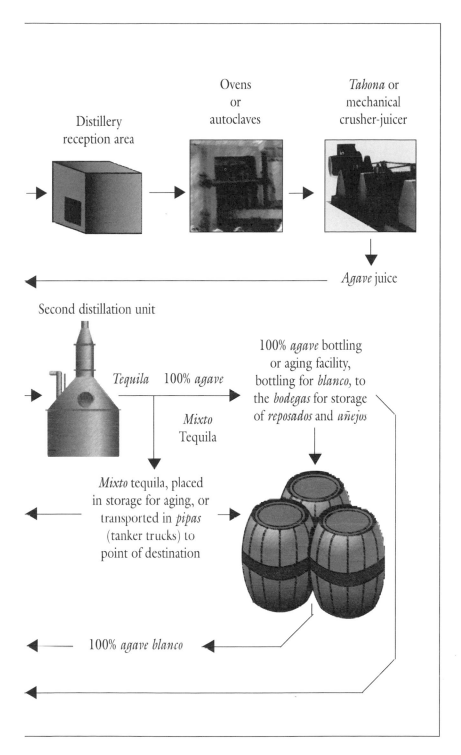

Distillery
reception area

Ovens
or
autoclaves

Tahona or
mechanical
crusher-juicer

Agave juice

Second distillation unit

Tequila   100% *agave*

Mixto
Tequila

100% *agave* bottling
or aging facility,
bottling for *blanco*, to
the *bodegas* for storage
of *reposados* and *añejos*

Mixto tequila, placed
in storage for aging, or
transported in *pipas*
(tanker trucks) to
point of destination

100% *agave blanco*

43

around 1,400 labels on a worldwide basis. Some of these are what are called 'illegal' labels, since they are bottled from exported bulk tequila that has been resold and do not have the NOM or distillery name on the label.

A Brief History of
Mexico and Tequila

Before the Spanish conquest in 1521, Mexico was the home of several high civilizations, many of whose achievements outstripped those of Spain. These ancient American cultures were all highly conscious of the *agave*, regarded as a 'gift of the gods' on account of its many uses.

The Aztecs (or 'Mexicas') were a literate people who painted many of their writings onto *agave* fiber, which served as a writing 'paper,' akin to papyrus in the Old World. The great majority of these prolific records and stories were quickly destroyed by the Spanish, who viewed the Mexican religions as devilish, but a few survived, and other records were made later by Catholic priests, who studied the conquered peoples, questioned them, and wrote books about them.

At least nine distinct types of *agave* were known from early times. The plants were classified by physical aspects such as size, stem, form, color, and width. Many uses are recorded, including food and medicine. *Agave* fiber yielded thread, cord, rope, clothing, rugs, footwear, and writing 'paper.' The leaves were used to provide thatching for roofs, and the thorns were used as needles for sewing, The fibers were also woven into coir mats, and finally the juice was allowed to ferment into the spirit *octili poliqhui*, or *octli*, a version of what is known today as *pulque*. Among the Aztec gods were Ometochtli, the god of *octli*, and Tepoztécal, the god of alcoholic merriment.

The alcoholic properties of the plant were discovered long before the rise of the Aztecs, probably in central Mexico around the year 200 C.E. or earlier. Exactly how the discovery was made is lost, but many stories and legends have survived.

One story tells of a grandmother who, while gathering food for her family, saw a bird acting very strangely near one of the sacred plants. The bird was flapping around on the ground and finally managed to fly up to a tree branch, but fell off and landed on top of the sacred plant. She went over to investigate this strange thing and, while looking at the bird, saw a bug scurrying around on the outside of the plant. It, too, was acting strangely and seemed to be lost, since it wandered aimlessly and at times almost seemed to dance.

She watched this strange behavior for a few minutes and soon saw another bug come from a small hole in the center of the plant. It acted just as strangely and could barely stand up. It seemed to have the same difficulty as the bird and the other bug.

To investigate further, she took her knife and cut into the plant where the bug had exited and was rewarded with a spurt of liquid which covered her hands. Licking it off her fingers, she found it to be delicious, and, taking her drinking gourd, caught some of it to take home to her family. Her son and daughter-in-law found it to be wonderful. It tasted delicious and eased the everyday pains of hard work. And it lightened your spirits and made you feel happy. This was no doubt a 'gift of the gods.'

The next day she showed her son where the plant was and how she had found the marvellous liquid. He probed the plant and finally found a cavity which had the liquid inside. The son collected this liquid and took it home to the rest of his family. Soon the word had spread to the friends and neighbors of the family, and eventually across the land.

We do not even know which of the Mexican cultures—the Olmec, Maya, Teotihuacán, Zapotec, or some other—made the discovery, but this delightful invention must then have spread from culture to culture fairly quickly, until it was known throughout what is now Mexico. The discovery of *octili poliqhui* must have had an impact on the pre-Columbian cultures comparable to the discovery of wine and beer upon the lives of people in the Old World.

Another old legend tells of a tribal chieftain who was partying with other chiefs at a gathering among the tribes. He drank too much *pulque* and became so uninhibited that he took off all his clothes and danced naked in front of the other chiefs. When he awoke the next morning and was told how he had misbehaved, he was so embarrassed that he and his entire tribe moved away from the area, never to return.

There is a tale from the Toltec city of Tula, about the founder of that city, King Topiltzin, who became identified in legend with the feathered-serpent god Quetzalcóatl. While in a struggle for power with the warrior-priests who worshiped Tezcatlipoca, the traditional god of the Toltecs, Topiltzin-Quetzalcóatl caught a cold. His rival Tezcatlipoca, in disguise, gained entry to the house of Quetzalcóatl and offered him medicine, which was in fact the alcoholic drink *pulque*, made from the juice of the *agave*. At first, Quetzalcóatl refused but was finally persuaded to take a sip and, liking the taste, asked for more. After five cupfuls, he was intoxicated and went to sleep. The next morning, he awoke to find himself on the sleeping pallet of his sister.

Believing himself to have broken his priestly vows by the sins of drunkenness and incest, he felt that he was disgraced. So, he and his followers moved away from the city. They went to the gulf coast and sailed away to the east. They are known to have landed in Yucatán and, joining with other Toltecs in the area, were apparently absorbed into the Mayan culture.

This legend of Quetzalcóatl had a remarkable sequel. Quetzalcóatl was bearded, and of comparatively fair complexion, and promised that he would return from the direction of the rising sun. When he and his people left for their journey in 987 C.E., they marked their way by shooting arrows through saplings, making signs that looked like crosses. Six hundred years later, the Aztec emperor, Montezuma II, was convinced by these remarkable coincidences that Hernán Cortés was Quetzalcóatl returning, and this contributed to Cortés's easy conquest of Mexico.

The discovery of *pulque* made the *agave* even more appreciated by the people of the land. Not only was it a staple of their lives, but now it supplied an easing of tensions and a form of relaxation that the people had never before experienced.

As political organization became more large-scale and more bureaucratic, priests and nobles enacted many rules of behavior; public drunkenness was frowned upon. As the the priesthood and aristocracy gained even more power, penalties were attached to misuse of the beverage, sometimes even death.

While some people were granted the right to consume the beverage for reasons of age or infirmity, the average person was allowed to drink this 'gift' only during the five-day period at the end of the calendar year known as 'The Days of the Dead.' During this holiday, huge stone bowls placed in the central plazas of the cities were kept filled with *pulque,* and the people were allowed to drink themselves into insensibility. But the warriors, aristocrats, and priests were allowed to drink it throughout the year.

They did, however, pay a price for this privilege. *Pulque* was considered to be the blood of the gods of the Earth, sent to the people through the gods' gift, the *agave*. The nobility was expected to guarantee the production and supply of *pulque* throughout the year. The manner in which they did this was to supply the gods with human blood in exchange for the blood of the gods. Aristocrats, priests, and warriors drew blood from their own bodies: men, by piercing their genitals with sea-ray spines, women and priests by drawing cords embedded with thorns through their tongues. The blood gathered this way was then offered to the gods to ensure good harvests of *agave*.

This seems to have been a standard practice in more than one of the cultures of the time. We do not know exactly how many of the societies adhered to this form of sacrifice, but archaeological research shows that it was widespread.

Pulque was also employed as a narcotic during the rites of human sacrifice practiced to appease the gods of the earth. War captives were allowed to consume great quantities of the beverage before they were brought out to have their throats cut and hearts removed as offerings to the gods.

The Spanish Conquest

The conquest of Mexico by Cortés is one of the most extraordinary and spectacular events in world history. The final capture of the city of Tenochtitlán (also known as 'Mexico'), capital of the Aztec empire and site of today's Mexico City, was accomplished by only 900 Spaniards, who had the support of 100,000 native allies during the final assault on the city. After the conquest was complete, the Spanish *conquistadores,* numbering just over two thousand, controlled a nation of 25 million 'Indians.'

After Cortés and his expedition landed in Mexico, and for the two years until the conquest was fairly complete, the country was in constant turmoil. Native tribes fought on both sides: some groups sided with the Aztecs, while others joined the Spanish out of hatred for the oppressive Aztec rule.

The Aztecs ruled only part of Mexico. The complete subjugation of all of Mexico took another ten to twenty years of warfare. Some of the tribes were not brought under control until the 1600s. There are still over 30 surviving Indian languages in various parts of Mexico. The thoroughness of the Spanish consolidation of power was inadvertently aided by the introduction of European diseases, such as measles and smallpox, to which the indigenous population had little natural resistance. Many more natives died from these illnesses than were killed in battle.

In 1519 there were an estimated 25,200,000 natives. Thirteen years later, following epidemics of smallpox in 1520 and measles in 1529, there were only 16,800,000. In 1548, following the typhus outbreak of 1545, the population had been reduced to 6,300,000. The native or 'Indian' population was reduced to its lowest level of less than a million in 1625. After that, the population began to recover slowly. The immense death toll from disease was neither intended nor welcomed by the Spanish, who reckoned their status by how many peasants they ruled, but it probably did snuff out resistance to Spanish rule, especially as no one had much understanding of the spread of infections. The comparatively high survival rate of the Spanish Catholics was perceived as a judgment from God.

The most richly rewarded and largest of the *encomenderos*, the new feudal ruling class, was Cortés himself. Upon his return to Spain in 1528, with many rich gifts and examples of the wealth of the new land, Cortés hoped to so impress the king, Charles I, that he would be made a duke and the governor of New Spain. When this did not occur he felt slighted, even though he was allowed to choose 22 of the richest towns and 23,000 natives as his personal vassals. This allowed him to become the wealthiest of the men who conquered the country of Mexico for the Spanish crown. But the king's fear that Cortés might seize Mexico for himself led to his being recalled to Spain, and he eventually died in greatly reduced circumstances, on his way to catch the ship for a final return to Mexico.

The first official government that Spain installed was a legislative court called the *audiencia*. This group of three appointed judges were the official rulers of Mexico from 1527 until the arrival of the first Viceroy, Don Antonio de Mendoza in 1535. The *audiencia* did a great deal of harm to the country through their mismanagement, graft, and corruption. The President of this three-man body was a judge named Nuño de Guzmán; he was eventually arrested and held by the courts in Spain until his death.

Prior to his capture, and knowing that he was going to be arrested, Guzmán led an expedition to conquer the western area of Mexico. While his brutality and cruelty were extreme, he did succeed in bringing a large area to the west and north of the Valley of Mexico under the control of the crown. This area, including Jalisco, was isolated from the rest of the country and was for a while an administrative territory separate from Mexico, called 'New Galicia.' Its capital was Guadalajara.

The economy of New Spain was controlled by representatives of the crown, with many taxes and restrictions imposed upon the people for the profit of the mother country. At this time, European monarchies considered that the sole purpose of distant colonies was to bring treasure into the 'mother country.' Many items which could have been easily manufactured or grown in the colony were forbidden for fear that they would compete with Spanish merchants and markets. For example, wine and olive oil, staples of the Spanish diet, had to be imported from Spain.

The Roman Catholic Church played a vital role in integrating the subjugated native peoples into the society of New Spain. While the bringing of Christianity to the natives helped Spaniards to justify their imperial expansion as a 'Great Crusade,' Catholic priests tended to be more sympathetic to the Indians, more prepared to appreciate their cosmological outlooks and to learn their languages. They often tried to defend the Indians against oppression by the government or by powerful individuals.

Mining and agriculture were the mainstays of the Mexican economy. The mines were often in areas where the Indians had not been pacified, and the pack or wagon trains were liable to be attacked. These dangerous trails led to the establishment of farms and cattle ranches close to the mines. Over time, these grew into the massive *haciendas* and *ranchos* of the nineteenth century. Over a 300-year period, from the early 1600s to the early 1900s, the families of the early Spanish settlers grew very wealthy; some owned millions of hectares of land.

From the time of the conquest, the Spanish had received gifts of women and girls from the Indian chieftains, or had simply taken them to serve as maids and bedmates. There were only six women of Spanish blood in all of Mexico at the time of the defeat of the Aztecs. A few Spanish women emigrated to Mexico to be with their husbands, but generally the Spanish who came were males. The arrival of entire families from Europe, so important in the colonization of British North America, was comparatively rare in Mexico. Today, at most 15 percent of Mexico's population are considered to be of purely European descent, and many of those are descendants of nineteenth-century arrivals.

People of mixed Spanish and Indian descent came to be classified by their skin tone and cultural training. Those who displayed more of the Indian traits were called *mestizo*; those with a more European appearance and education were called *criollos* (creoles). As the years passed and more colonists came from Spain, the mixing of strains became more prevalent, and eventually led to 16 different popular classifications of racial status based on skin color, the lowest stratum of society being the natives and those imported as Negro slaves. Moving up the social ladder, one encountered an increasingly lighter skin tone, with the highest social group being the *peninsulares*, Spaniards who were born in Spain and emigrated to Mexico as bureaucrats for the Crown. Today, most Mexicans are described as *mestizos*, though their ancestry is more heavily Indian than European.

The Evolution of *'Mezcal* Wine'

The Spanish conquerors soon took to the *agave* in all its uses. In his *History of the Indians of New Spain* (1541), Father Antonio Toribio of Benavente-Motolino talks of how the Spanish liked slices of the well-cooked heads of the *maguey* "more than candied-citron."

The Spanish enjoyed *pulque,* but they soon began to look for something a little stronger than the native beverage. With the exception of *pulque*, all alcoholic beverages had to be imported from Spain and were heavily taxed by the royal government. Later, the sugar plantations were set up on the islands of the Caribbean and rum production began, but the Spanish were in Mexico for 50 years before Caribbean rum became widely available.

As supplements to the beverage market, beer was brewed in Mexico as early as 1544, and *pulque* was made and consumed on a regular basis. Distillation had also been introduced into the area by the Spanish conquerors early on, and some manufacture of the product known as *'mezcal* wine' was begun in the period immediately after the conquest. But all other spirits had to be imported through the Spanish factors and were taxed by the Crown.

While the exact date of the introduction of distillation is unknown, it probably occurred in the 1520s. The way that the spirit *mezcal* is produced today is probably very similar to the way that all of the *'mezcal* wines' were produced then. The *agave* was cooked over wood fires, or baked in underground ovens, milled by pounding with wooden mallets to squeeze the juice from the fiber, and distilled in clay pots, only once, over wood fires. The more modern production of *mezcal* still includes the cooking and distillation over burning wood, and this imparts a taste of wood smoke to the modern spirit.

The evolution of what was to become tequila was gradual. *Mezcal* wine was produced all over the country from many different types of *agave*. Production in the area around Tequila village probably began on a small scale during the sixteenth or seventeenth century. It was certainly well established in the early eighteenth century.

In 1608, the Royal Governor of New Galicia, Juan de Villela, imposed the first taxes on *mezcal* wine. In 1636, Don Juan Canseco y Quiñones, Governor of New Galicia, authorized the distillation and manufacture of *mezcal* wine—apparently he believed that this would be healthier for the Indians than *pulque*. This move allowed the government to control the quality of the spirit and made it easier to collect taxes. Communications were evidently a little slow back then, since the decree was ratified by Charles II in 1671, a delay of only 35 years.

In 1656, the community of Tequila was elevated to the status of a village and called by the name of La Torre Argus De Ulloa y Chavez, the name of the then Governor of New Galicia.

Writing in 1742, Don Matias de la Mota y Padilla, in his *History of the Conquest of New Galicia*, mentions the "monopolies of coconut wine and *mezcal*." He also speaks of the Indians' preference for *mezcal* over *pulque*, because of *mezcal*'s strength and flavor.

The production of alcoholic beverages continued apace as the economy grew; in 1786–89, sales of *pulque* accounted for a large portion of the colony's payments to the Crown. The tobacco monopoly contributed the largest amount, 16,000,000 pesos, but the *pulque* monopoly added 3,500,000 pesos. The production of *mezcal* wine was forbidden by the crown in 1785, hoping to increase the importation of wines and spirits from Spain. But the people who could afford to drink the imports were far fewer than those who could afford the local spirit, so the *mezcal* wine trade went underground for a while. There was a loss of tax revenue, and the import trade did not increase enough to cover the losses. When Charles III died in 1792, the new king, Ferdinand IV, lifted the ban on spirit production in Mexico. He also granted a license to produce *mezcal* wine to one Jose Maria Guadalupe Cuervo, in 1795, and from that time we have an unbroken chain of records attesting to the continuing production of the beverage that was to evolve into tequila.

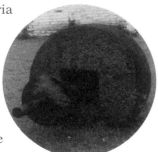

Prior to the granting of the license, Jose Maria Guadalupe's father, Jose Antonio de Cuervo, had purchased some land, the Hacienda de Cuisillos, in 1758. This property had been given to one Vicente de Saldivar by a land grant from

At Centinela, a ten-ton stone wheel used long ago for crushing agave

the Audencia de Guadalajara, on the 3rd of June, 1573, and passed down through heirs until purchased by Sr. Cuervo. The property had a distillery already present when it was purchased, and we can presume that some *mezcal* wine was made there. In combination with the property that his father had purchased and some land belonging to his brother, on which were grown large numbers of *agave*, Jose Maria began production of *mezcal* wine which was a close ancestor of tequila.

This arrangement proved to be quite a profitable venture for both the Crown and Sr. Cuervo. Ten years later, he was able to declare himself the owner of the distillery, his family house, and twelve fields planted with hundreds of thousands of *agave* plants, mostly the varieties *chinos azules* and *manolargo*. At that time, he claimed to be producing 4,000 barrels or about 800,000 liters of *mezcal* wine per year.

After his death in 1812, all of his property passed to his children, Jose Ignacio Faustino Cuervo and Maria Magdalena de Cuervo. Maria married one Vicente Albino Rojas and offered all of her goods and chattels to him. Rojas already owned other distilleries and was a very proud man who could not stand having the distillery named 'Taberna de Cuervo.' He changed the name to 'La Rojeña,' increased production, and began exporting his product to fairs and fiestas as far away as Aguascalientes, Zacatecas, and San Luis Potosí. In the mid-1800s, La Rojeña was the most respected of the distilleries in Tequila and had three million *agave* plants under cultivation.

During this period, the distilleries were set up in a manner similar to the brew-pubs of today. They had a tavern on the grounds of the distillery which served the locals and exported varying amounts of tequila to different areas close by. Tequila at this time was sold only in barrels and not bottled, though some of the patrons brought their own bottles for filling (a practice still followed today). Since the largest city in the area was Guadalajara, that city was responsible for most of the consumption of the local product in the early days.

Many others were also building new distilleries and going into the business of making and selling *mezcal* wine during the 1800s. In the first decade, Father Mariano Ramirez, started a distillery that disappeared about 1850. Between 1810 and 1820, three other distilleries were founded in Tequila, by José Maria Zamudio, Esteban Mayoral, and José Maria Ballesteros. All three distilleries disappeared during the middle of the nineteenth century. In the 1820s Justo Casteñeda started a company that joined with Don Felix López and disappeared about 1850.

Not all of the new enterprises were failures. In 1805, Sr. Jose Maria Casteñeda founded a distillery which he named 'La Cruz'. In 1835, his son, Cruz Casteñeda, inherited the business, and in 1850, joined with Don Felix Vargas, who owned another *taberna*. They then made the two companies into one. In 1862, Don Felix's brother Rafael acquired the company, and in 1869, passed it to Don Andrés Martinez Caras. In this same year, it was sold to Don Felix López, who, in 1872 sold it to a Sr. Justo Rufino Flores.

In 1873, the distillery was resold to Don Cenobio Sauza, who renamed it 'La Perseverancia'. It has remained in the hands of the Sauza family until today, though a part of the business was sold to the Spanish corporation Pedro Domecq in the 1970s. It is still the main fabrication plant for 'Tequila Sauza,' though it has been rebuilt and modernized many times.

Another distillery, 'San Martin,' was started in the 1830s by José Antonio Gómez Cuervo. He served as Governor of the state of Jalisco in 1867–68, and the distillery at Hacienda San Martin became the property of Vicente Orendain in 1889. He immediately sold it to Don Cenobio Sauza.

During the years between the purchase of his first distillery in 1873 and the turn of the century, Don Cenobio Sauza purchased no less than fourteen other distilleries, plus numerous fields of *agave*, and many houses in the city of Guadalajara.

Mexican Independence

The revolution against Spain began in 1810 and lasted for eleven years. The first leader of the rebels was a priest named Miguel Hidalgo y Costilla, whose proclamation *El Grito de Dolores* ('the cry of Dolores') of 16th September, 1810, is the occasion now celebrated as Mexican Independence Day. After almost a year of fighting, Hidalgo was captured by the Spanish. He was executed by firing squad at dawn on the 31st of July, 1811. Following his death, the leadership role of the independence movement fell to one José María Morelos y Pavon, another priest.

After almost surrounding Mexico City, the rebels lost a number of battles, and Morelos was captured in the fall of 1815, defrocked, and executed by firing squad. The revolution slowed for lack of dynamic leadership and fell into a guerrilla mode, with the rebels able to strike against the Spanish only on rare occasions.

Actual independence was the achievement of upper-crust *criollos* who feared the advance of liberal constitutionalism in Spain itself. With the King's giving in to demands for personal freedom and civil rights in Spain, the *criollos* in Mexico judged that the time was right to support the bid for independence. Instead of fighting each other, the armies of the royalists and the republicans, under Augustín de Iturbide and Vicente Guerrero, united under the 'three guarantees' (independence, union of all races, and Roman Catholicism).

At first, newly independent Mexico was an 'empire,' with Iturbide as emperor, but a military revolt led to his ouster, and a republic was proclaimed by General Antonio López de Santa Anna Perez de Lebron, better known to the world merely as 'Santa Anna.' After switching sides in 1821, and helping in the ejection of the Spanish Crown from Mexico, Santa Anna seemed to be involved in most of the military conflicts of the developing country, usually switching sides and ending up on the winning side.

From the beginning of independence until 1876, the presidency of Mexico changed hands 36 times, the average term being seven and a half months, the shortest term being about six hours. Santa Anna himself held the office on eleven different occasions. In 1836, he marched into Texas (recognized by the U.S. as a Mexican possession) to quell a rebellion by settlers from the U.S., and was twice victorious, at the Alamo and then at Goliad. The execution of Texan prisoners on orders from Santa Anna resulted in a public outcry in the United States, and men and supplies were rushed to help the rebels. General Sam Houston caught the forces of Santa Anna by surprise and routed them at San Jacinto. Santa Anna was taken prisoner, shipped to Washington for an interview with President Jackson, and then returned to Mexico.

Texas became an independent republic, but was annexed by the United States in 1845. Furious Mexican reaction to U.S. territorial expansion led to war, the outcome of which was foreordained and disastrous for Mexico. Besides confirming Mexico's loss of Texas (which included Oklahoma and portions of Kansas, Colorado, and New Mexico), the area seized by the United States included the rest of New Mexico, California, what is now Arizona, and portions of Nevada and Utah. Mexico was reduced in size by half of its total land area.

One event during the rule of Santa Anna gives some insight into his megalomaniacal ways. In a battle against an invasion of Veracruz by the French in 1838, Santa Anna had his horse shot from under him and was severely wounded in the left leg, resulting in its amputation below the knee. After returning to power, Santa Anna issued a proclamation in the fall of 1842, ordering that his amputated leg be given a state burial. The funeral was attended by the Legislature of Mexico, and amid speeches, a parade of cadets from Chapultepec castle, and band music, the leg was placed inside an urn, atop a huge stone pillar, in the Cemetery of Santa Fe, in the heart of Mexico City.

Santa Anna's swan song came when, as president in 1854, he sold a large chunk of territory in southern Arizona and New Mexico to the United States for $10,000,000. This 'Gadsden Purchase' was motivated in the U.S. by the desire for a southern transcontinental railroad. The sale of Mexican territory, following the loss of so much territory in war with the U.S., so outraged Mexican patriotic sensibilities that the unprincipled Santa Anna was never again called on to save the Republic.

The next major conflict in Mexico was called the War of Reform. Mainly between the traditional political opposites, the liberals and the conservatives, this conflict also involved problems between the constitution and the Church. The fighting began in 1858 and lasted three years, culminating in victory for the liberals and the installation of Benito Juárez as president in 1861.

Exiled Mexican conservatives enlisted the support of the French emperor, Louis Napoleon (Napoleon III), for an invasion of Mexico to restore the monarchy. Louis Napoleon wanted to set up a 'Latin League,' uniting the Mediterranean countries and Spanish and Portuguese America. The term 'Latin America' derives from this idea.

The French invasion could never have occurred but for the fact that the United States was embroiled in a war of its own, the Civil War. If the American conflict had not been in progress, the Europeans would never have attempted such an invasion, for the U.S. would not have tolerated this incursion on the American Continent. While the United States government could not supply troops to aid in the coming battles, they did allow the out-of-power Mexican resistance to purchase arms and ammunition to carry on the fight against the invaders.

Mexico was invaded by the military forces of France, Britain, and Spain, but Britain and Spain soon withdrew from the alliance. French troops marched on Mexico City, but were halted at Puebla on 5th May, 1862—the origin of the *Cinco de Mayo* holiday. A year later, a reinforced French army again attacked Puebla and, after a siege of two months and reduction of the city to rubble, Puebla surrendered. The French occupied Mexico City, and installed as emperor of Mexico the Austrian Archduke Ferdinand Maximilian.

Maximilan turned out to be a moderate constitutionalist, so he lost the backing of the church and the army. But he also declared the republican guerrillas, and all who assisted them, bandits to be executed, thus losing any support he might have had from the liberal republicans.

With the end of the American Civil War, the U.S. put pressure on Louis Napoleon to withdraw French forces from Mexico, leading to the rapid downfall of Maximilan. He was executed by firing squad, ending all hopes for the restoration of a monarchy in Mexico.

The republic returned to power when Juárez entered Mexico City on July 15th, 1867, in a black coach. After being re-elected for his fourth term, Juárez died of a heart attack on July 19th, 1872, and was succeeded by Sebastián Lerdo de Tejada, who defeated Porfirio Díaz for the Presidency, and, in 1876, decided to run for a second term. But Díaz, a military man, declaring himself against re-election on principle, staged an armed revolt, and assumed the presidency in November 1876.

Porfirio Díaz, originally a poor Indian from Oaxaca, was to remain firmly in control of the direction and fate of Mexico for the next 35 years, until he stepped down on the 25th of May 1911. This exceptional period of peace and stability in Mexican life is known as the *Porfiriato*.

The Emergence of Tequila

For the *mezcal* wine distilleries, the nineteenth century was one of great hazard and insecurity. With all of the revolts and the continuous fighting, it was not at all unusual for a party of men from one side or the other to ride up to a *taberna* and ask the owner for a contribution to the cause. Whether money, men, or *mezcal*, it could be dangerous to refuse when these groups were all heavily armed and ready to kill.

A common sight in the various military camps was wagons loaded with barrels. The barrels were often full of *mezcal* wine, normally confiscated, for the troops of both sides liked to drink tequila mixed with fruit juice. Such confiscation could gravely hurt a small *taberna*. Many of the closures and disappearances mentioned earlier were undoubtedly caused by just such events during the conflicts.

The establishment of the *Porfiriato* steadied the national economy and allowed the distilling companies the stability necessary for growth. The policy of Díaz was to keep all the democratic reform laws on the books, and observe them where convenient, but to operate in practice a highly authoritarian system in which every influential group in society was given a stake. An elite police force, rather like the Texas rangers, the *rurales*, successfully stamped out brigandage. Díaz believed that the Mexican people needed slow preparation for a liberal society, which they were not yet educated to maintain, but the pattern of liberal laws alongside actual authoritarianism and corruption was one that has exercised a grip on Mexico until today.

Many members of the upper crust of society took advantage of the situation to become rich, and the perception was that this enrichment took place at the expense of the people, especially since the rich aped European ways, and tried to appear as un-Mexican as they could. This contributed to the downfall of Díaz in 1911.

As the distillation of various kinds of *mezcal* wine spread throughout the country, there were experiments with different varieties of *agave*, and different combinations of these. Eventually, in one branch of the evolution of *mezcal* wine, the *agave* was narrowed down to the species now called *Agave tequilana Weber*, blue variety. One story is that the final determination that this was the best type of *agave* for producing tequila was made by don Cenobio Sauza in the 1890s. The plant was classified and named by the botanist Weber in 1902.

The first to export outside the country was don Cenobio Sauza, who, on the 7th of August 1873, sent three barrels and six *botijas* (earthenware jars) across the border at El Paso del Norte, today's Ciudad Juárez. In the fiscal year 1873–74, alcoholic beverages made in Mexico were exported to England, Spain, France, the United States, and Nueva Granada. The products included wine, rum, and *mezcal*. The amounts were small. Total value of exported products was only 2,628.50 pesos. The new idea of looking for

*Front gate of Villa Sauza,
home of the Sauza family*

markets outside the country for *mezcal* wine showed the foresight of Cenobio Sauza and opened new vistas for expansion.

Other companies were also arising, and new companies were being founded on a regular basis with exports growing slowly. Twenty-five years later, in 1899, exports of tequila totalled 9,539 kilograms at a value of 3,062 pesos. One year later, exports had grown by a little over 20 percent, the total being 14,030 kilograms of tequila with a value of 5,664 pesos.

While the external market was growing, so was the internal, but, if the numbers can be believed, growth was really erratic. In 1889, production of *mezcal* and tequila in the state of Jalisco totalled 111,535 hectoliters with a value of 1,166,240 pesos. In 1895, production was 68,873 hectoliters, value 1,369,175 pesos. In 1897, 79,317 hectoliters, 1,600,898 pesos. In 1901, 99,441 hectoliters, 1,998,978 pesos. In 1905, a drastic decrease to only 2,023 hectoliters, worth 38,068 pesos. In 1906, a slight recovery to 16,196 hectoliters, valued at 541,950 pesos.

The nature of the distilling industry was transformed during the first decade of the twentieth century. In Jalisco between 1900 and 1910, the number of distilleries making *aguardiente*, or alcohol made from sugarcane, fell from 38 to 27, whereas the number of distilleries producing *mezcal* wine rose from 68 to 87.

The Mexican Revolution

During the first portion of his time in power, Díaz held to his original reason for throwing out Lerdo, the no re-election policy. So,

61

after his first term, he stepped aside peacefully and threw his support to his good friend and ally, Manuel González, a renowned military man and his secretary of war—also the great-grandfather of the current owners and operators of the distillery, La Gonzáleña. González won easily and made no changes in the Díaz policies.

When Díaz again ran for the presidency in 1884, he swept to a landslide victory and, setting aside his prior conditions of no re-election, remained in the office of president until he was removed in 1911.

A statement by Díaz in 1908, that he would step down in order to help Mexico advance to genuine democracy, was mistakenly interpreted as a promise not to run for re-election in 1910. This stimulated the growing opposition to the *Porfiriato* to mobilize. Armed bands were formed, and clashes with federal troops began in 1910.

The overthrow and expulsion from office of Díaz began another period of instability, with the leader of the victorious rebels, Francisco I. Madero, becoming the leader of the liberal cause. His trials and tribulations just began with the victory over Díaz, however. As he attempted to re-stabilize the country, he alienated many of his former allies, among them the leader of the rebels in Chiapas, Emiliano Zapata.

Over the next ten years, the country returned to the warring ways of the different factions from the previous century. It seemed that everyone was in revolt against the government, no matter who was in charge. At various times, Pancho Villa, Emiliano Zapata, Bernardo Reyes, and Pascual Orozco waged war on the Madero government. Madero's biggest mistake was appointing Victoriano Huerta commander of his government's military. Huerta switched sides and had Madero and his vice-president arrested. They were later assassinated

Huerta managed to secure the presidency, but Zapata in the south and the 'Constitutionalists' in the north, declared themselves to be in revolt. Huerta managed to hold them off for a while, but was unable to get recognition for his regime from the United States. When Woodrow Wilson became U.S. president, he was determined to oust Huerta, and landed U.S. troops in Veracruz.

Huerta resigned the presidency, and the Constitutionalist leader, Venustiano Carranza, called a convention of the disparate anti-Huerta forces to appoint an interim president. The convention dissolved in chaos, with each group setting its own goals and, for the most part, refusing any compromise. Each of the groups went its own way, and the country fell apart. Each group issued its own money and had its own military forces.

Carranza did win the presidency in a special election held in March, 1917. He was still opposed by Zapata and Villa, and in 1919 arranged the murder of Zapata by government troops during a ceremony supposed to honor him. The Carranza government was then attacked by the remaining opposition, and when Carranza fled into the countryside to avoid impending capture, he was killed by one of his own bodyguards in May of 1920. The election of Alvaro Obregón that year marked the decline of violence and the commencement of rebuilding the country.

What emerged from the Mexican revolution was a one-party state, which permitted competing political parties, but rigged things so that the ruling party alone had any possibility of election. After World War II, this party changed its name from the Party of the Mexican Revolution to the Institutional Revolutionary Party (PRI). It is still in power, but has gradually liberalized so that Mexico is coming to approximate a genuine democracy, with a real chance of the PRI's being ejected from power by the voters. Despite some upheavals, the general social life of Mexico has been more stable, for a longer period, since the revolution than at any time since the Spanish conquest. Mexico has been transformed from a predominantly rural and agricultural economy into an overwhelmingly urban and industrial power. Rural Mexico is still there, but it now accounts for less than a quarter of the population.

The Triumph of Tequila

At the start of the twentieth century, the area around the village of Tequila was still the major contributor to the tequila industry, but some new entrepreneurs had begun growing *agave* in the

Highlands around the village of Arandas. The first was Porfirio Torres Pérez, who began growing *agave* there before the turn of the century, and founded his distillery, 'El Centinela,' in 1904.

There has been an enormous expansion of tequila output, and mechanization has also affected the industry. While many of the manufacturing stages of tequila are still performed by hand, many more have been either mechanized or eliminated. The methods of cooking the *agave* has moved from ovens to auto-claves. The crushing and juice extraction methods have moved from beating the *agave* with mallets, to the *tahona,* and then to mechanical grinders.

Scientific advances which resulted in the introduction of com-mercial yeasts and chemical accelerators to hasten the fermenta-tion process have reduced costs but have also changed the taste of the tequila. Other innovations have been made for health and safety reasons.

The first of the organizations designed to advance the tequila industry was founded in 1928, but it dissolved in arguments and bickering. Another group was founded in 1933, and it survived for a longer period of time. With some changes in makeup, members, and rules, *La Cámara Regional de la Industria Tequilera* is still much the same as that organization.

The Lisbon Accord of 1958 allowed the signatory countries to designate certain products as coming from specific points of ori-gin within those countries. Such products as cognac, scotch whisky, and American bourbon were protected by this recogni-tion, so it was expected the same would apply to tequila. But Mexico never became a signatory of this treaty, since at the time of the signing, there was a large distillery in northern Mexico which was making a product they called 'bourbon.' For political reasons it was judged that this company was too important to close in order to come into compliance with the requirements for signing. A separate agreement was later signed with the U.S. and the distillery closed, but it was too late for Mexico to sign the Lisbon Accord. International agreement on recognition of tequila as coming exclusively from the designated areas within Mexico had to wait until 1996.

The registering of the industry with SECOFI and the founda-tion of the first Norm for Tequila in 1947 played a large part in the stabilization of industry conditions. The Norm is updated and modified every few years, the last major modification taking place in 1978, with a change in the requirements for *mixto* in 1995.

The *Consejo Regulador del Tequila, A.C.,* the Tequila Regulatory Council, opened for business in May of 1994. All regulatory rights have been assigned to this organization, and the *Consejo* appears to be leading the industry in a more outward-looking direction, designed to improve the image of tequila and gain recognition on the international scene.

All of these factors have played a large part in the evolution of the tequila industry, but none more than the decision, in the 1930s, to adulterate tequila with sugars other than those from the *agave*. This fateful step may, however, be gradually reversed in the future.

The introduction of individual bottles around the turn of the century helped increase sales in Mexico, especially the flat bottle with curved sides which fit so well into the large pockets of the baggy work trousers that were worn at that time.

Another very important influence on the growth of the tequila industry was its presentation in the Mexican media of the 1930s, 1940s, and 1950s. During the *Porfiriato*, imported wines and liquors had been the rage. Most of the aristocrats of the 600 families who controlled Mexico at that time (and still retain some influence) considered the native Mexican beverage less chic than imported wines and spirits.

Mexican movies helped to reverse this attitude by instilling national pride. The portrayal of the heroic *ranchero* usually showed him, at some point in the picture, enjoying the camaraderie of his friends and neighbors, with a glass or bottle of tequila. This glamorization of the native product was effective, and consumption increased. Even the tragic figure of *film noir* was seen in a more positive light when drinking tequila.

But the most important factor in the growth of the tequila industry in the last 40 years has been the growing popularity in the United States of the margarita cocktail, which I discuss in Chapter 9. While the precise origins of this cocktail formula are controversial, some mixture of *mezcal* wine with fruit juice has been popular on both sides in Mexico's many civil conflicts over the past couple of centuries.

65

4

A Bird's Eye View of Tequila Country

Mexico—or the United Mexican States, to give the country its official name—comprises 31 states and one federal district which encompasses the capital, Mexico City, the world's most populous city. Mexico's land area is about one-fifth that of the United States, but its population is rapidly approaching one-half, and is expected to overtake the U.S. in the first half of the twenty first century.

In most countries, including Europe and the U.S., anything sold under the name 'tequila' can legally be made only in Mexico, and under Mexican law can only be made in certain limited areas within the country (the precise delineation of these areas is given in Appendix E).

The heartland of tequila production is the western state of Jalisco (pronounced 'Haleesco'). Tequila may be produced anywhere within Jalisco, a state which includes Mexico's second largest city, Guadalajara, the village of Tequila, and the popular coastal resort of Puerto Vallarta.

Seven states border Jalisco, and tequila may be produced in limited areas within three of these states: Nayarit, Guanajuato, and Michoacán, though currently only one distillery operates in Guanajuato, none in Nayarit or Michoacán.

Finally tequila may be produced in a limited area in the state of Tamaulipas, far away from Jalisco in the Northeast of Mexico. How tequila came to be manufactured there is a story in itself, recounted in Chapter 5 under Distillery #44. La Gonzáleña is the only distillery in Tamaulipas which produces tequila.

The state of Jalisco begins at the Pacific Ocean on the west and rises into the Sierra Madre Occidental mountains as you travel east. The state capital, Guadalajara, is located at 5,092 feet above sea level and sits in a bowl-like valley surrounded by higher peaks. The highest of the mountains approaches 9,500 feet, with the Highlands to the north and east of Guadalajara forming a plateau, with an average elevation of approximately 7,500 feet (this is significant because the main concentration of *agave* is now grown in this region).

Jalisco has a wide variety of economic activities, including mining, manufacturing, agriculture, and arts and crafts. Tlaquepaque, a suburb of Guadalajara, is well known for its stores and its workshops producing ceramics, wooden artifacts, jewelry, copperware, glassware of many kinds, and many other forms of decorative art. Jalisco is the leading producer within Mexico of many important agricultural products, including corn and beans, as well as of the blue *agave*. As you travel around Jalisco, you can easily observe the large tracts of land set aside for *agave* farming.

Within Jalisco, the tequila factories are primarily located in two geographic areas: the Tequila village area, to the west of Guadalajara, comprising the villages of Tequila, Amatitán, Arenal, Antonio Escobedo, and Santo Tomas; and the Highlands area, to the east, which has the villages of Arandas, Atotonilco el Alto, Capilla de Guadalupe, Jesus Maria, Tepatitlan, Tesistan, Tototlan, and Zapotlanejo. There are also two distilleries in Guadalajara itself, and a new distillery at Ciudad Guzmán in the south of Jalisco.

Before giving a brief account of all these distilleries, I must issue a warning. *Please do not go to Jalisco expecting to make a tour of tequila distilleries,* in the way that you would in Scotland or Kentucky. You can, of course, see and photograph the distilleries from outside, and this in itself will make a fascinating trip

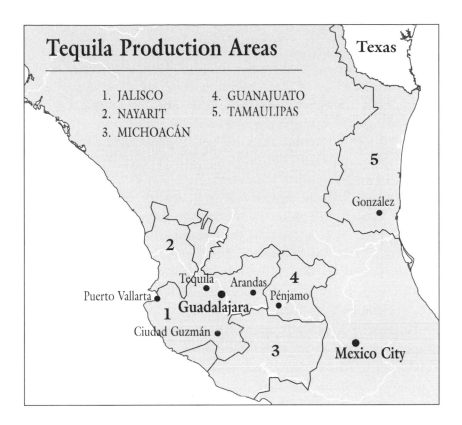

Tequila Production Areas

1. JALISCO
2. NAYARIT
3. MICHOACÁN
4. GUANAJUATO
5. TAMAULIPAS

Texas

5

González

2

Tequila   Arandas   4
Puerto Vallarta   Guadalajara   Pénjamo
1
Ciudad Guzmán

3   Mexico City

through an enchanting part of Mexico. But in many cases you will not be permitted inside the distillery.

Although some distillery staff will be glad to show you around, this accommodating policy is something quite new and exceptional in Mexico, and you should not be surprised if other distillery managements are frankly hostile to the idea. This is still a comparatively poor country, and these are, in many cases, essentially small, struggling factories, whose managers would no more think of showing strangers around, on a regular basis, than they would in factories producing stoves or car batteries.

The owners and managers do not welcome the interruption of work and the distraction presented by groups of people asking questions in a foreign language, not to mention the liability problem, for these are often cramped and dangerous places. Furthermore, there is, here and there, a certain amount of secretiveness and suspicion of anyone who wants to find out what goes on in the distilleries. Are these enquirers snoopers working for competitors, or are they government spies looking for tax or regulatory violations? A number of distillery companies were opposed to the idea of being mentioned in this book, and others, while not actively resisting it, would do nothing to help, even to the extent of answering a few questions.

Eventually, no doubt, attitudes will change, as the distilleries come to see the public relations benefits, and even the immediate marketing opportunities, in encouraging visitors. There will one day be a 'tequila trail' comparable to Scotland's highly successful Whisky Trail. But, to date, distilleries where you can expect anything approaching a 'tour' in the American sense are still in a minority. I mention some of these exceptional distilleries in Chapter 5, and, if you really want to push the envelope, you can enquire in Guadalajara—the great majority of distillery companies maintain offices there.

We now move to a brief survey of each distillery in its geographic context. Let me explain three numbers you will find associated with distilleries. In Chapter 5 I have listed all the companies alphabetically, and numbered them from #1 to #46. So 'Distillery #—' refers to my own listing in Chapter 5 of this book, a listing which is, incidentally, currently the only complete listing of operational tequila distilleries available anywhere. Each company is required by Mexican law to place a recognition number, called a NOM, on the label or bottle, to allow instant determination of liability. A new number, also now being placed on tequila products, is the DOT, which means 'Denomination of Origin, Tequila'. Many companies have this number, but some do not. The letters 'S.A.' or 'S.A. de C.V.,' which follow the company names in Mexico, refer to incorporation, so they are roughly similar to the 'Inc.' or 'Co.' at the end of American company names.

Distilleries near Tequila Village

The oldest distillery companies are located in the production area around the village of Tequila, and it is here that the spirit began. The name of the drink is taken from the name of the village. There are at least six stories explaining how the village got its name, and I will here mention the two most likely. One is that the name derives from an indigenous tribe known as *tecuilas* who lived on the sides of the volcano now called Tequila mountain. Another possibility is that 'tequila' derives from a combination of two Náhuatl words, *tequitl*, meaning work or employment, and *tlan*, which means place.

Tequila village sits at the base of a volcanic cinder cone which the locals call Tequila Mountain. The mountain rises about 3,500 feet above the surrounding terrain at 9,580 feet above sea level and dominates the scenic area for miles. The surrounding area is rolling hills, periodically separated by small valleys. These valleys are full of fields of *agave* and other crops, mainly corn, but including beans and citrus fruits. There are spectacular panoramic views, with the mountains soaring above the valleys and everything covered in green vegetation.

In the Tequila village region, the distillery farthest west is Distillery #14, 'Hacienda Santo Tomas,' located just outside the town of Hostotipaquillo, and owned and operated by Industralización y Desarrollo, Santo Tomas, S.A. (NOM #740). This distillery produces the tequila 'Los Valientes.' It has its own off-ramp from the *autopista* (freeway toll road, MX 15) and has been standing for well over 200 years, though for part of that time it was abandoned and declined into a near-ruin.

Travelling east, we come to the main production center for tequila, the village of Tequila itself. Tequila is on the *Carretera*

Above the entrance gate at El Llano, where Tequila Arette is produced

Front of the visitors' center at La Rojeña in Tequila village

Internacional highway, and contains eleven distilleries, with twelve company names credited to them. Most of the larger companies producing bulk *mixto* for export are located here.

Distillery #7 is 'El Llano,' owned and operated by Destiladora Azteca de Jalisco, S.A. de C.V. (NOM #1109; DOT #98), which belongs to two sons of one of the brothers Orendain. El Llano produces 'Tequila Arette', a 100 percent *agave* product available only in Mexico.

Distillery #16, 'La Martineña,' is currently involved in a legal dispute, with the following two companies battling for possession: Destiladora de Occidente, S.A. de C.V. (NOM #1173; DOT #108) and J. Jesus Reyes Cortes, S.A. (NOM #856 and NOM #1154; DOT #114). Occidente is also building a new distillery in the village of La Laja, a suburb of Zapotlanejo.

The distillery 'La Guarreña' (#17) is owned and operated by Jorge Salles Cuervo y Succesores, S.A. de C.V. (NOM #1108; DOT #87). It produces only *mixto* under the label 'Tequileño,' all of which is consumed in Mexico.

Founded in 1992, 'La Cofradia' (#19), is owned and operated by La Cofradia, S.A. de C.V., (NOM #1137; DOT #111), which produces both *mixto* and *cien por ciento de agave* tequila.

'La Areñita' (#21), owned and operated by the company Productores Especiales de Tequila, S.A. de C.V. (NOM #1196), was inactive in 1996, and produced only 15,049 liters in 1995. There are rumors that this company and J. Jesus Reyes Cortes (#16) may be contemplating a merger.

The largest of the bulk exporters is 'La Rojeña' (Distillery #27), owned and operated by Tequila Cuervo La Rojeña, S.A. de C.V. (NOM #1104). Cuervo accounts for more than 35 percent of the total industry output of bulk *mixto*. Their tequila is made for a number of different brands, all of which are owned by the liquor conglomerate Grand Metropolitan of Great Britain, which employs various subsidiaries such as Heublein Imports and Carillon Imports to bring the tequila into the United States.

'Santa Cruz' distillery (#29) is owned and operated by Tequila Eucario Gonzalez, S.A. de C.V. (NOM #1113; DOT #109). This company changed ownership in 1994 and is now operating at a reduced level of export, producing both *mixto* and 100 percent *agave* tequilas.

The fourth largest manufacturer of tequila is 'La Mexicana' (Distillery #31), owned and operated by Tequila Orendain De Jalisco, S.A. de C.V. (NOM #1110; DOT #95). This parent company has a second NOM, #1172, which is registered to their other totally owned company, Compania Orendain, S.A. de C.V. (Distillery #5). This is why there are twelve companies in this locality, but only eleven distilleries.

'La Perseverancia' (Distillery #35) is owned and operated by the second largest of the tequila exporters Tequila Sauza, S.A. de C.V., (NOM #1102; DOT #88). It manufactured 16 percent of all *mixto* and 20 percent of all 100 percent *agave* tequila produced in 1995.

The distillery for Tequila Viuda de Romero, S.A. de C.V. (Distillery #41; NOM #1111; DOT #83) has the same name as the parent company and dates from the nineteenth century. It is currently owned by Grupo Cetto, based in Tijuana, and produces both *mixto* and 100 percent *agave* tequilas.

Our final distillery in Tequila itself is #42, 'La Tequileña', owned and operated by the company Tequileña, S.A. de C.V.

(NOM #1146; DOT #102), which is owned, in turn, by a major *agave*-growing company named 'Grupo Foncer,' whose offices are in Guadalajara. This company produces both types of tequila.

The next village in the Tequila village region which produces tequila is Amatitán, a small village about ten kilometers east from Tequila in the direction of Guadalajara. It contains two distilleries. 'La Regional' (#12), owned and operated by Empresa Ejidal Tequilera Amatitán, S.A., (NOM #1121; DOT #117), a co-operative distillery which makes tequila for its members and also sells to certain outside tequila bottlers and rectifiers in Mexico.

The other distillery in Amatitán is the 'Ex-Hacienda San Jose del Refugio' (#30), the ancestral home of the Romo de la Peña family, who own and operate the company Tequila Herradura. S.A. de C.V. (NOM #1119), the largest company that produces the full spectrum of only 100 percent *agave* tequilas. It has a wide market in the United States.

There is a second company name which is a totally-owned subsidiary of Herradura, Destilados de Agave, S.A. de C.V. (Distillery #10; NOM #1359), which is now being used to market the brand name 'El Jimador.' All of this tequila is made at the Ex-Hacienda San Jose del Refugio. The name was changed from Hacienda to Ex-Hacienda in 1996 for tax purposes.

Between the villages of Amatitán and Arenal is a distillery which uses both villages for its company address. This company is J. Jesús Partida Melendez (Distillery #15; NOM #1258). It produces the tequila labelled 'Tres Mujeres'.

Another ten kilometers down the Carretera Internacional from Amatitán towards Guadalajara is the village of Arenal, which contains three distilleries. The first is 'La Fortuna' (#11), a very small distillery first opened around the turn of the century, formerly owned by the company Destiladora de Arenal, now owned and operated by the company, Elaboradora y Procesadora de Agave y sus Derivados, S.A. de C.V. (NOM #1141) This company makes only 100 percent *agave* tequila and is currently exporting its total output to France.

The second Arenal company is 'El Cascahuin' (#23), owned and operated by the company Tequila Cascahuin, S.A. de C.V. (NOM #1123; DOT #106) This company makes and exports

Distilleries by Area and Town

Tequila area

Amatitán
#10 Destilados de Agave
#12 Empresa Ejidal Tequilera Amatilán
#22 Tequila Cabillito Cerrero
#30 Tequila Herradura

Antonio Escobedo
#33 Tequila Santa Fe

Arenal
#11 Elab. y Prod. de Agave y sus Deriv.
#15 J. Jesus Partida Melendez
#23 Tequila Cascahuin
#32 Tequila Parreñita

Santo Tomas
#14 Indus. y Dillo. Santo Tomas

Tequila
#5   Compañia Orendain
#7   Destiladora Azteca de Jalisco
#16 J. Jesus Reyes Cortes
#17 Jorge Salles Cuervo
#19 La Cofradia
#21 Productos Especiales de Tequila
#27 Tequila Cuervo La Rojeña
#29 Tequila Eucario González
#32 Tequila Orendain de Jalisco
#35 Tequila Sauza
#41 Tequila Viuda de Romero
#42 Tequileña

Guadalajara
#9   Destiladora González González
#36 Tequilas del Señor

Distillery #44 La Gonzáleña is located in the state of Tamaulipas.
Distillery #37 Tequila Sierra Brava had not finished their *fábrica* by January 1997.

Highlands area

Arandas
#13 Fáb. de Agard. de Agave
#18 La Arandina
#25 Tequila Cazadores
#26 Tequila Centinela
#39 Tequila Tapatio
#46 Tequilera Rustica de Arandas

Atotonilco el Alto
#28 Tequila El Viejito
#38 Tequila Siete Leguas
#40 Tequila Tres Magueyes

Capilla de Guadalupe
#2   Agroindustrias Guadalajara

Ciudad Guzmán
#3   Agroindustrias Santa Clara

Jesus Maria
#1   Agave Tequilana Prod. y Com.
#24 Tequila Catador Alteño

Tepatitlan
#34 Tequila San Matias de Jalisco

Tesistan
#45 Tequila Newton e Hijos

Tototlan
#20 La Madrileña

Zapotlanejo
#4   Casa Cuervo
#6   Corporación Ansan
#8   Destiladora de Occidente

Pénjamo, Guananjuato
#43 Tequilero Corralejo

mixto, but received its license to make 100 percent *agave* tequila in 1996.

The third distillery in Arenal is 'La Parreñita (#32), owned and operated by the company Tequila La Parreñita, S.A. de C.V. (NOM #1115; DOT #105), which produces both *mixto* and 100 percent *agave* tequila.

The last distillery in the 'Tequila' area is Distillery #34, located southwest of the town of Tequila, in the village of Antonio Escobedo. It is owned and operated by Tequila Santa Fe, S.A. de C.V. (NOM #1112; DOT #112), a company formed in 1992 which produces both *mixto* and 100 percent *agave* tequila.

Two distilleries are located in the city of Guadalajara itself: Tequilas del Señor (#36; NOM #1124; DOT #97) and González González (#9; NOM #113). Both produce *mixto* and 100 percent *agave* tequila.

Distilleries in the Highlands of Jalisco

A distillery which I have included in the 'Highlands' area, though it is located just to the north and a little west of Guadalajara, is Distillery #45, owned and operated by Tequilera Newton e Hijos, S.A. de C.V. (NOM #1173; DOT #115). It's in the village of Tesistan. It could be included in either of the two areas, but I have placed it in the Highlands.

Besides that village, there are seven villages in the Highlands area which contain tequila manufacturing facilities. They are Arandas, Atotonilco el Alto, Capilla de Guadalupe, Jesus Maria, Tepatitlan, Tototlan, and Zapotlanejo. The town with the most distilleries is Arandas, which has six.

The first of these is a company that was authorized to make tequila in 1996, Fábrica de Aguardientes de Agave la Mexicana, S.A. de C.V. (Distillery #13; NOM #1333; DOT #124).

The second company in Arandas is 'La Arandina,' owned and operated by the company La Arandina, S.A. de C.V. (Distillery #18; NOM #1131; DOT #100), which makes both *mixto* and 100 percent *agave* tequila.

Next is 'El Gallito', owned and operated by the company Tequila Cazadores de Jalisco, S.A. de C.V. (Distillery #25; NOM

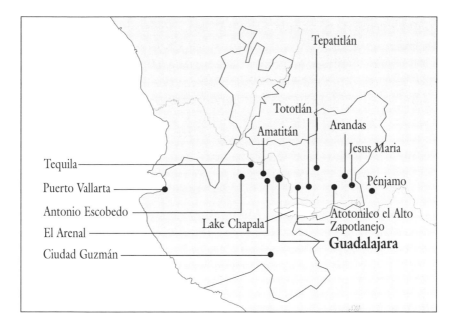

#1128), which produces only a *reposado* tequila of the same name.

Also in Arandas is 'El Centinela' (Distillery #26), owned and operated by Tequila Centinela, S.A. de C.V. (NOM #1140; DOT #86), which produces only 100 percent *agave* tequila.

Then there is 'La Alteña' (Distillery #39), owned and operated by the company Tequila Tapatio, S.A. de C.V. (NOM #1139; DOT #101), one of the most traditional of all the distilleries, and producing only 100 percent *agave* tequila.

Finally in Arandas, there is Distillery #46, the company Tequilera Rustica de Arandas, S.A. de C.V. (NOM #1235), who received their licenses and began production in 1996.

A new distillery is being built in Arandas by Seagram de México. Located on the same road as Cazadores and La Arandina, it is scheduled to begin production in 1997. It will be fairly large, with initial output of around two million liters per year.

Two other companies may be opening facilities in Arandas. The old Cazadores distillery on the main road into town has been sold to another company, and a new facility is nearing completion on the highway leading into town from the west. Neither had applied for its operating license prior to January 1997.

The regulatory council, El Consejo, is also in the process of opening a second office in the town of Arandas.

The next village in importance in the Highlands area is the town of Atotonilco el Alto, located about two kilometers from the main *autopista*, MX80. This village contains three distilling companies. First is the company Tequila El Viejito, S.A. de C.V. (Distillery #28; NOM #1107; DOT #94), which operates two plants, 'El Viejito' and 'El Papagayo', and produces both *mixto* and 100 percent *agave* tequilas.

Second is Tequila Siete Leguas, S.A. de C.V. (Distillery #38; NOM #1120; DOT #105), which also operates two plants and makes only *cien por ciento de agave* tequila. This company makes, bottles, and exports the tequila known in the U.S. as 'Patrón'.

Last is 'La Primavera' (Distillery #40), owned and operated by the company Tequila Tres Magueyes, S.A. de C.V. (NOM #1118; DOT #84), which produces the 100 percent *agave* tequila 'Don Julio,' and used to produce some *mixto* for export. This company now produces only 100 percent *agave* tequilas.

'Satisfactores,' a distillery located in Atotonilco, is now closed due to the death of the owner. This distillery is still fairly complete and previously had production levels in the area of two million liters of *mixto* per year. The estate is currently being settled, but the distillery has reportedly been sold to the children of the previous owner, and could reopen at any time,

The village of Jesus Maria contains two small distilleries. The first, Agave Tequilana Productores y Comercialzadores, S.A. de C.V. (Distillery #1; NOM #1179), opened for business in January of 1995, and is producing only 100 percent *agave* tequila, under the labels 'Oro Azul' and '1921'.

The other is the small 'Rancho Los Ladrillos' (Distillery #24), owned and operated by Tequila Catador Alteño, S.A. (NOM #1105), producing only 100 percent *agave* tequila, a *reposado* labelled 'Tequila Catador.'

The village of Capilla de Guadalupe contains the manufacturing facility for the company Agroindustrias Guadalajara, S.A. de C.V. (Distillery #2; NOM #1068), which makes only 100 percent *agave* tequila and is located about twelve kilometers west of Arandas on the same highway. They began production in October

Behind an agave *field, the big new Seagram distillery in Arandas*

of 1994 and produce four labels, '30-30,' 'Jaliscience,' 'Ambarfino,' and 'El Amo Aceves.'

The village of Tototlan contains the distillery 'La Madrileña, the third largest manufacturer and exporter of tequila. While this company makes both *mixto* and 100 percent *agave* tequila, this is a recent development. Prior to 1995, it made only *mixto*. Owned and operated by La Madrileña, S.A. de C.V. (Distillery #20; NOM #1142; DOT #82), its offices are located in Mexico City.

The village of Tepatitlan contains the distillery 'La Argentina' (#33), owned and operated by Tequila San Matias De Jalisco, S.A. de C.V. (NOM #1103; DOT #93), which manufactures both *mixto* and 100 percent *agave*.

The second Cuervo distillery, 'Los Camachines' (Distillery #4; NOM #1122), is located in Zapotlanejo, and is currently making and exporting the tequila 'Gran Centenario' with Carillon Imports, as a 100 percent *agave* product.

A distillery is also being built in La Laja, a suburb of Zapotlanejo. At the time of the completion of this book, Corporación Ansan, S.A. de C.V. Distillery #6, NOM #1360, is in the construction phase, and production is expected to begin in the spring of 1997. Once in production, they will also probably be making tequila for the company Destiladora de Occidente.

Of the two regions, the 'Highlands' region is about 1,500 feet higher than the Tequila village region and most of the *agave* used for tequila production is now grown in the Highlands. Many people in the industry now say that the *tierra rojo* of the Highlands region and the greater elevation make for better growing conditions.

Whatever the reason, the companies in the Highlands area seem to adhere to the traditional methods of making tequila more closely than those in the Tequila region. The factories in the Tequila region tend to be larger, to use more heavily mechanized processes for manufacture, and to be more geared to the export of bulk *mixto*.

The companies in the Highlands area tend to use more traditional methods of manufacture, some even still using the *tahona*, or stone grinding wheel, to crush the *agave* after cooking and to separate the fiber from the juice. Most use ovens rather than autoclaves to cook the *agave*, and many use their own natural yeast cultures rather than commercial ones.

This is just a tendency, of course. Herradura in Amatitán, in the Tequila area, makes only 100 percent *agave* tequila and has never made any *mixto*. They have been exporting to the U.S. since the 1940s, when Bing Crosby and Phil Harris first discovered this fine tequila and arranged for its distribution north of the border.

And the company La Madrileña, located in the Highlands, has been a major producer and exporter of bulk *mixto* for many years. They only began making 100 percent *agave* tequila in 1995, but have plans for greater expansion in this area of the market.

The general point holds, however. The student or visitor should not be misled by the glamour of the name 'Tequila'. Tequila is the main center for the mechanized production of the least expensive tequilas. The authentic, traditional production methods are most often to be found in the Highlands, to the east.

A new distillery, not completed when this book went to press, is Distillery #3, owned by Agroindustrias Santa Clara de S.P.R. de R.L. (NOM #1384). It's to be found in the village of Ciudad Guzmán, way to the south of all other distilleries in Jalisco.

Another distillery is currently being considered for construction by the company Destilera Porfidio. Rumors say that it too will be located in the south, near Lake Chapala, so perhaps the south of Jalisco will become a new center of tequila production.

A Complete Guide to
Tequila Distilleries

This chapter gives information on all the tequila distillery companies currently operating. I have provided a description, wherever possible, of each company's history, equipment, products, and philosophy, along with personal impressions of my visits to the distilleries.

I have listed the companies in alphabetical order, and numbered them; the numbers are used elsewhere in this book—especially in the tasting notes in Chapter 7 and in the appendixes. Directly under each company name I provide: the NOM of that company, the name of the distillery which makes the tequila, and the DOT number (wherever I could determine these).

Also included are some of the proprietary label names of the distillery companies and cross-references to the companies that import their products into the United States, if applicable (Appendix A is a list of labels). Many of the companies are small and do not export their products. Some do not wish to have anyone outside their locality even be aware that their company exists.

Strictly speaking, this chapter lists distillery companies rather than distilleries, but it is very rare for a tequila distilling company to operate more than one distillery. Where this does occur, it is of course pointed out.

As mentioned in Chapter 4, it is not traditional in Mexico to offer tours of distilleries to the general public, any more than you would expect any other kind of factory to encourage a constant stream of sight-seers. This is changing now, but it remains true that most distilleries will not welcome you if you show up as a tourist. One of the new companies, Tequilera Corralejo, does cater for tourists, and plans to offer tours exhibiting the historical evolution of tequila. This distillery is located in a colonial hacienda. built before 1800 and has been designed from the outset for the accommodation of tourists.

The newly remodeled Tapatio distillery in the village of Arandas has also been designed to allow demonstrations of how tequila is made. This demonstration area will be separate from the normal working area, and located in the front portion of the distillery.

DISTILLERY #1

Agave Tequilana Prod. y Com., S.A. de C.V.

NOM #1179

Founded in March of 1995, this company produces only 100 percent *agave* tequila under the labels 'Oro Azul' and '1921'. The *blanco* has been available since September, 1995. The reposado was released in January of 1996, and the *añejo* in January of 1997.

The distillery is very small, having only ten 5,000-liter fermentation tanks and two stainless steel pot stills. The first-run still has 1,500 liters capacity, and the second still has 750 liters capacity. The company employs all the traditional methods of manufacture, even to the point of using a *tahona,* or stone grinding wheel, to crush and juice the *agave*, and leaving the *agave* fiber in the must until time for distillation.

The company is owned and operated by a brother and sister team, Sr. Juan de Dios López Garibay, production manager and general director, and his sister Señorita Roxana López Garibay, director of administration. They are cousins of the operators of

Distillery #39, Tequila Tapatio, which is owned and operated by the Camarena family.

This company does not currently export its product, which is available only in Mexico, though eventual export was contemplated.

DISTILLERY #2
Agroindustrias Guadalajara, S.A. de C.V.
NOM #1068

This fairly new company, formed in October of 1994, released its first offering of tequila in September of 1995, a 100 percent *agave blanco* under the label of '30-30' (in Spanish, the name is 'Treinta y Treinta'). The company has built a new distillery on the edge of the village Capilla de Guadalupe, in the Highlands of Jalisco. This village is located on the highway to Arandas and seems to have a growing economy, with a new food processing plant as well as the distillery.

My visit to the distillery began by being picked up at the hotel by Horacio Gomez, one of the office managers and a nephew of the managing director. During the drive from Guadalajara, we learned a little about one another. He spoke a little English, was 32 years old with two children, both boys. He had been a loan officer for a bank in Mexico City prior to joining this new company and was excited about the opportunity afforded him by his new job in the tequila industry.

We went to the company office in Capilla de Guadalupe and met his uncle, Heriberto Gomez, president and administrative director of the company. Sr. Gomez speaks very good English and helped me get pictures of 'los jimadores'. One of his associates, Sr. Juan Manuel Trujillo, the treasurer of the company, took me to the *agave* fields to photograph the process of harvesting.

We drove to a *rancho* with a very nice house and yard, plus a house for the caretaker. Along one edge of the yard was a row of *agave* that was the largest that I had yet seen. The central *pencas*, or leaves, were over eight feet high. I asked the variety and was amazed to hear that they were *Agave tequilana Weber, variedad azul*, the same as those used in making tequila. Apparently, the continual watering and fertilization of the lawn has allowed these *agave* to reach unusual proportions. These individual plants are as yet immature, but if harvested upon maturity, each could easily produce a *piña* weighing 200 to 250 kilos, or around 500 pounds.

We drove on to the fields, picking up two workers, one Juan Perez, *el jimador,* and his helper Salvador, on the way to cut the *agave.* The process has been described in Chapter 2, and Juan harvested the plants with impressive facility. The *rancho* is owned by Sr. Trujillo, who has grown *agave* for many years, just recently investing in this new tequila company.

Upon my return to the office, Heriberto drove me to the distillery, about a mile away on the edge of town. The compound is very new and clean, with all of the usual accoutrements. The *fábrica* has two 30-metric-ton autoclaves with room for another in the same building. A large mechanical crusher-juicer also stands in this building, with twelve 28,000-liter stainless steel fermentation tanks in a connected building. Across a courtyard, in another building with open sides, are located three 3,500-liter stainless steel pot stills, with room for five more alongside. At my visit, the maintenance shed was constructing another still, with the cut out pieces being welded together.

The company has room for growth, with another five hectares or so available for expansion. The *bodega* (storage warehouse), has about 1,500 barrels in place, and another 530 have been ordered to expand the storage capacity for the *reposado*. At the time I visited, they were limited by lack of storage space, having to use a large stainless steel fermentation tank to hold the tequila until the new barrels arrived. Current production is between

The new distillery at Capilla de Guadalupe, producing Jaliscience and 30-30

5,000 and 6,000 liters per day, but will rise as more storage space becomes available.

After my tour of the distillery compound, we met a couple who had come to the office to investigate the new tequila. The gentleman was an importer-exporter in the liquor industry who just happened to be out of his business cards, and the same was true of his female associate. But they were very nice people and since they were very knowledgeable about the liquor industry in Mexico, I have attempted to find out who they were and to contact them. But, not at all unusually for Mexico, this proved impossible.

My overall impression was of a company on the move. The management is young, enthusiastic, and dedicated to making a superior product. They appear well in control of their finances and have bold new ideas about the tequila industry. The product is attractively packaged, and new distinctive bottle designs are being considered.

Currently, the company is producing and marketing three tequilas under two separate labels. Under the label '30-30,' they make a *blanco* and a two-month *reposado*. Under the 'Jaliscience' label, they are marketing a five-month *reposado*. All three products are of excellent quality and flavor. The company produces only 100 percent *agave* tequila and believes very strongly that this is the future of the industry. They were also considering making an *anejo*.

This tequila was available only in Mexico, but the company Tequila Imports of Houston, Texas, was planning to import a version of this distillery's tequila, in all three types, under the label 'Ambarfino.'

DISTILLERY #3
Agroindustrias Santa Clara de SPR de RL
NOM #1384

I was informed that this company was scheduled to begin operations in 1996. Its distillery is located in the area of the village of Ciudad Guzmán, with offices in Guadalajara. The registered label names for the company are 'El Nativo' and 'La Cava de los Beas.' The owner is Sr. Jaime Beas Arenas.

DISTILLERY #4

Casa Cuervo, S.A. de C.V.

NOM #1122   'Los Camachines'

This distillery is a totally-owned subsidiary of Tequila Cuervo, and until recently all of its production was included in the parent company's output. In 1995 it produced only *mixto,* but in July of 1996, Carillon Imports of Teaneck, New Jersey, announced that they were importing a new tequila named 'Gran Centenario.' This tequila had previously been imported as a *mixto,* as one of the versions of Cuervo, by Heublein Imports, but is now a 100 percent *agave* tequila. The NOM on the bottle is #1122 which means that the tequila is made at this distillery. The name for this *fábrica* is listed with La Cámara as 'La Florida,' but press releases for the new tequila state that the tequila is made at 'Los Camachines'. The distillery's name must have been changed for some reason.

This new tequila is presented in the same bottles as the Cuervo tequila, 'Dos Reales,' with much the same style of label. It is available as both a *blanco* and a *reposado*.

DISTILLERY #5.

Compañia Orendain, S.A. de C.V.

NOM #1172

The second company name owned by the brothers Orendain, this company is totally owned by Tequila Orendain de Jalisco, but is almost never used. A small amount of product is available that uses this company name and NOM, but it is normally encountered only in Mexico.

DISTILLERY #6
Corporación Ansan, S.A. de C.V.
NOM #1360

While this company was not in operation at the beginning of 1997, it was expected to come on line later that year. A new distillery was under construction in La Laja, a suburb of Zapotlanejo, and will probably become the primary *fábrica* for Distillery #8, Destiladora de Occidente, and the related company, Tequila Viuda de Martinez, as well as for its own output.

Current labels registered to this company include 'Sublime,' 'Honorable,' and 'Zafarrancho.' The CEO is Sr. Santiago Gomez Martinez, who also runs Viuda de Martinez, which has been affiliated with the noted Destiladora de Occidente.

DISTILLERY #7
Destiladora Azteca de Jalisco, S.A. de C.V.
NOM #1109   'El Llano'   DOT #98

This second Orendain company is owned and operated by Eduardo and Jaime Orendain Giovannini, sons of Jaime Orendain González. When the new Orendain factory was

The small, busy distillery of Azteca de Jalisco in Tequila village

87

constructed, their father bought the old factory from the family company, Orendain de Jalisco, and gave it to them to run. The two brothers are assisted by their sister, Marcela, who also helps her father in the main offices of Orendain, located in Zapopan, a suburb of Guadalajara.

Visiting the factory, 'El Llano', I found a small plant with two autoclaves, four pot stills, the usual fermentation tanks, a small storage area and bottling plant, and the office with Eduardo working inside. He encouraged me to tour the factory and take some pictures. A very small *tahona* was on the property, though it had not been used for 14 years, since the mechanical crusher/juicer had been installed.

The company is in the throes of change, with the young Orendain brothers looking toward the future. They are currently changing from *mixto* to 100 percent *agave* production. This transformation was taking place slowly but was expected to be fully consummated by the end of 1996. The brothers plan to make only the best-quality 100 percent *agave* tequila and find a niche in the super-premium market.

Their main label, 'Arette,' is gaining recognition in the domestic market. The product is not yet available outside Mexico, but will probably be exported within the next few years, as their supplies of all types of tequila become stable.

Currently they are producing about 300,000 liters per year under the 'Arette' and 'El Gran Viejo' labels. Arette is available only in Mexico as a *blanco*, and a four-month *reposado*. They are not currently producing an *añejo*.

DISTILLERY #8
Destiladora de Occidente, S.A. de C.V.
NOM #1117   DOT #108

Founded in the 1860s by Sr. Francisco Quintanar and don Aurelio G. Martinez, this is a small company that made only *mixto* tequila, approximately 200,000 liters per year. It uses the proprietary labels 'Tequila Viuda de Martinez' and 'Sin Rival' ('without rival'). The company is owned and operated by Sr. J. Donato Ruiz Sanchez.

I visited with Sr. Ruiz at his combined office and home in downtown Guadalajara. The house was a magnificent gray stone structure facing on one of the busiest streets in the city, though inside it was very calm and quiet. There was a beautiful interior garden, open to the sky, with flowers in bloom in the patio. Sr. Ruiz was in his late fifties and in frail health, but very graciously showed me around his home, of which he was rightfully proud.

The house is about 100 years old and was given to Sr. Ruiz by his father when he was only five years old, apparently to guarantee that he would always have a place to live. Sr. Ruiz's family have been part of the tequila industry since his grandfather, Sr. Donato Ruiz Savala, entered the business in the early 1900s. The distillery, 'La Martineña,' had been founded in 1840 and was purchased by the elder Ruiz before the turn of the century.

The various branches of the Ruiz family have continued to be involved in the tequila business over the decades. The company 'Tequila Parreñita,' is owned and run by the present Sr. Ruiz's cousin, Sr. Jorge Ruiz Ibarra. Another distillery, 'Satisfactores,' in Atotonilco el Alto, was owned and operated by another cousin, Jaime Ruiz Llaguno, who died in 1995.

Sr. J. Donato Ruiz currently owns and operates two tequila companies. 'Destiladora de Occidente' produced 529,656 liters of *mixto* and 3,656 liters of 100 percent *agave* tequila in 1995. The second company, 'Viuda de Martinez,' produced no tequila at all during 1994 and 1995, though the company has still been selling from previously manufactured stock.

Señor Ruiz is currently involved in a legal battle with the company 'J. Jesus Reyes Cortes' over possession of the distillery 'La Martineña.' The conflict is rather complex, but involves leases as well as the actual ownership of the factory.

Both of Sr. Ruiz's companies manufacture primarily *mixto* for both domestic and export markets, with Cabo Distributing of Los Angeles being the main exporter for Occidente.

A new *fábrica* is also under construction in the village of La Laja, in concert with Distillery #6, Corporación Ansan.

DISTILLERY #9
Destiladora González González, S.A. de C.V.
NOM #1143   'La Peregrina'

This was the fifth largest exporter of bulk tequila in 1994, with 3,700,000 liters of bulk tequila being shipped to David Sherman Corp. in St. Louis, and it retained the same position in 1995 by manufacturing and exporting 3,327,834 liters of *mixto* and making 24,586 liters of 100 percent *agave* tequila. They had previously manufactured only *mixto*, but introduced a *cien por ciento de agave* tequila, 'El Mayor', in 1995. This tequila is currently available, as a *blanco* and a *reposado*, only in the Jalisco area. The company was founded in 1984 by Sr. Rudolfo González who remains owner and CEO.

Prior to his founding of this company, Sr. González worked for his uncle, Sr. Eucario González, who had founded the company of the same name, Distillery #29. Sr. Rudolfo González left that company and started his own when the company 'Eucario González' was sold to Cabo Distributing of Los Angeles.

On my visit to the plant I met the distillery manager, Sr. Miguel Cedeño, an intelligent man who holds a master's degree in microbiology and appeared to be in his mid-thirties. He gave me some of his time and an English translation copy of a paper he had written, 'Tequila Production' (listed in the Bibliography), which was a great help in increasing my initial understanding of how tequila is made.

He speaks excellent English, and answered all of the questions that I then knew enough to ask. An interesting side note is that he and another distillery manager, Sr. Marco Cedano of 'Tres Magueyes,' are good friends and have similar mindsets about the future of the tequila industry. They, and others like them, are the future of the tequila industry. Both exude a calm inner confidence and look forward to forthcoming developments in the industry. They are aware of the needs and purposes of both *mixto* and 100 percent *agave* tequila, and appear to consider both to be equally important, though they do lean in the direction of 100 percent *agave* for the long term.

DISTILLERY #10

Destilados de Agave, S.A. de C.V.

NOM #1359

This company, founded in 1996, is wholly owned and controlled by Distillery #30, Tequila Herradura, and is used solely for the marketing of the tequila labelled 'El Jimador.'

DISTILLERY #11

Elab. y Proc. de Agave y sus Derivados, S.A. de C.V.

NOM #1141   'La Fortuna'

Formerly known as 'Destiladora de Arenal,' this company has recently recommenced production. The owners of the re-organized company include some of the previous owners, but the management is completely new.

Trying to find the factory 'La Fortuna' was not plain sailing. It is located in an industrial portion of the town of Arenal that seemed bereft of street signs. My driver, Rudy Vasquez, and I finally found it by asking an older woman in the area, who told us it was the "first white door on the street around the corner."

All the tequila made here is drunk in France.

Once we had found the proper location, it turned out to be a very small distillery of only two ovens with a very small column still about eight feet high and four inches in diameter. There are two pot stills on the property, but these are no longer used. Total daily production is in the neighborhood of 750 liters of *cien por ciento de agave* tequila under the label of 'Revolucionario 501'; currently it is all exported to France.

The tequila was sampled at the factory, only the *blanco* being available, and it was found to be a representative 100 percent *agave* product, perhaps a little light in its presentation of *agave* flavors. It also leaves a slightly bitter aftertaste, and gives the impression of a raw potato flavor. The production manager told me that they use only one distillation with the column still and this did seem to be their usual process, though two distillations is usual and called for in the NORMA.

The factory dates from the early 1900s, but has periodically been refurbished and updated. This is one of the smallest of all tequila distilleries both in physical size of the plant and in output of tequila. This product will probably not be available anywhere but in France for some time to come, since the new company does not appear to have plans to expand. They also do not seem to be trying to make any inroads into the domestic market and appear content with their current export niche.

DISTILLERY #12

Empresa Ejidal Tequilera Amatitán, S.A.

NOM #1121   'La Regional'   DOT #117

This is a co-operative distillery which produces different tequilas for its members. Founded in December, 1973, the company began production of tequila on the 25th of October, 1975. The company is registered under the name 'Alfredo V. Bonfil' with the organization of regional unions, and has a registration number of 584/75. The director of the company is Sr. Mario Gomez Vasquez, who is registered with the national agrarian record.

The primary proprietary label used by the company, 'Regional,' is available as a *blanco*, a *reposado*, and an *añejo*. The company also makes and bottles 'La Nueva Reforma'. Some other labels

La Regional in Amatitán

made at this plant are 'Caballito Cerrero', an impressive tequila now available only in Mexico, and the *añejo* tequila in the cactus bottle of 'Porfidio.'

The factory is equipped as follows:

One scale of 50,000 kilograms capacity, two autoclaves of 13,000 kilograms capacity each, one autoclave of 18,000 kilograms. capacity, one crusher-juicer with four 20-inch grinding wheels, two 22,000-liter tanks to mix and homogenize the juice, two 3,750-liter tubs for culturing yeast, two 16,750-liter stainless steel tubs for fermentation, one 22,000-liter stainless steel tank to feed the stills, three 2,700-liter stainless steel pot stills, two 150-horsepower boilers for steam generation, a deep well for water supply, a high-water tank of 30,000 liters capacity for the plant, and one cooling tower for the three stills, to condense the tequila faster.

The plant also has nine stainless steel storage tanks for finished tequila with a capacity of 273,000 liters, plus four wooden tanks with total capacity of 85,000 liters for aging *reposado*, and 834 barrels with a capacity of 129,517 liters for storing and aging *reposado* and *añejo*.

In 1995, the company manufactured 65,618 liters of *mixto* tequila of all types, and 17,689 liters of 100 percent *agave* tequila of all types, according to the figures of La Cámara.

Agauardiente de Agave la Mexicana, where they make El Corral

DISTILLERY #13
Fáb. de Aguard. de Agave la Mexicana, S.A. de C.V.
NOM #1333   DOT #124

This small company began production in mid-1996, with a plant that is located about eight kilometers outside of Arandas on the way to the village of Jesus Maria. They are currently producing a tequila labelled 'El Corral,' which is available in Jalisco. One other label, 'Don Benito,' is registered to this company.

The plant is down a side road, and this was the first of three companies that saw me taking pictures and actually asked me what I was doing. The two previous ones had ignored me.

DISTILLERY #14
Industrialización y Dllo. Santo Tomas, S.A. de C.V.
NOM #740   'Hacienda Santo Tomas'

Located on the western side of the village of Tequila, close to the village of Hostotipaquillo, this tiny company is based at Hacienda Santo Tomas. The hacienda was first built in the 1600s as a protective fortress to support agricultural and mining activities in the area, though a distillery was also begun on the property at about that time.

After many ownership changes, the hacienda served a spell as the retirement home for General don Manuel M. Diguez, former governor of the state of Jalisco. After his term as governor and following his subsequent retirement from political life, he had a road built connecting the hacienda to the highway between Guadalajara and the port of San Blas, so that he could use his car for travel. His was the first automobile ever seen in this area.

The hacienda was completely abandoned from 1938 until 1954, when the buildings were reduced to little more than ruins. The efforts of the then governor of Jalisco, Sr. Jose de Jesus Limon Muñoz, in 1965, saved the hacienda and brought it back to life by restoring many of its previous agricultural activities.

In 1988, Sr. Limon's son, Alvaro Limon Torres, and his childhood friend, Alvaro Martinez Ramos, took over the responsibility of restoring and rehabilitating the tequila production facilities. Their efforts have resulted in a fine quality product being brought back to the marketplace.

The tequila currently marketed is named 'Los Valientes,' available only as a 100 percent *agave reposado*. The packaging certainly makes this product stand out from its neighbors, by placing the clear glass bottle inside a canvas sheath, with the sheath glued to the bottle and the label information printed on the canvas.

This distillery still uses most of the old production methods, including a 'tahona' or stone *agave* crusher, and has only one oven and one pot still. The company is currently producing about 20,000 liters per year (1995 production was 23,600 liters of 100

The village of Santo Tomas

percent *agave* and 600 liters of *mixto*) but some modest expansion is planned.

This tequila is available in Mexico and certain areas within the United States. It is imported by Parliament Import Co. of Atlantic City, New Jersey, and distributed in about six areas, including California and New York.

DISTILLERY #15
J. Jesus Partida Melendez
NOM #1258

This company applied for their operating licenses in February of 1996, and began making tequila immediately. They produce a *reposado* under the label of 'Tres Mujeres,' currently marketed in Jalisco, with plans to begin exporting to the U.S.

Another label registered to this company is 'Miramontes', listed as belonging to a Sr. Alberto Miramontes Arana. Tres Mujeres is stocked at the Sam's Club in Guadalajara, but I discovered it on the highway between Amatitán and Arenal. As Rudy and I were returning from taking pictures in Amatitán, we stopped at a road-side stand that was advertising and selling the tequila 'Tres Mujeres,' of which I had no previous knowledge. We each bought a bottle of the tequila and then visited the distillery, which was down a dirt road, through the *agave* fields behind the stands.

The distillery is very small, having only one still of 750 liters capacity. Expansion is planned, but will be slow. The owner, Sr. J.

Rudy, holding a bottle of Tres Mujeres at the roadside stand between Amatitán and Arenal

Jesus Partida Melendez, named the tequila after his mother and her two sisters, who work in the roadside stands.

DISTILLERY #16

J. Jesus Reyes Cortes, S.A.

NOM #856   'La Martineña'   DOT #114

This small distillery in the town of Tequila has four ovens, four stills, and open concrete fermentation tanks. The distillery was built about 1900, but I have been able to establish very little about the company's history. The company has a retail store on the main highway through the town of Tequila, and the distillery has been under a partial sublease to the company 'Destileria Porfidio', making that company's triple-distilled *blanco*.

This company is presently involved in a legal dispute with the owner of Distillery #8, Destiladora de Occidente, Sr. J. Donato Ruiz Sanchez, over a lease agreement for the operation of the distillery 'La Martineña.' The company currently manufactures very inexpensive tequila under the labels 'RB D'Reyes,' 'J.R. Jesus

Though this was 1995, it could have been any time in the past 150 years.

Reyes,' and 'R.B. Rey.' It also produces other labels, 'La Areñita,' 'Virreyes,' and 'Viva Miguel Villa,' for Compania Tequilera, S.A. de C.V., a rectifier and distribution company based in Mexico City. No production figures are available for this company, since they are not members of La Cámara, the organization which keeps those figures.

DISTILLERY #17

Jorge Salles Cuervo y Sucs., S.A. de C.V.

NOM #1108   'La Guarreña'   DOT #87

Sr. Jorge Salles Cuervo had worked in the tequila industry for 18 years when he founded this company in 1959. He had begun working for the Sauza company in 1941, mainly as an inside man. Sr. Salles was still active in his company in 1996, at the age of 77. He now mainly works in the fields overseeing the growth and production of *agave,* but also supervises the manufacturing plant.

The plant has five autoclaves and two large and two small alembic stills (pot stills). It produces about 400,000 liters of *mixto* annually (output in 1995 was 356,819 liters). They produce no 100 percent *agave* tequila and do not export. The office and administration is operated by the founder's son, Sr. Antonio Salles, who is assisted by his nephew.

The company both purchases *agave* on the open market and grows some of its own, holding approximately 400 hectares of

La Guarreña, the Salles distillery in Tequila

Piles of agave cabezas *outside La Arandina in Arandas*

agave fields. They manufacture only their own brands, 'El Tequileño,' a *blanco,* and 'El Tequileño Especial,' a *reposado*.

DISTILLERY #18

La Arandina, S.A. de C.V.

NOM #1131   'La Arandina'   DOT #100

A medium-sized distillery in the village of Arandas, La Arandina produces *mixto* for sale to Mexican distributors and for bulk export. The company is owned by a branch of the Camarena family, cousins to the owners of 'Tapatio.' They sell under the proprietary labels 'Dos Amigos' and 'Hipodromo' as 100 percent *agave reposados*, and 'Casca Viejo' as a *mixto* white tequila. They hold rights in another label, 'Camarena', but are not producing under that name at present. All proprietary labels are sold only in Mexico.

In 1995, output of all types of *mixto* totalled 684,781 liters, and production of all types of 100 percent *agave* tequila came to 66,049 liters.

DISTILLERY #19

La Cofradia, S.A. de C.V.

NOM #1137   'La Cofradia'   DOT #111

A medium-sized company located in Tequila, La Cofradia was founded in 1992 by two cousins, Sr. Carlos Hernandez Hernandez, the owner of record, and Ing. Carlos Hernandez Ramos, the general manager and operator of the distillery.

Gate maintenance at La Cofradia in Tequila

The plant is set up to produce a maximum of 9,700 liters per day, or 3,123,400 liters per year total capacity of *mixto*. The company also produces 100 percent *agave* tequila, normally sold under the label 'Tres Alegres Compadres.' From January through October, 1995, the company exported 994,663 liters of all types of tequila from a total output of 1,329,294 liters. For 1995 as a whole, total output of all types was 1,568,671 liters.

This company is aggressively seeking growth opportunities. In their first year of production, 1993, they produced 70,200 liters; in 1994, 201,000 liters; and in 1995, 1,568,671 liters.

The proprietary brand names they use are 'La Cofradia', 'Los Cofrades,' 'Tres Alegres Compadres,' 'De Los Dorados,' and 'Cava del Villano.' They also supply twelve other companies with tequila for export purposes, some in bulk, but most of the companies purchase La Cofradia tequila under their 100 percent *agave* label, 'Tres Alegres Compadres'.

Other labels which may use tequila produced by this company are 'Cancún,' 'Don Salvador's,' 'Hot Jalisco Tequila,' 'Hussong's,' 'Santos,' 'Tequila Jalisco,' and 'Toltec.'

They are currently under contract to supply Cabo Distributing, Los Angeles, and expect to ship about 2,000,000 liters per year to that company. They shipped the first container load (1,330 cases) of bottled 100 percent *agave* tequila to McCormick Distilling in Missouri, which markets under the Hussong's label.

DISTILLERY #20
La Madrileña, S.A. de C.V.
NOM #1142   'La Union'   DOT #82

The fourth largest manufacturer of bulk export tequila in 1994, La Madrileña moved up to third in 1995, with total output of 5,534,970 liters of all types of tequila. The company was founded in 1911 by Sr. Pedro Velasco Calle, grandfather of the current general director, Sr. Luis Velasco Jr. The main offices are in Mexico City, and the company operates two different manufacturing facilities.

The main plant for bulk export tequila at 55 percent alcohol is in Tototlan, Jalisco, and makes only *mixto*. In 1994, this facility manufactured and exported 3,854,000 liters in bulk to such customers as Barton Brands, Frank-Lin Distillers, Hiram Walker, and Paramount Distillers.

The plant in Tototlan has seven autoclaves—one with a capacity of eight metric tons, one with a capacity of ten metric tons, and five with eighteen metric tons capacity; eight fermentation tanks of 139,230 liters each; one continuous action distillation column; and four pot stills of 10,500 liters each, with seven storage units that can hold a total of 447,000 liters. The capacity figure for the eight fermentation tanks seemed improbably large to me. I asked the company about it, and they insisted the number was correct. It amounts to slightly more than 35,000 gallons of liquid, more than a standard-sized swimming pool.

Current production levels are about 65 percent of a maximum of 40,000 liters per day. If operating at full capacity, annual production would be in the area of 6,760,000 liters for both the

La Madrileña, a major producer of exported mixto

domestic and export markets. Both white and gold tequilas are made in and exported from this plant.

The second plant is in San Juan del Rio, Queretaro, where all products are bottled for the domestic and export market, including the recently introduced 'Jarana,' a *mixto* available in *blanco* and *reposado*, only in Mexico

This company has historically produced tequila only for bulk export, and 'Jarana,' their own new proprietary label, was introduced in May of 1995. The company is considering the growing international market for 100 percent *agave* tequila and is formulating plans to become part of that trend.

In 1995, the production lists of La Cámara show that the company made 26,138 liters of 100 percent *agave* tequila, though a company representative stated that they had made none for the year. Where it went, nobody seems to know.

DISTILLERY #21
Productos Especiales de Tequila, S.A.
NOM #1196   'La Areñita'

Owned by Sr. Ramiro Orendain González, a cousin of the brothers who own and operate Tequila Orendain de Jalisco, S.A. de C.V., Distillery #31, this is a medium-sized company which in 1994 made 524,017 liters of *mixto* tequila and exported all of its production. In 1995, the company produced only 15,049 liters

The front gate at La Areñita in Tequila

during the early part of the year and apparently shut down production for the remainder of the year.

Tequila Caballito Cerrero, S.A.
NOM #1114

This company has been producing tequila for about 25 years. They have a distillery that has been closed down for the last four years. Rumors state that the tequila they currently market is produced by Distillery #12, Empresa Ejidal Tequilera Amatitan.

I have spoken with one of the primaries of this company, and his statement was that the company produces about 40,000 liters per year.

Rudy took me to a storefront in downtown Guadalajara, a factory-owned outlet for this company, and I purchased a 750 ml bottle. When I got back to the hotel, upon closely checking the bottle and label, I could find no 100 percent *agave* designation. I opened and smelled the product, decided it was a *mixto*, and gave it away the following day.

Tequila Cascahuin, S.A. de C.V.
NOM #1123   'El Cascahuin'   DOT #106

This is a small company in the village of Arenal, located on the street next to the railroad tracks, with a blue door. A liquor store is located next door to the factory selling the products of the plant.

Rudy and I arrived at lunch time, about 2:30 P.M., so of course no one was in the factory. The liquor store was open, but the factory was closed. About 3:15, the workers returned, and we managed to rouse someone inside and gain entry for a cursory examination.

The factory is small to medium, with four ovens and two pot stills. The production averages 2,000 liters per day of *mixto*; the company was not then licensed to produce 100 percent *agave*. The company currently produces and markets tequila under two

Only mixto; *El Cascahuin in Arenal*

proprietary labels, 'Cascahuin' and 'Cuernito'; they also manufacture for three export companies: Javier Ohrner Co. under its own label, 'Ohrner Co.'; Bacardi y Compañia, under the labels 'Camino Real' and 'Poncho Rojo'; and Tequila Cerro Viejo, under the label 'El Herradero'.

This factory's annual total output is approximately 400,000 liters (1995 production was 507,350 liters) and the proprietary company labels are sold only in Mexico.

DISTILLERY #24
Tequila Catador Alteño, S.A. de C.V.
NOM #1105   'Rancho Los Ladrillos'

This tiny company sells only in Mexico. The management evidently has no desire to give out any information. When I called, they hung up on me. The only sources of information were La Cámara and the other companies. This is what little I could glean from them:

The introverted Catador Alteño in Jesús María

The company produces tequila under three labels, 'Catador', 'Barrancas', and 'Barranca de Viudas.' The distillery is located in the village of Jesus Maria in the Los Altos region of Jalisco. They manufacture only 100 percent *agave* tequila, with an output of 81,900 liters in 1995, and they do not export any of their product.

DISTILLERY #25
Tequila Cazadores, S.A, de C.V.
NOM #1128   'El Gallito'

One of the largest distillers in Mexico, Cazadores was founded by the Banuelos family group of six brothers on November 7th, 1973. They initially used an older distilling plant on the edge of the town of Arandas. A new distillery was constructed and opened for operation in early 1994. It has seven 60-ton auto-claves, a fully automatic grinder-juicer, and 52 fermentation tanks of 30,000 liters each. It uses a seven-day fermenta-tion cycle and has 30 stainless steel pot stills of 5,000 liters capacity each. Simple arithmetic shows that this dis-tillery is capable of producing about twelve million liters of tequila per year.

The pleasantly outgoing Cazadores in Arandas

Their year-to-date production through September 1995 was slightly over 4,000,000 liters. They are growing at the rate of about 1,000,000 liters per year. Some confusion apparently exists here since the production figures from La Cámara for 1995 show 2,640,897 liters of 100 percent *agave* production through the end of 1995.

This company produces only *reposado* tequila and is one of the top three selling brands in Mexico. They started exporting their tequila to the United States in January of 1995.

My tour through the distillery was conducted by the adminis-trative director, Sr. Gustavo Hernandez Godinez, a very helpful gentleman who answered all questions openly and even volun-teered information. The company is planning a new building to house their bottling and labelling plant, and will be increasing their stock of barrels for aging from 4,000 to 7,000 white oak barrels. The current aging cycle is 70 days, which puts it just over the requirement for *reposado*. They are quite content in their location within the tequila market and have no plans to move into any of the other areas such as *blanco* or *añejo*. Formerly one of the better *mixtos*, Cazadores was changed to a 100 percent *agave* tequila in January of 1997.

DISTILLERY #26
Tequila Centinela, S.A. de C.V.
NOM #1140   'El Centinela'   DOT #86

Founded in 1904 by Sr. Pofirio Torres Perez, this was the first producing distillery in the Highlands of Jalisco. It is a small distillery that produces about 200,000 liters per year (1995 production was 341,556 liters) under two brand names, 'Centinela' and 'El Cabrito.' The label 'El Cabrito' was, at one point, another distillery company and was acquired by Centinela.

'Centinela' is exported to the United States as a premium 100 percent *agave* tequila. It comes as a *blanco*, six-month *reposado*, one-year *añejo*, and three-year *añejo*. 'El Cabrito' is a 100 percent *agave* product that has been sold only in Mexico as a *blanco* and

The company offices of Tequila Centinela in Arandas

four-month *reposado* (Cabrito began being imported into the U.S. by Paramount in 1996).

The distillery is located about two miles outside the town of Arandas, down a dirt road off the main highway. The office is on the main city plaza in Arandas, with a storefront selling the products of the company. The administrative offices are behind and upstairs from the retail operation.

I spent a day in August of 1995 visiting this company. I was picked up at my hotel in Guadalajara at 8:00 in the morning by 'Pepe,' Sr. José Luis Sánchez Rojas, the Director de Zona, and we drove to Arandas, arriving about 10:30 A.M.

Going first to the office, we passed an *iglesia* on the way. The most interesting thing about this church is a large bell sitting in front on braces. It seems that the bell was ordered a number of years ago and was planned to be the largest bell in the state of Jalisco, but when delivered, it was discovered that the bell tower was not strong enough to hold such a massive bell. The bell was hoisted up for placement once, and when the bell was rung the first time, the vibrations almost caused the tower to crumble. The bell was brought down to await strengthening of the tower, and it has been sitting ever since.

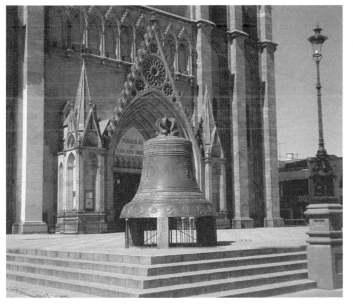

The biggest bell in Jalisco

Upon arrival at the office, I was introduced to Sr. Juan Leonardo Hernandez, the administrative manager of the company, and his son, also called Leonardo. After a small attempt at conversation, a party of three others was put together, and we went out to the distillery for a short tour.

Upon arrival at the plant, we were greeted by Sr. Jaime Torres, one of the partners in the company and a descendent of the founder. Our group entered the plant through a small door in the large red delivery gates and found the plant in full operation. As in all the distilleries, there was a guard at the gate, though there was no signing in and out of the plant. We went through to the work area. The reception area had a large pile of freshly harvested *agave* waiting for the ax and the ovens, of which there are four. A mechanical crusher-juicer is in use but has only been in place for the last ten years. Two stone wheels from the *tahona*, which was formerly used, are sitting in the interior yard as decorations.

There are 14 stainless steel fermentation tanks varying in size from 8,000 to 10,000 liters, and four stainless steel pot stills. There are also two *bodegas* on the property, plus the laboratory which most distilleries have. The on-property storerooms contain about 1,000 barrels, and the company has two more *bodegas* in town that have another 1,000 barrels for storage and aging of the *reposado* and *añejo*. They have ordered another 2,000 used barrels from the whiskey distilleries in Kentucky and Tennessee, and are planning on doubling their production of *reposado* and *añejo* over the next two or three years.

The company at present has 400 hectares of their own *agave*, or about 1,000,000 plants in the ground, and also buys on the open market. They have a bottling and labelling plant located in Arandas in conjunction with one of their *bodegas*.

After the tour, we returned to the office and talked with the office staff until we left for lunch. About 2:30 P.M., everyone left the office and went out to the cars to head for the restaurant, named 'Las Terrazas,' located on the highway just outside of town. It was owned by the owner of Centinela, another Pepe, Sr. José de Jesus Hernandez M.

We were joined at the restaurant by the members of the office staff and about four others I had not previously met, only men.

Women were not yet generally included in Mexico's business world.

Since this restaurant was owned by Pepe Hernandez, it only served Centinela tequila. We sat down at a table and were served salsa and chips, with tequila being brought in very small snifters, about two ounces capacity. First 'Salud,' a small sip of the spirit, with a little sangrita as a chaser, and some mineral water to cut the heat from the sangrita. Then the *carnitas*, slender strips of barbecued pork with garnish, *nopal*, the inside of the new leaves of the prickly pear cactus, some sliced tomatoes, onions, tortillas, and the ever present *chiles*, four different kinds, including *habaneros*. If you don't already know, the *habanero* is the hottest pepper in the world. When made into a salsa, it appears yellow in color, and if you aren't used to hot peppers, it will take the skin off the inside of your mouth.

Lunch started at about three o' clock, with people coming and going from the table. Everyone wanted to see or talk to the *gringo* writer. The first question was invariably, 'Why are you writing a book about tequila?' My answer: 'Because there isn't one.'

As lunch continued, the tequila flowed, and everyone tried to pour just a little more into my glass. After four glasses of about two ounces each, I started trying to say, 'No more, I've had enough'. The people at the table kept filling my glass and proposing toasts. It's strange, but after about eight of the small glasses of tequila, my Spanish improved enormously.

About 5:00 P.M., the entertainment arrived, a guitarist, a real *mariachi*, who played songs and encouraged singing from the patrons. Much of the office staff had to go back to work by about 6:00, but many of the others stayed to keep the party going. Pepe and I finally left around 8:00 P.M., heading back to Guadalajara and my hotel.

You may forgive my apprehension at the thought of travelling over rough, back-country roads in Mexico with a driver who had matched me drink for drink, and had a few more on the side, but we arrived at my hotel in good time and one piece, and I gratefully went to bed. I awoke the following morning with no hangover.

Centinela is a very good 100 percent *agave* tequila, and is a little more reasonably priced than some of the currently modish tequilas, averaging around $30.

DISTILLERY #27
Tequila Cuervo La Rojeña, S.A. de C.V.
NOM #1104   'La Rojeña'

This is the largest tequila company, with bulk exports in 1994 of 19,800,000 liters of *mixto* at 55 percent alcohol. It is also the oldest continuously running company for which there are definitive records. There is another wholly-owned distillery named 'Casa Cuervo' in the village of Zapotlanejo.

Both distilleries are under the control of Heublein Corp., which is owned by the international conglomerate Grand Metropolitan of Great Britain. The United States corporate offices of Jose Cuervo are located in Hartford, Connecticut, and I could not get their marketing or public relations people to respond to repeated letters, faxes, and phone calls. The only contact that I was able to make was with their public relations office in Guadalajara, where someone told me to read *Artes de México*, Volume 27, to get the approved history of Tequila Cuervo.

Here is a summary of what I found in that article: In 1758, Sr. Jose Antonio de Cuervo purchased a piece of land in the village of Tequila named the Hacienda de Cuisillos; the property included a distillery. In 1785 King Charles III of Spain banned all production of alcoholic beverages in Mexico in an attempt to increase taxes on imported wines and brandies. After his death in 1792, the new ruler, Charles IV, lifted the ban and in 1795 issued a permit to Jose Antonio's son, Jose Maria Guadalupe Cuervo, allowing for the manufacture of *mezcal* wine.

The property and fortunes of Sr. Cuervo prospered and grew so that in 1805 his inventory for taxes listed the distillery, the family house, twelve fields of *agave*, mostly *chinos azules* and *manolargo* varieties, with the plants numbering in the hundreds of thousands, as his property. He also declared that his average production level for the five years between 1800 and 1805 was 400,000 *cribas* (receptacles), of which we don't know the size.

When Jose Maria Guadalupe died, he left all of his property to his son and daughter. The girl married one Vicente Albino Rojas, and gave control of her properties to him. His ego was such that he could not bear owning a company called 'Taberna de Cuervo,'

The truck entrance for agave *delivery at La Rojeña*

and changed the name of the distillery to 'La Rojeña.' He modernized the plant and began boosting production and selling his product over a wider area, shipping to fairs and fiestas as far away as Aguascalientes, Zacatecas, and San Luis Potosí.

In the nineteenth century, three men controlled the fortunes of Cuervo: Vicente Albino Rojas, Jesus Flores, and Jose Cuervo Labastida. After the death of Rojas, his will left everything he owned to his two daughters who passed control to Sr. Jesus Flores, who already owned two other distilleries in Tequila. How Sr. Flores arranged the production schedules and balanced the levels between the three factories is unknown, but he did greatly increase production and sales.

Jose Cuervo Labastida didn't actually take over management of the company until 1900, but he had worked inside the distillery for years and had influenced production and quality levels before he rose to managerial level by marrying the widow Flores. He ran the company until his death in 1921, when a series of administrators took over. These were Guillermo Freytag Schreir and his son, Guillermo Freytag Gallardo. Subsequently, administration was placed in the hands of the Cuervo heirs, Juan Beckmann Gallardo and Juan Beckmann Vidal, who currently operate the company.

111

Cuervo has mainly concentrated on the production of *mixto* tequila. Aside from their product called 'Tradicional,' they did not make a 100 percent *agave* until 1995. They do have a new 100 percent *agave* offering, released under the label 'Reserva de la Familia.' The company at first stated that this was to be a limited release tequila, a three-year *añejo* with a release volume of only 3,000 liters. The volume seems to have increased to at least 30,000 liters and to have now become a staple of Cuervo's line.

Having tasted this tequila, I found that, in my opinion, it was lacking in the qualities that make tequila what it is, the freshness and flavor of the *agave*. There is a strong impression of charred oak in the liquid, perhaps because of the use of new heavy-char barrels, and the nose and initial taste is reminiscent of bourbon. This has affected the spirit to such an extent that it lacks certain flavors of the *agave*, or they barely come through because of the overpowering effect of the wood. If you are an aficionado of both bourbon and tequila, you may find this a charming intermediate form. Unfortunately, I have been unable to discuss the theory or the intentions behind this product with anyone at Cuervo.

DISTILLERY #28
Tequila El Viejito, S.A. de C.V.
NOM #1107   'El Viejito' and 'El Papagayo'   DOT #94

The sixth largest exporter of bulk tequila, this company was founded in the 1930s by Sr. Jose González Estrada and Sons. It is currently run by Sr. Antonio Nuñez Hurtado and his family.

I met Sr. Nuñez in his office in Guadalajara. His father, Sr., Indalesio Nuñez Muro, was introduced to the tequila industry when he began working for Sauza in 1914. The elder Nuñez took over management and ownership of El Viejito in 1937, and his son Jorge (Antonio's older brother) became president of the company in 1963. The current CEO is Sr. Antonio Nuñez Hurtado, who assumed overall management duties in 1973. His sister Elena Nuñez Hurtado, serves as corporate secretary on the board of directors, and both Sr. Nuñez' son, Juan Eduardo Nuñez Eddings, and his nephew, Francisco Torres Nuñez, have positions within the company organization.

El Viejito distillery gates in Atotonilco

El Viejito exported 1,774,000 liters in bulk to numerous recti-fiers in 1994, and 1,851,054 liters in 1995. The largest receiver is in Minnesota, but they also export to a company called 'Guadalajara Imports' in St. Louis, which bottles a tequila labeled 'Aguila'. In 1995, the company produced approximately 200,000 liters of *mixto* tequila for export per month.

This company is one of the largest 100 percent *agave* produc-ers for other labels and also produces under their own label. 'El Viejito,' currently being imported by 'Frank-Lin Distillers Products,' as well as the tequilas sold under the following labels: 'Distinqt', formerly imported by Munico International of San Antonio; the new release, 'J.R. Jaime Rosales,' imported by Franzia of Calexico, California; 'Las Trancas,' a tequila which has been sold in Mexico for a number of years but is only now begin-ning to find a niche in the U.S. market; 'Sierra,' sold only in Germany, a label which is the leader in 100 percent *agave* tequilas in that country; 'Los Cinco Soles,' a label sold only in Mexico.

The company until recently also produced a large portion of, and bottled all of, the tequila sold under the 'Porfidio' label, though that practice has now been changed.

Among tequila industry watchers, there are constant rumors of future brands and labels being introduced to the 100 percent *agave* market segment, and Tequila El Viejito frequently features as the producer in such rumors.

Tequila Eucario Gonzalez, S.A. de C.V.
NOM #1113   'Santa Cruz'   DOT #109

Tequila Eucario Gonzalez was founded in the 1940s and named after its founder. The company was in operation under the same management until 1982, when it was sold to Federico Cabo of Los Angeles, and managed by him and his sister until they sold it to the current owners. A new partnership, under the management control of Dr. Sergio Flores y Nava, purchased the property in 1994.

In that year the company exported 2,193,000 liters of *mixto* in bulk to Cabo Distributing, who marketed it under their own labels and resold a portion to other companies, including McCormick Distillers. This made them the seventh largest exporter of bulk tequila for that year.

In 1995, total output of this company was 1,765,479 liters of *mixto* and 294,046 liters of 100 percent *agave*. Unfortunately, the new owners do not respond to telephone calls, faxes, or enquiring letters, and the Cabo siblings no longer have access to the necessary information. So all my information about this company has perforce come from sources other than the current management.

DISTILLERY #30
Tequila Herradura, S.A. de C.V.
NOM #1119   'Hacienda San Jose del Refugio'

This distillery makes only 100 percent *agave* tequila and has never made any other kind. Founded in the 1860s, and having the paperwork for an unbroken chain of events from 1870, this company has always taken pride in the products that it makes. When the adulteration process began in the 1930s, Herradura did not follow the easy road but instead held to the old values.

The company has remained under one or another branch of the Romo de la Peña family almost since its inception and has always followed traditional methods of manufacture. Currently in use at the Hacienda are eight large ovens, a mechanical grinder-juicer, numerous fermentation tanks of differing sizes, and 14 stainless steel pot stills of about 1,500 liters capacity each.

Only natural yeasts are used in the fermentation process, the company having isolated 15 different strains; they feel that each imparts its own flavor to the tequila. No accelerators are used, with the full fermentation cycle normally taking six to eight days. The company currently produces two different labels, 'Herradura' and 'El Jimador.' Herradura offers a *blanco*, a six-month *reposado*, and a three-year *añejo*. El Jimador offers a *blanco* and a four-month *reposado*.

Herradura has historically been the largest selling manufacturer of 100 percent *agave* tequila in both Mexico and the rest of the world. In 1994, their total production was 4,634,000 liters for all types of tequila bottled under both labels, but in 1995, output decreased to 2,856,000 liters. The company grows all of its own *agave*, buying none on the open market; this allows them to state that their tequila is "estate bottled."

After having toured the distillery in the morning and having lunch with the International Export manager, Ms. Louise Walsh, I met with Sr. Guillermo 'Bill' Romo de la Peña at the company offices in Guadalajara. While talking in a conference room, Sr. Romo showed me a video that the company had produced,

The front gate at Ex-Hacienda San Jose del Refugio in Amatitán

picturing a re-creation of the way tequila had been produced in the past, including a reproduction of the crushing process using the old *tahona* which still exists on the property.

During our meeting, 'Bill' told a story that illustrates how dangerous life used to be in the old days. During the revolt against Diaz, a group of revolutionaries, led by a former worker of the company, came to the hacienda and took away the owner, Sr. Aurelio Lopez Rosales. All of the family left at the property feared that the group intended to kill Sr. Lopez. Imagine their surprise when soldiers of the government arrived the very next day with orders to arrest and execute the *Patrón*. He had been saved by his former workers and fled the country in fear for his life. He eventually died in Paris in 1926.

At the Hacienda, I was struck by the beauty of the grounds and the buildings. The old distillery was preserved as a remembrance, but has been closed for many years. It is so dark inside that it is almost impossible to make out any details of the interior, and it is not served by electric light.

The mother of the current owners, 'La Señora' de la Peña, had lived in the Hacienda for her entire life, raising both of the boys, Pablo and Guillermo, on the property. She is now greatly missed, having passed away in December of 1994.

The two labels produced by this company are basically the same tequila, except that 'El Jimador' was sold only in Mexico until 1996, when it began being imported into the U.S., and 'Herradura' is distributed worldwide. This tequila was discovered and introduced to the United States market in the 1950s by the American entertainers Bing Crosby and Phil Harris. Import and distribution have since passed to Sazerac Company Inc. of New Orleans.

DISTILLERY #31

Tequila Orendain de Jalisco, S.A. de C.V.

NOM #1110   'La Mexicana'   DOT #95

Company Orendain was the third largest exporter of *mixto* tequila in bulk in 1994, with 4,634,000 liters of production. In 1995, they produced 5,423,864 liters, but were surpassed by

La Mexicana, distillery for Orendain de Jalisco in Tequila

Distillery #20, 'La Madrileña,' and are therefore now in fourth position despite increasing sales.

They currently supply Le Vecke and Glenmore with tequila, and manufacture and export all of the tequila for Seagram de México. Their product is also bottled under the U.S. labels of 'Pepe Lopez,' 'Puerto Vallarta,' 'Gavilan,' and others.

The Orendain family has been involved in the tequila industry for well over a hundred years, with historical notes being available from the 1870s, when the family was comparable to the Cuervo or Sauza families in their size and the number of their activities relating to the 'Industria Tequilera.' Around the turn of the century, an entire generation dropped out of the industry, selling all of their interests and moving to other areas of enterprise.

Not until Sr. Eduardo Orendain began the new company, Orendain de Jalisco, in 1935, did the Orendain family return to the tequila business. The company is currently operated by four of don Eduardo's six sons. The two oldest sons have a financial interest in the company and serve on the corporate board of directors but leave the operation to the four younger brothers. Jaime is president and CEO; Carlos is the director of operations; Alfonso is director of distillery production; and the youngest, Juan Jose, is director of sales.

Another factor in the business is the separate but related company, Azteca De Jalisco (Distillery #7), run by two of Jaime's sons. President of that company is Eduardo Orendain Giovannini, and he and his brother Jaime Orendain Giovannini handle most of the promotion of the business. Both are assisted by their sister, Marcela, who also acts as secretary to her father. Azteca de Jalisco makes some bulk tequila which is included as part of the export of the parent Orendain company, but it is an independent entity.

Orendain de Jalisco exported 4,634,000 liters of tequila in bulk in 1994, and through July of 1995, had exported 3,177,389 liters in bulk. They also exported 182,777 liters in bottles. Year's end showed production levels for 1995 of 5,423,864 liters of *mixto*, and 81,123 liters of 100 percent *agave*. All of Tequila Orendain's product is *mixto* except for their 'Ollitas' *reposado*, which is 100 percent *agave* and is rested for six months.

They consider 'Anniversario' to be their premium tequila and state that it is an eight-year *añejo*, but it is not a 100 percent *agave* tequila.

DISTILLERY #32
Tequila Parreñita, S.A. de C.V.
NOM #1115   'La Escondida'   DOT #105

A small- to medium-sized producer, this company produced 129,394 liters of all classes of tequila in 1994. The following year they produced 165,833 liters of *mixto* of all types, and 16,165 liters of 100 percent *agave* tequilas of all types.

Their proprietary labels are 'Parreñita,' 'Penca Azul,' 'La Parreñita y Dis.,' 'Arenal,' and 'Caballo Moro.' They also produce

Parreñita's La Escondida in Arenal

118

for the Mexican company, 'Bodegas Queretanas, S. de R.L.,' under the labels 'Peneranda' and Peneranda Especial.'

Parreñita is owned and operated by Sr. Jorge Ruiz Ibarra, a cousin to the owner of Distillery #8, Sr. J. Donato Ruiz Sanchez. When I was contacting all the various tequila companies to gain the information needed for this book, Parreñita would not make any comments, and the company attorney stated that, for political reasons, they did not wish to be mentioned in the book.

DISTILLERY #33
Tequila San Matias de Jalisco, S.A. de C.V.
NOM #1103   'La Argentina'   DOT #93

This is a medium-sized company whose distillery is located in the town of Tepatitlan in the Los Altos region to the East of Guadalajara. The factory, sometimes called 'Ojo de Agua de Latillas,' is fairly large, with 13 ovens each having a capacity of 20 metric tons, 28 fermentation tanks with capacities of 20,000 liters each, and five alembic stills that can each distill 3,500 liters of 55 percent alcohol tequila daily.

The company was founded in 1886 by Don Delfino González in the village of Magdalena, close to the town of Tequila. Don Delfino started the original distillery on his Rancho, San Matias, and sold the products of his *taberna* in the surrounding area. The product slowly gained recognition, became accepted as a good tequila throughout Jalisco, and gained strong support in the state of Zacatecas, just to the north of Jalisco.

In 1912, Don Delfino acquired some property in the town of Tequila and built a factory called 'El Chiripa' in the Latillas zone. He also bought another factory named 'El Tigre' a few years later. During this time, Tequila San Matias had become well-known in the northern part of Mexico, and during the 40 years following 1912, began exporting tequila to the United States.

Don Delfino took a partner in 1958, one Sr. Guillermo Castañeda Peña, and began plans to move the company from the area of Tequila to the new premium area for the growth of *agave* in 'Los Altos de Jalisco.' The new association built a modern distillery named 'La Argentina' at a location in the village of

119

*Offices of
San Matias in
Guadalaja*

Tepatitlan that had good water supplies, excellent areas for the growth of *agave,* and all other things necessary for the making of good tequila.

Sr. Casteñada directed the company for 27 years, gaining nationwide acceptance for its products. He decided to retire in 1985 and sold the company to the current owner, Sr. J. Jesus Lopez Roman.

Sr. Lopez Roman has launched the brand 'Pueblo Viejo' as a 100 percent *agave* tequila, and is currently constructing a new distillery in the village of Acatic, which will double the production capacity of the company. In 1995, Tequila San Matias de Jalisco, S.A. de C.V. manufactured 440,000 liters of 100 percent *agave* tequila and 1,780,000 liters of *mixto*. Of the output, 98 percent was consumed in Mexico, and the remaining 2 percent was exported to the United States, France, and Greece.

DISTILLERY #34
Tequila Santa Fe, S.A. de C.V.
NOM #1112   DOT #112

This recently-formed medium-sized company is located in the village of Antonio Escobedo, about 30 kilometers southwest of the village of Tequila. Begun in the early 1990s, the company is owned by Sr. Salvador Valenzuela Foster, but daily operations are conducted by Sr. Con Pablo Joa.

Production for 1994 was 47,063 liters of all types of tequila, and for 1995, they produced 93,806 liters of *mixto* and 27,453 liters of *cien por ciento de agave* tequila. Their 100 percent *agave* label is '1,000 Agaves,' and for *mixto* they use the labels 'Santa Fe' and 'Revolución.' None of their tequila is exported.

DISTILLERY #35
Tequila Sauza, S.A. de C.V.
NOM #1102   'La Perseverancia'   DOT #88

Tequila Sauza is the second largest producer of bulk export tequila, trailing only Cuervo in volume of production. The company is owned by the very large liquor company, Pedro Domecq, which is based in Spain. This company is now a part of the international conglomerate, Allied Domecq, of Great Britain.

Sauza was originally founded by Don Cenobio Sauza in 1873, with his purchase of a distillery which became 'La Perseverancia'. During the following years until his death in 1906, Cenobio Sauza purchased no fewer than 13 other distilleries in the state of Jalisco, for the purpose of increasing his power of production, and also in an attempt to decrease the competition. If he owned the fabrication plants, they didn't cause him any problems by making or selling competitors' tequila.

La Perseverancia; despite my perseverance, this was all I could see of it.

After his death, his son, Eladio Sauza, took over and ran the company until the 1940s, when Eladio's son Javier assumed control and ran the business until the company was acquired by Domecq.

In 1994, Sauza exported 5,800,000 liters of tequila in bulk at 55 percent alcohol. The company also produces a 100 percent *agave reposado* called 'Hornitos,' which is claimed to have spent a year in the wood.

Domecq in the United States has been helpful, but I was unable to gain entry to the distillery in Tequila, or talk to anyone there, on either of the two occasions when I tried. Sauza products are, for the most part, attractively packaged and marketed well, but excepting 'Hornitos,' all of them are *mixtos*.

DISTILLERY #36
Tequilas del Señor, S.A. de C.V.
NOM #1124   'Rio de Plata'   DOT #97

The ninth largest exporter of bulk tequila, this company sells to many different labels in the U.S. and Mexico. The company also makes many other types of spirits, including an excellent coffee liqueur, 'Café XO', which uses tequila as the base spirit.

Calderas *(steam boilers) used to cook the* agave, *heat the stills, and purify the water at Tequilas del Señor*

The distillery shipped 1,619,000 liters of *mixto* in 1994, at 55 percent alcohol by volume, to various rectifiers in the United States. The distillery consists of four autoclaves of differing sizes, an automatic grinder-juicer, numerous fermentation tanks of various volumes, three stainless steel pot stills of about 4,000 liters each, and eight wooden *reposado* tanks varying from 13,000 to 18,000 liters capacity. The total capacity of the distillery is approximately 7,000,000 liters per year; when I visited, it was running at about 40 percent of capacity, or about 2,800,000 liters per year of all types of tequila.

I was picked up at my hotel by the export manager, Blanca Delia Ramirez, and transported to the distillery which is in an area now completely surrounded by the city of Guadalajara. When the company was founded in 1943, by Sr. Cesar Garcia Fernandez, the plant was out in the country. In the past 52 years, the city has swallowed up the surrounding countryside until the factory is ten miles inside the city.

Blanca took me on a tour of the distillery and showed me the plant, explaining how the different machines functioned (this was the first distillery I visited in Mexico) and the reasons for some of the practices, and helpfully pointing out aspects that might be different from other *fábricas*. One point of interest was the cellar where a *solera* for the aging of *mixto* had been set up. The *solera* was constructed in 1970 and comprises five levels of barrels.

The company was run by a cousin of Sr. Garcia for the first 30 years, with Sr. Garcia visiting the plant a couple of times a month, while he and his family continued to live in Mexico City. In 1968, his son, Manuel Garcia Villegas, began working and living at the plant, and in 1973, took over the operation of the company. He continued to live on the plant property until 1980, when he purchased property and built a home in Guadalajara.

The company currently exports in bulk to companies whose labels include 'Torada,' 'Jose Cortez,' 'Jose Gaspar,' 'Clamantini,' and 'Pecos Heat.' The company bottles its own labels mainly for sale in Mexico and operates both an automatic bottling and labelling machine and a manual bottling and labelling line. Some of the proprietary labels the company uses are: 'Reserva del Señor,' 'Diligencias,' 'Cesar Garcia,' 'Huerto Vieja,' 'Maragalime,' 'Rio de Plata,' 'Ora Viejo,' 'Castilla,' 'Herrencia del Señor,' 'Sombrero Negro,' and 'Herrencia de Plata.'

When I met with Sr. Garcia, his son, and the marketing manager, Mr. Hendrik Nollen, I learned something of their future plans. Expansion of this plant is not now feasible, since it is surrounded by the city, and the cost of buying more land would be prohibitive. Sr. Garcia does have some 400 hectares (about 1,000 acres) of land under cultivation, with about 1,000,000 *agave* in the ground, and the company also buys *agave* on the open market.

The company is thinking of adding even more and differing types of spirits and liqueurs. Their new 100 percent *agave* tequila, Herrencia del Señor, is a very smooth, flavorful tequila that should do well, but has appeared on the market in Mexico only fairly recently. The company plans to export the product to the United States through Sun Imports of Winston-Salem, under the label 'Authentico', and on the west coast through Frank-Lin distributors under the label 'Rio de Plata'.

DISTILLERY #37
Tequila Sierra Brava, S.A. de C.V.
NOM #1298

This company had not begun production at the end of 1996, and little information was available. The labels that will be used have not yet been registered and distillery construction was not finished on schedule. However, it was still being predicted that the company would begin operating during 1997.

DISTILLERY #38
Tequila Siete Leguas, S.A. de C.V.
NOM #1120   'El Centenario' and 'La Vencedora'   DOT #105

Founded in the 1920s by Sr. Jose González Estrada, the company passed to his son, Ignacio González Vargas, in 1944, and is currently being managed by Amparo De Anda, Ignacio's widow, and their sons. One of the sons, Fernando González de Anda, is taking a strong management position and helps his mother run the company.

Of the two distilleries, one is a small, totally traditional *fábrica*, and the other is a small, fairly modern facility. The older plant still uses a *tahona* when it operates, which is mainly to provide an educational exhibit for visitors, as most of the output comes from the other distillery.

Siete Leguas is generally acknowledged to manufacture one of the best of the super-premium tequilas. In Mexico, it is considered among the top five and is imported into the United States as the boutique tequila, 'Patrón,' a major player in the fast-growing upper-end market for tequila. The brand owner and importer of 'Patron' into the United States is St. Maarten Spirits located in Culver City, California, which is owned by Martin Crowley and John Paul de Joria of the Mitchell hair care products company. Worldwide distribution rights for 'Patrón' are held by Seagram International.

The name 'Siete Leguas' means 'seven leagues,' or a distance of 42 miles. This was the name of Pancho Villa's favorite horse, a mare with enormous energy, who reputedly never tired.

The company manufactures only 100 percent *agave* tequila, and in 1994 exported 128,073 liters, comprising their *blanco* and a two year *añejo* in hand blown glass bottles. In 1995, they exported 203,191 liters out of 338,340 manufactured.

The owners are relatives of the family that owns 'Tequila Tres Magueyes' (Distillery #40) and the founders of both companies may have been brothers. Sr. Jose González Estrada, the founder of 'Siete Leguas' may have been the older brother of don Julio González Estrada, the founder of 'Tres Magueyes.' Don Carlos González Estrada, who also founded a distillery of aguardiente (raw brandy), named 'Arroyo Bonito,' in the village of Atotonilco el Alto in the 1930s, is also a brother of don Julio.

There were at one time five distilleries in Atotonilco el Alto, and the González Estrada family founded four of them, the fourth being the El Viejito distillery, purchased by Sr. Indalesio Nuñez Muro in the early 1940s, and currently operated by his second son, Sr. Antonio Nuñez Hurtado, and his family.

DISTILLERY #39

Tequila Tapatio, S.A. de C.V.

NOM #1139   'La Alteña'   DOT #101

Founded in 1937 by Sr. Felipe Camarena Hernandez, this company was originally named 'Camarena Hermanos,' meaning 'Camarena Brothers.' The company passed to his son, Felipe J. Camarena Orozco, in 1971. While the current Don Felipe, now in his late sixties, still takes a great interest in the company and its methods of manufacture, he does most of his work in the area that he loves best, supervising labor in the fields and watching the *agave* grow to maturity.

His son, Carlos Christian Camarena Curien, handles most of the administrative work of the company, much to his chagrin: he went to four years of college and graduated with a degree in agriculture, and now finds himself sitting behind a desk all day. He and his father are assisted by Carlos's two sisters, who also serve on the corporate board of directors, Lilianna Maria as secretary and Gabriela as treasurer.

The company currently produces two brands of tequila, 'Tapatio' and 'El Tesoro de Don Felipe.' The name 'El Tesoro' ('the treasure') is a created label name which was reached after much discussion between the Camarenas and their exporter, Robert Denton and Co. A number of names had been proposed and rejected, but both could agree on this one, though for different reasons. Bob Denton regarded it as a tribute to the skill of the current 'Don Felipe,' but the Camarena family saw the name as a tribute to the original, their father and grandfather, the founder.

La Alteña is one of the few distilleries that still uses all of the old methods to produce tequila. They harvest the ripest and best *agave*, from their own fields, currently owning approximately 1,000 hectares of *agave*, or about 2,500,000 plants in various stages of maturity. The *agave* is transported to the distillery in the bed of a four-wheel drive pickup, or on a larger truck, and cut up for placing in the ovens. Tapatio has two firebrick ovens of 16 metric tons capacity each. They are expanding the manufacturing facility and plan four additional ovens of 40 metric tons each (40 metric tons is 88,000 pounds).

After the *agave* has cooked for 48 hours and cooled for 24 hours, it is removed from the oven and placed in one of the few *tahonas* (stone crushing pits) still in constant use (Tapatio's expansion plans include three more *tahonas*). A small tractor is used to pull the massive stone wheel around the circle, crushing the agave into a stringy pulp and releasing the sugary juice to form puddles upon the surface. The juice is removed by hand, in long-handled ladles and placed in buckets, in which it is conveyed by hand to the fermentation tanks (it is carried in wooden buckets on the heads of three workers and dumped into the tanks).

After all of the juice has been extracted, the pulp is packed into the buckets, and a portion is placed into each tank prior to beginning the fermentation process. This is done because the family believes that leaving the fiber in the juice as long as possible imparts the very best *agave* flavor to their products.

Once the juice and fiber has been distributed and the tanks are filled, the yeast is introduced. This yeast is a strain that has been kept alive and used in the making of their products for the last fifty years. After each 3,000-liter wooden tank receives its ladle of the yeast and is well mixed, one tank is set aside to be the repository of the yeast for the beginning of the next fermentation cycle.

After the must or juice is fully fermented, it is removed from the tank by hand and carried to the first run still, where it is placed in the still with the fiber in place. Following the first fermentation run, the remainder, or *bagasse*, is carried into a nearby field to dry and is ground up and used as fertilizer on new fields. The *ordinario* is distilled a second time in a smaller pot still and comes out at approximately 42 percent alcohol (Tapatio has two pot stills, the first run still about twice as large as the second). When completed, the new tequila is piped into a large wooden holding tank to await shipment to the bottling plant or storage area in Arandas.

The fabrication plant is currently running at capacity of about 300,000 liters per year. Of the different types and brands marketed, Tapatio and El Tesoro *blanco* are the same; about 30,000 liters per year are produced. Tapatio also produces 200,000 liters of *reposado* a year with the new El Tesoro *reposado* being eight months old. Seventy thousand liters of *añejo* are also produced: Tapatio *añejo* is a one-year and El Tesoro a 30-month *añejo*.

After the tour, Carlos took me to the obligatory lunch at a local restaurant, one that served Tapatio tequila, of course. Lunch is the main meal of the day in Mexico, and one or two glasses of tequila is required (especially when you make tequila—you must continually monitor the product). Tapatio *añejo* is a very smooth tequila, with a dry tartness to its herbaceous flavor and a flowery aroma. It makes an excellent complement to spicy food.

The three tequilas made by this company are justly considered among the loftiest achievements of the tequila maker's art.

DISTILLERY #40
Tequila Tres Magueyes, S.A. de C.V.
NOM #1118   'La Primavera'   DOT #84

Tres Magueyes was the sixth largest exporter of bulk tequila in 1994, shipping 2,703,000 liters of *mixto* to Barton Brands of Chicago, who bottled the product under the label 'Montezuma', but Tres Magueyes slipped to ninth in 1995, with exports of only 1,398,938 liters of *mixto*.

This company is wisely expanding its production of 100 percent *agave* tequila, while slowing its bulk exports. They have been very successful with their premium product, 'Don Julio', in Mexico, where it is marketed as both a six-month *reposado* and a three-year *añejo*. They also market another *cien por ciento de agave* product under the 'Tres Magueyes' label as a *blanco* and a *reposado*. Recent levels of 100 percent *agave* tequila production have been approximately 500,000 liters per year and are steadily expanding. Tres Magueyes is currently in negotiations with the Rémy-Martin company of France for worldwide distribution, and the tequila should be making an appearance, in certain areas, about the middle of 1996.

My first meeting with the international manager of Tres Magueyes, Eduardo González Garcia, was at a luncheon with him and a couple of associates at one of the newest restaurants in Guadalajara. We had seafood, talked about the tequila business, and why I would want to write a book about tequila. I gave my stock answer, "Because there aren't any books on tequila." The conversation continued from there, with constant interruptions from Eduardo's cellular phone (the smallest I'd ever seen, no more than two inches square and one inch thick).

Next day I arrived at the distillery and was introduced to don Carlos González Estrada, the younger brother of Don Julio and Eduardo's uncle, and the distillery manager, Sr. Marco Cedano. I remarked upon the similarity between the spelling of his name, Cedano, and that of the distillery manager of González González , Sr. Miguel Cedeño As it turns out, the two men are good friends and talk often, having many similar interests besides their not-the-same names.

Marco took me through the plant and showed me the operation from beginning to end. By this time, I had already toured

Front entrance of La Primavera in Atotonilco

five other distilleries, but the plant was still fascinating. The distillery is currently operating with four 40-ton ovens, and Marco feels that they need a large autoclave to speed the cooking process. An automatic grinder-juicer extracts the *agave* juice, and after fermentation is complete, using commercial yeasts, the alcohol is concentrated in five stills.

One still is a copper pot still, smaller than the others, now used to purify water for the boilers. The other four are stainless steel pot stills used to concentrate the alcohol into tequila. While checking the stills and watching the *ordinario* flow from the still-pipe, I made a comment that I could smell the agave in the liquid. Marco said that after ten years, he was so used to it he never noticed it, and, dipping his finger in the liquid flowing from the pipe and tasting it, made the comment that it was about 20 percent alcohol. Looking at the stillman, Enrique Abarca, Marco told me that Enrique could tell the percentage of alcohol in the clear liquid simply by looking at it. Enrique could only explain this

129

ability by saying that it was the way the liquid flowed from the pipe. Perhaps it has something to do with the 25 years that he has been a still master at Tres Magueyes. Enrique is the middle one of three brothers, who have together had over 100 years with the company. Enrique's older brother had been with the firm 37 years, Enrique had 34 years, and the youngest had worked there for 32 years.

After the tour, Raul and I headed back for the office in Guadalajara. He wanted to stop for lunch at the restaurant of a friend in Chapala so I could sample Mexican caviar. From the outside, the building looked like a small walk-in restaurant, but once through the doors, a staircase led down the side of a hill into a very large room and on down through a series of open areas, until we reached a large area resembling a Hawaiian long-house, overlooking Lake Chapala. It was beautiful, with a soft breeze blowing in from the lake following an afternoon shower.

We ate the fish eggs on small fresh corn tortillas and had small whitefish fried crisp. You put them in a tortilla and add a little salsa—not too much, or you would need more 'Negro Modelo' beer to cool down your throat. After the fish, a little Don Julio to soothe our nerves for the drive back into Guadalajara.

My next visit to Guadalajara fell on the 12th of October—it was Columbus Day in the United States, but in Guadalajara it was the feast day of the Virgin of Zapopan. The entire city was shut down for the fiesta, so we went to the distillery in Atotonilco el Alto, to meet with some friends and business associates of the González family.

We drove up the mountainsides to look at the *agave* fields, checking out areas where harvesting was going on and looked at the growth patterns in the different fields, with don Carlos talking, telling the others what was going on, and me catching a word here and there. The side of the mountain behind the town of Atotonilco was covered with *agave* on what appeared to be a slope of about 45 degrees. I made the comment to Eduardo that when the *agave* were cut, all you would have to do was let them roll down the side of the mountain. He laughed and said that it could sometimes be a problem. During the harvest season just such things as this happened if you weren't careful. Imagine a 200-

pound *agave cabeza* rolling down that steep a slope, gaining speed all the way. It could be dangerous.

After a couple of hours of this, we stopped at the municipal swimming pool in Atotonilco and had a beer, returned to the plant, and after changing cars, drove up to the home of Eduardo's brother, Francisco, the CEO of Tres Magueyes and currently the Director of the National Social Security System for the State of Jalisco. Francisco's house sits on top of a ridge alongside the main highway, looking over the valley of Atotonilco. We all went into the courtyard of the house, where one side of the yard had the tables set for lunch, and the other had three horses staked out in a corral for the guests to ride. Talking and eating and drinking: *Hablando y comiendo y bebiendo*. It was a beautiful day.

Eduardo and I talked at some length about the business and the future growth of the industry. Rumors had it that a portion of the company had been sold to another family company in Mexico City—Eduardo confirmed this and showed me the new composition of the board of directors. My impression of this company is that they are on the right track, while still searching for new opportunities. The connection with Rémy-Martin should allow for excellent opportunities in worldwide distribution and will allow the company to grow at an appropriate pace.

'Tequila Don Julio' and 'Tequila Tres Magueyes' should both be available in the United States by the time this book is released, or shortly thereafter.

DISTILLERY #41
Tequila Viuda de Romero, S.A. de C.V.
NOM #1111   'Viuda de Romero'   DOT#83

The history of Tequila Viuda de Romero began in 1852, when Don Epitacio Romero began producing *mezcal* wine, or what was at the time called 'tequila wine', in the state of Jalisco. When he died in 1873, he left his property and estate to his son, Francisco Romero.

Don Francisco Romero González had married Doña Catalina Aguilar Madrileño, and his uncle, Eduardo González, the brother of the mother, had died and left him 12,000 agave plants. When his father died, Francisco found himself in possession of two *tabernas*, or manufacturing plants, both in the village of Tequila. The plants were named 'La Quintaneña' and 'El León.'

In 1888, Don Francisco formed a partnership with Don Cenobio Sauza plus others and founded Compania Minera de Tequila. By the year 1902, his companies had grown to include four *tabernas*, 'La Quinteneña' and 'El León', plus 'Las Fuentes' in Teuchitlan, and 'San Ignacio' in Hostotipaquillo.

Don Francisco died in 1906, and the properties passed to his wife, Doña Catalina Aguilar Madrileño, Viuda de Romero, and were administered by his son, Ignacio Romero Aguilar. *Viuda* means 'widow.'

During the time that Don Ignacio ran the company, the properties were dispersed in a manner that left little in the way of historical record, but it is known that he transferred ownership of the *taberna* 'Las Fuentes' to his nephew, Tomas Romero Montero. At the time of the transfer, the distillery was making a product known as 'Tequila Romero.' Don Tomas opened a new production facility in the village of Ahualco, near to the 'Las Fuentes' *taberna*, and in 1906, changed his product name to 'Tequila de la Viuda de Francisco Romero.' This name was used until the year 1918, when it was changed to 'Tequila Viuda de Romero.'

From 1918 to 1983, the brand changed hands four times and was made in a number of different distilleries. In 1935, the brand was administered by the Velasco family, and it was purchased by a company named González y Noriega in 1943. Through a number of mergers and partnerships, the brand was managed by that company until 1978, when the Spanish company Cavas Bach

Viuda de Romero in Tequila

assumed control. They closed their Mexican operations in 1983 and sold the company to the Luis A. Cetto group.

The Cetto group built a new production facility and began producing tequila under the name 'Tequila Viuda de Romero' in 1985. Currently, the company produces a *blanco*, a gold, a six-month *reposado*, and a two-year *Añejo Inmemorial* under the Viuda de Romero name, as a *mixto*.

Cien por ciento de agave tequilas are made and sold by the company under the names of 'Real Hacienda', as a *blanco, reposado,* and *añejo,* and another *reposado* under the name 'Alteño.'

The present distillery is of medium size and is capable of producing 2,000,000 liters per year of *mixto*. For 100 percent *agave* the figure would be half of that volume.

DISTILLERY #42
Tequilena, S.A. de C.V.
NOM #1146   'La Tequileña'   DOT #102

Originally founded by Sr. Robert Orendain in 1967, this was a small distillery with an annual output of 300,000 liters of *mixto*. At that time, the official norm for bulk tequila was 70 percent *agave* and 30 percent other sugars at 55 percent alcohol.

In 1981, the company was purchased by Bacardi, the giant rum manufacturer based in Puerto Rico, and thoroughly rebuilt and expanded over the next few years. The annual production capacity of the company reached a high of 3,300,00 liters of *mixto* at 55 percent alcohol. *Cien por ciento de agave* capacity would be half that figure.

While the proprietary brand 'Xalixco' was established in the domestic market by Barcadi, the main sales thrust was for the export market, with 80 percent of production being shipped to other countries. Because of Bacardi's new growth strategy and recommitment to the rum market, the company was sold to 'Vinicola del Vergel,' a leading Mexican brandy manufacturer, in 1987.

The new owners seemed to lack firm knowledge of the tequila market or to be unable to determine the direction in which that market was moving. They failed to produce a tequila which found

On the right track: La Tequileña in Tequila

favor in the domestic market, and the company was again sold in 1990, to Sr. Enrique Fonseca, since 1978 the largest *agave* farmer in Jalisco. He has been growing *agave* for over 50 years and sells it to all of the major distillers, with production varying between 17,000,000 and 25,000,000 kilograms of *agave*, mainly from the Los Altos region.

The company now quickly got on the right track. They began producing 100 percent *agave* tequila and completely refurbished their storage units for *reposado* and *añejo*, finally reaching a total of 412,400 liters capacity for storing and aging tequila.

In 1992, Tequileña began marketing their current labels: a 100 percent *agave* tequila under the label 'Pura Sangre', and a *mixto* of 70 percent *agave* and 30 percent other sugars under the label 'Xalixco.' This spelling is the seventeenth-century original of 'Jalisco.'

The company is very proud of the continuous action copper still that they use for the first concentration of alcohol from the *mosto* to the *ordinario*. The second still is a copper pot still used to further concentrate the alcohol in the *ordinario* to tequila.

Tequileña has correctly analyzed the likely direction of future changes, and appears well-situated in the expanding market for quality tequila.

DISTILLERY #43

Tequilera Corralejo, S.A. de C.V.

NOM #1368

This is a new distillery in the village of Pénjamo, in the state of Guanajuato, just across the border with Jalisco, making it the second distillery not located in Jalisco. It was opened in June of 1996, as the very first distillery to be designed with tourism in mind.

Located on the grounds of a small colonial hacienda, and using many traditional methods to demonstrate how tequila was formerly made, this company will produce five brands of tequila, mainly *reposados*, under different labels: 'El Sol de Pénjamo,' which will be bottled in a special rustic-looking container, 'Tequila Corralejo,' La Quita Peñas,' 'Leyendas de Guanajuato, and a special brand, 'La Cucaracha,' which will be made exclusively for a wine company based in Cancún.

This company is owned and operated by a glass and bottle maker, Sr. Leonardo Rodriguez, and the company is also in the process of constructing a restaurant in Spain which will be used to promote the new tequilas in Europe. Since sales are expected to be brisk, the current plans of the company are that most production will be exported to Europe.

The plant will have two alembic stills of a new type, made in Spain, the first ones of this type in Mexico, and eleven twelve-thousand-liter *reposado* casks for aging the spirit. There are currently no plans to export any of this company's tequilas to the U.S.

DISTILLERY #44

Tequilera La Gonzáleña, S.A. de C.V.

NOM #1127   'La Gonzáleña

One of only two distilleries outside the state of Jalisco currently producing tequila, this *fábrica* is located in the state of Tamaulipas in the eastern part of Mexico. It makes a very fine and what was a very rare tequila.

During the war of reform in 1850 and the French intervention in 1863, a group of wealthy landowners banded together, and with their workers, joined in the fight for the Mexican regime. These men were known for their dashing elegance and bravery. They were the 'Chinacos.' One of these Chinacos, Manuel González, was destined for great prominence. After the wars he returned to his birthplace, the northern state of Tamaulipas, with the military rank of General and began buying up extensive tracts of land from Tamaulipas to Mexico City. Because of these actions, he became deeply involved with the Department of Agriculture.

In 1880, He was elected president of Mexico. During his four years in office, Manuel González accomplished many things. He directed the foundation of the first Mexican-owned bank, Banco Nacional de México, brought electricity to Mexico City, and was responsible for the construction of half of the railroad system still in use, earning him the distinction of being called the 'Father of the Railroad'.

After leaving the presidency in 1884, he was elected governor of the state of Guanajuato, a position he held until his death in 1893. When he died, he was interred in the federal Rotunda, a place of honor where other distinguished citizens have since followed him.

Manuel González's great grandson, Guillermo González began his career as a lawyer in Mexico City. He also farmed land inherited from his great-grandfather in his home state of Tamaulipas. After his cotton crop in 1952 was destroyed by an unusual frost, he announced in a newspaper interview that he and the new president of Mexico were going to start a national agricultural insurance program. Though the president was only made aware of this program by reading about it in the newspaper, he installed Guillermo as the Secretary of Agriculture.

After hurricane Beulah devastated southern Tamaulipas in 1965, González went there to survey the damage and found that the only plants which had survived were wild *agaves*. He contacted one of the large tequila producers in Jalisco, who offered attractive prices for any *agave* that the farmers in Tamaulipas could grow. But eight years later, when the first crop was ready for harvest, the tequila producer came in with an offer of less than half the originally-mentioned price.

Refusing this offer, Guillermo burned his crop, and decided to build his own distillery. He bought an old cotton gin that had been abandoned and brought in engineers from Jalisco with experience in designing and building a tequila distillery. A year later he applied for his licenses and a trademark. Several large tequila producers fought his application, quoting laws stating that tequila could only be produced in Jalisco and certain bordering states. Starting a legal battle to change the law and allow manufacture of tequila in his home state, he found some friends in government and on October 13th, 1977, the NORMA was amended to include eleven municipalities in Tamaulipas as legally permitted to manufacture tequila.

After he had won his battle against the larger producers, he began producing tequila under the name 'Chinaco' as a reminder of the odds over which he had triumphed. For seven months he ran the plant at full production, storing all of the tequila in barrels for aging. After this first frenzied production period, Guillermo limited production to under 1,500 cases per year (About 13,500 liters). The tequila was never available on the open market in Mexico, being reserved for private clubs and 'those in the know'. In 1983, the first shipment of Chinaco *añejo* was sent to Robert Denton and Company in Michigan.

In 1993, Guillermo's four sons bought the company, and are still continuing in the tradition of excellence begun by their father. The first shipment of Chinaco *blanco* produced by the sons, crossed over into the U.S., in November of 1994. Sadly, Sr, Guillermo González Diaz Lombardo, the founder of Chinaco, died on February 3rd, 1996. The letters G.G.D.L. now appear on all labels of Chinaco as a tribute to his memory.

Making only 100 percent *agave* tequila, this small distillery exports everything to the United States via Robert Denton and Company. As this book goes to press, the company offers only *blanco* and *reposado,* but I have tasted a pre-release sample of the forthcoming *añejo,* and it is excellent.

DISTILLERY #45
Tequilera Newton e Hijos, S.A. de C.V.
NOM #1173   DOT #115

A small tequila company founded in the 1980s, Newton e Hijos manufactured 513,901 liters of *mixto* and 46,653 liters of 100

The office of Newton e Hijos in Guadalajara

percent *agave* tequila in 1995. They sell their tequila under the labels 'Especial Newton,' 'Los Corrales,' 'Newton (Diseño),' 'El Destilador,' and 'Puente Viejo.' They also sell tequila to Ohrner Company, HCJ.

I once came across a one-liter bottle of Tequila Newton in a Guadalajara liquor store with a price tag of six pesos. At the time, the monetary exchange rate between the U.S. and Mexico was about 6.50 new pesos to $1.00 U.S. Unless this tequila was selling below cost, it must have been able to show a profit for both the distillery and the retail store at a price of about 95 American cents, which would be disquieting.

DISTILLERY #46

Tequilera Rustica de Arandas, S.A. de C.V.

NOM #1235

This company began production in mid-1996, and produces the tequila labelled 'El Charro,' its primary brand in Mexico. Also registered to this company are the brand names 'Hacienda de Tepa,' 'Tres Caballos,' 'Tepa,' and 'Tres Reyes.'

This is a small distillery, located some ten kilometers outside of Arandas on the highway to Léon. The buildings are partially concealed behind a beautiful villa right on the highway. It is fairly

Rustica de Arandas, actually just outside Arandas

small, producing approximately 1,500 liters a day, and can be difficult to find.

Rustica de Arandas is actively pursuing the possibility of exports and hopes to sell into the U.S. market soon.

That concludes the complete listing of all 46 distillery companies which could be considered operational by January, 1997.

More New Distilleries

As this book went to press, 13 additional companies were expected to open for production before long. They are as follows:

DISTILLERY #A

There is a newly-built distillery on the main highway into Arandas. I believe it may belong to Destiladora de Los Altos, S.A. de C.V., which has applied for licenses to operate a tequila distillery in Arandas.

DISTILLERY #B

A new distillery for Seagram de México is under construction in Arandas and was expected to begin operations by July of 1997. They will presumably continue using their own brand names of

This new distillery on the road into Arandas is probably owned by Destiladora de Los Altos (#A)

'Los Ruiz,' 'Mariachi,' 'Olmeca,' and 'Coyote,' and will probably also add others.

DISTILLERY #C

The Satisfactores distillery in the town of Atotonilco el Alto has been closed for some years due to the illness and subsequent death of the owner, but rumor has it that the plant has been sold to the children, and could re-open for production.

DISTILLERY #D

Compañia Destiladora de Acatlan has applied for licenses to operate a tequila distillery in Acatlan. This distillery has been pro-ducing *mezcal*. I doubt very much that anyone would try to pro-duce *mezcal* and tequila in the same distillery, so I'm sure the distillery will be completely converted to tequila production.

DISTILLERY #E

A company calling itself Tequilera La Tapatia plans to open a tequila distillery in the village of Cuquio. This company name is so close to that of Tequila Tapatio that efforts will undoubtedly be made to persuade the new company to change its name.

DISTILLERY #F

Compañia Destiladora de Los Altos plans to open a distillery in the village of San Ignacio. My information is that this distillery

140

will be ambitious—not quite as big as the new Seagram distillery, but big.

Of the remaining proposed distilleries almost nothing is known except the company name and the town in which they plan to operate:

DISTILLERY #G
In Amatitán, Mextlalla, S.A. de C.V.

DISTILLERY #H
In Arandas, Feliciano Vivanco e Hijos.

DISTILLERY #I
In Arenal, Jose A. Sandoval.

DISTILLERY #J
In Tepatitlan, Industrializadora San Isidro.

DISTILLERY #K
In Tequila, CIA, Internacional Tequilera.

DISTILLERY #L
In Tequila, Tequila, R.G.

DISTILLERY #M
In Tlaquepaque, Industrialización Integral del Agave.

They Keep On Coming

When, after years of research, I finally began writing this book, there were 32 tequila companies. Within six months this had grown to 35, and it is now 46, with the likelihood of the 13 listed above being added soon. There are also around five other projected new companies who are working discreetly on their plants and have not yet applied for licenses, which would bring the number of producing distilleries to 64. For comparison, 64 tequila distilleries would still be well below the number of scotch whisky distilleries in the tiny country of Scotland.

Who knows how many more can be added, before a shake-out occurs among tequila companies? There are already qualms about the fight for retail shelf space, and some sort of correction may occur within the next few years. More hopefully, the expected move to 100 percent *agave*, with increased emphasis on the super-premium or boutique labels, and the coming growth of a large population of tequila connoisseurs outside Mexico, could favor an increase in the number of tequila producers and a reduction in their average size.

Tequila Importers and Distributors

This chapter gives some idea of the system that moves tequila from the distillery, via a retailer, to the ultimate consumer. As this system is complex and constantly evolving, I cannot hope to present a complete account within such a short space. More information is provided in the appendixes.

Since the U.S. consumes more tequila than the rest of the world put together, and since most readers of this book will be U.S. residents, this chapter concentrates heavily on the United States, but at the end I give a little information about distribution in Mexico and other countries around the world.

Some companies buy and sell bulk tequila all over the world. Others bottle under their own labels or may use the labels of either the manufacturer or the retailer. There are over 3,500 U.S. companies, classed as manufacturers, wholesalers, importers, or distributors of alcoholic beverages, listed with the BATF, so it's clear that the totality of all the pathways of commerce between these entities is too complex for any individual to grasp.

The U.S. Distribution System

The distribution system inside the United States works in different ways within different areas, partly because state and local regulations differ considerably. I will give an informal description of the system in the area I am most familiar with, Northern California. Many aspects will be similar in some other areas of the U.S.

In California there are currently two major, two medium-sized, and 14 smaller wholesale distributors handling spirits or wine. There are also 18 distributors who primarily distribute wine; they may also handle minor specialty items but are mainly in the wine business.

There are over 30 beer distributors in Northern California, most covering imports or smaller breweries. Domestic beer sales and distribution for major brands such as Anheuser-Busch or Coors are handled by direct licensed-dealer representatives of the brewers.

Each company handles specific brands and labels and provides those products to the retailer, whether on- or off-sale establishments. The largest wholesalers tend to handle the most popular brands of spirits, and the more esoteric brands are usually distributed by the smaller companies, normally on an exclusive basis, though a brand may occasionally be channelled through more than one distributor.

Importers tend to prefer larger, more well-known distributors to distribute their products. If a new high-quality product is just coming onto the market and is not affiliated with an established group of brands, it can be very difficult to get shelf space in the local liquor store, or to get the distributors to place that product in local bars and restaurants. If you are an importer and one of your competitors is larger and better known than your company, you may come to believe that they make demands upon the distributors not to handle or promote your product.This can make it very difficult to gain market share when your product is consigned to the back room or not properly represented. There are many companies who have started to import quality spirits or other products, only to feel that they were frozen out of the market by such policies.

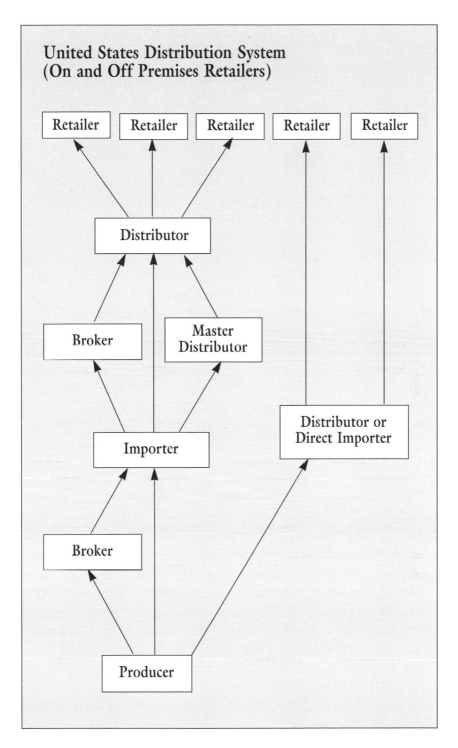

United States Distribution System
(On and Off Premises Retailers)

Since there are currently over a thousand different labels of spirits available in Northern California, plus something approaching three thousand different labels of wines, it is obvious that few stores can stock all of the wines and spirits available in the marketplace. I'm not sure how many different beers are manufactured, but since Mexico alone makes well over 50 different brands, and the U.S. hundreds, there must be at least a thousand in the world as a whole.

In California alone, there were, as of June 1995, 841 winegrowers, 40 distilleries, half of which made only brandy, and eight major breweries, with 129 small beer manufacturers, including brew-pubs. Further licensees include 164 general beer and wine importers, 43 general distilled spirits importers, 1,217 beer and wine wholesalers, and 255 distilled spirits wholesalers. If you are looking for a rare or unusual product, you need to know how to get in touch with the importer, supplier, or wholesaler.

If you want to get information by contacting any of the liquor distributors in your area, you will normally find them listed in the yellow pages, or any tavern or liquor store can give you the address of a local liquor industry publication that can provide you that information. In California, the primary source for such information is a monthly publication called the *BIN merchandiser*, ('BIN' stands for Beverage Industry News). This publication has listings for all distributors in the area, plus the local addresses for the supply companies and regulatory agencies. All parts of the United States have similar publications, which usually appear monthly, and are aimed exclusively at liquor businesses in the area, but most liquor license holders will subscribe, and back copies will usually be easy to obtain.

Of the many fine, superior-quality alcoholic beverage products manufactured around the world, the proportion available in any area within the U.S. is certainly less than 50 percent, probably substantially less than 25 percent. Most of the major American and Canadian whiskey companies are well represented, with a dozen major manufacturing companies supplying the majority of the whiskeys on the market. Imports of other brands may face a hurdle in that members of the public may be unaware that they exist. The fact that they may be more expensive than the well-known brands, and that liquor advertising is restricted, makes it hard to spread the good news about superior quality.

This is not a problem confined to tequila. The best of such beverages as the fortified wines—the ports, sherries, madieras and marsalas—or the French brandies like cognacs, armagnacs, and calvados, are not very well known, or are ridiculed as being too pretentious for regular people. Nothing could be further from the truth. These products are merely misunderstood or overlooked, very much as tequila has been until recently. Many of the best Caribbean rums, the ones produced in small, highly traditional pot stills, are also difficult to find in the U.S. There may be a revival in the consumption of superior spirits in years to come. Rising incomes lead to more discriminating tastes and the search for higher-priced, better-quality varieties of all kinds of consumer goods.

Government Involvement

The liquor import and distribution system of the United States is a labyrinthine system made more difficult by the fact that each state controls the sale and availability of alcohol in different ways.

Federal government control comes primarily through the BATF enforcement arm of the Treasury Department. Federal controls not being enough for the states, each state has many additional laws. Eighteen states (and one county in Maryland) are classed as 'control states', with the state government controlling all aspects of importation, distribution, and sales of that old bugaboo, 'demon rum', or in our case, possibly *tequila del diablo*.

These unfortunate states are: Alabama, Idaho, Iowa, Maine, Michigan, Mississippi, Montana, New Hampshire, North Carolina, Ohio, Oregon, Pennsylvania, Utah, Vermont, Virginia, Washington, West Virginia, and Wyoming, with the addition of Montgomery County, Maryland.

All of those states have government bodies that play an unusually intrusive role in the retail sales area, and enforce price controls for the entire alcohol sales market. Some go so far as to own the entire distribution system, Pennsylvania even owning the retail stores. In that sorry state, all liquor stores are owned and operated by the state government.

In the other states listed, the main disturbance in the liquor industry comes from price controls imposed on the retail market by state alcohol control boards. In all the states not mentioned above, prices are basically allowed to move up or down according to supply and demand, though all states have a governing board which controls the issuance of licenses for on-sale bars, taverns, night clubs, and off-sale 'package' stores. (In some parts of the country, people never speak of 'package stores', whereas in some states this is the common way of referring to liquor stores.)

To give some idea how these licenses work, again taking California as an example, there were, in July 1995, 71,554 licenses of all types issued by the state ABC (Alcoholic Beverage Control) Commission. The licenses range from manufacturers and blenders to restaurants and liquor stores. They are broken down into two groups, wholesale and off-sale licenses, and on-sale licenses. The off-sale segment has 28 categories; the on-sale has 29. The largest groups in the off-sale segment are beer and wine, with 14,809 licenses, and off-sale general with 12,664 licenses, for a total of 27,473 licenses out of 30,772 within that group. The on-sale segment has 20,682 beer and wine eating places, 1,441 on-sale beer and wine public premises, 10,863 on-sale general eating places, and 3,592 general public premises, for a total of 36,578 licenses out of 40,782 on-sale licenses in all categories.

While this merely shows some of the categories into which the state has split the liquor business in order to better control sales, taxes, and license fees, it is interesting to look at the approximate amounts they can collect in these licensing fees. A general on-sale license has a one-time fee of $6,000 paid to the state, with beer and wine eating establishments paying $2,000 for their licenses. Simple multiplication shows that the license fees rise into the hundreds of millions of dollars, with general on-sale eating establishments alone paying $65,178,000 in license fees in California.

These figures should help the reader to understand why the various types of beer, wines, and spirits cost what they do in the retail market. In addition to the licensing fees charged, a large but varying rate of taxation is imposed on each type of alcoholic beverage sold within each state, and sales figures are checked and taxation rates enforced by investigators within the state bureaucracy.

While there are no longer, thank heaven, any states that are totally 'dry' (my native state of Oklahoma was the last of the states to be totally 'dry', and Oklahoma went 'wet' in 1959) there are certain counties, parishes, cities, and other political divisions within states that do prohibit the sale of alcoholic beverages within their boundaries.

United States Tequila Importing Companies

Currently, only two of the tequila manufacturing companies are owned by international companies. All of the other distilleries are controlled by Mexican entrepreneurs, most often families with a traditional involvement in tequila.

The United States imported 43 million liters of tequila in 1995, almost twice as much as that consumed in Mexico. I present below a list of tequila importers, in alphabetical order, with the labels they sell, and the distilleries from which they purchase their tequila.

Some of these companies handle the worldwide distribution of their respective spirits, while others serve only as U.S. importers, enlisting the aid of larger, more diverse companies within the alcoholic beverage industry to help in distribution.

As examples, the label 'Patrón' is a proprietary name owned by the St. Maarten Spirits Company, but the worldwide distribution of that label is handled by Seagram. 'Chinaco' and 'El Tesoro de Don Felipe' are imported by Robert Denton, with national distribution handled by Jim Beam. 'Don Julio', made by Tequila Tres Magueyes (Distillery #40), will soon be available worldwide, with international distribution handled by the well-known French cognac company, Rémy-Martin.

The 100 percent *agave* tequilas are mainly handled by smaller import companies, whereas the very large import companies are mainly involved in the importation of *mixto* in bulk. This is not always the case, but it is the dominant pattern, and this is one rea-

149

son why those interested in the best tequila find that they have to know about importers.

The following list does not include all of the importers of tequila into the United States, but it includes all the most important ones. It is, of course, purely a coincidence that there are just 46 importers here, the same number as the tequila distilleries. More information on the importers can be found in Appendix D.

IMPORTER #1
Barton Brands, Ltd

Based in Chicago,this company imports from a number of different tequila distilleries, including Tres Magueyes (Distillery #40), Orendain De Jalisco (Distillery #31), and Tequila La Madrileñe (Distillery #20). They bottle all of the tequila from the above companies under their own proprietary label, 'Montezuma'.

IMPORTER #2
Black Prince Distillery

Black Prince is currently importing tequila from Tequilas del Señor (Distillery #36), under the label 'Tlamitini'.

IMPORTER #3
Brown-Forman Beverage Company

Brown-Forman imports tequila under the label 'Pepe Lopez', from Tequila Orendain de Jalisco (Distillery #31).

IMPORTER #4
Cabo Distributing Company

This company owned the distillery company Eucario González from 1982 to 1994, but now imports most of its tequila from La Cofradia (Distillery #19). Cabo also handles the label 'Sin Rival' from Destiladora de Occidente (Distillery #8), and own the labels 'Aztlan', 'Black Death', 'Black Hat', 'Caballo Negro', 'Don

Federico', 'Eucario González', 'Limitado', and 'Portales' from their years of owning the above mentioned Tequila Eucario González (Distillery #29).

IMPORTER #5

Carillon Imports

A subsidiary of Grand Metropolitan and sister company of Heublein Imports (Importer #16), Carillon is located in Teaneck, New Jersey, and is importing the tequila labelled 'Gran Centenario', made by 'Casa Cuervo' (Distillery #4) and using the NOM #1122.

IMPORTER #6

Chatham Imports, Inc.

Chatham imports the label 'Casteneda' from Tequila La Madrileña (Distillery #20), in concert with Distillerie Stock USA Ltd (Importer #10).

IMPORTER #7

Consolidated Distilled Products Inc.

Based in Chicago, Consolidated import the tequila 'Tres Alegres Compadres' from the manufacturer, La Cofradia (Distillery #19).

IMPORTER #8

David Sherman Corp.

David Sherman imports most of their bulk tequila from Tequila González González (Distillery #9), including label names, 'Azteca', 'Casa Gallardo', 'Centennial', 'El Cid', 'Fonda Blanca', 'Gavilan', 'Hacienda', 'Juárez', and 'Rio Baja'.

IMPORTER #9

Distillerie Stock USA Ltd

This company imports the label 'Casteneda', in concert with

Chatham Imports (Importer #6), from Tequila La Madrileña (Distillery #20).

IMPORTER #10
Domecq Imports Co.

The sole importer for Tequila Sauza (Distillery #35), Domecq Imports is owned by the international conglomerate Allied Domecq and is a sister company of Hiram Walker and Sons (Importer #16).

IMPORTER #11
El Dorado Importers

Importer for Tequila Centinela (Distillery #26), El Dorado is owned by the Campos family of three brothers in the Santa Fe, New Mexico, area.

IMPORTER #12
Florida Distillers Co.

A branch of Todhunter Imports Company, this company imports Albertson's Tequila in the eastern U.S. from Tequila Eucario González (Distillery #29).

IMPORTER #13
Frank-Lin Distillers Products, Ltd

Frank-Lin imports from a number of different distilleries, and is now bringing in 100 percent *agave* tequila from Tequila El Viejito (Distillery #28). Frank-Lin also imports 'Potter's', from La Madrileña (Distillery #20), and labels 'Albertson's', 'Save-On'; and 'Juárez' from Tequila Eucario González (Distillary #29). They are also in negotiations with Tequilas del Señor (Distillery #36) to import their 100 percent *agave* tequila under the label 'Rio de Plata'.

IMPORTER #14

Franzia Importing Co.

This company imports the tequila 'J. R. Jaime Rosales', which has been manufactured by Tequila El Viejito (Distillery #28). In 1996, the company La Parreñita (Distillery #32), began making this tequila and is now listed as the manufacturer. J. R. Jaime Rosales is currently available in certain areas of Texas.

IMPORTER #15

Guadalajara Imports

Based in St. Louis, Missouri, Guadalajara Imports is a partnership owned by David Kay and Lynn Pilz. They are currently importing the label 'Aguila Tequila', made by El Viejito (Distillery #28), both as a *mixto* and a 100 percent *agave*.

IMPORTER #16

Heaven Hill Distilleries, Inc.

Also a major producer of American whiskey, Heaven Hill imports the labels 'Aristocrat' and 'Distiller's Pride', from Tequila Orendain de Jalisco (Distillery #31).

IMPORTER #17.

Heublein Inc.

Heublein is the owner and worldwide importer for Jose Cuervo Tequila, which is owned by the international conglomerate Grand Metropolitan of Great Britain, and manufactured either at the distillery Casa Cuervo (#4) or at Tequila Cuervo La Rojeña (Distillery #27). Heublein is a sister company of Carillon Imports (Importer #5).

IMPORTER #18

Hiram Walker and Sons, Inc.

Owned by Allied Domecq Corporation and a sister company of

Domecq Imports, Hiram Walker imports the label 'Two Fingers' from La Madrileña (Distillery #20).

IMPORTER #19
Hood River Distilleries, Inc.

Hood River Distilleries imports the 'Monarch' label from Tequila Orendain de Jalisco (Distillery #31).

IMPORTER #20
Illva Saronno Corp.

Illva Saronno imports the label 'Fandango' into Italy and the U.S., from Tequila Orendain de Jalisco (Distillery #31).

IMPORTER #21
Jenkins Spirits Corp. Ltd.

This company imports the labels 'Mexican Silver' and 'Mexican Gold' into the U.S. from Tequila Orendain de Jalisco (Distillery #31).

IMPORTER #22
Jim Beam Brands Co.

Jim Beam is the importer for labels 'Beamero' and 'Tempo' from Tequila Tres Magueyes (Distillery #40) and is also U.S. distributor for the very fine tequilas 'Chinaco' and 'El Tesoro de Don Felipe', imported by Robert Denton and Company (Importer #36).

DISTILLERY #23
Joseph E. Seagram and Sons Inc.

Originally a Canadian firm, Seagram's is the parent company of Seagram de México. It imports the brands 'Coyote', 'Los Ruiz Blanco', 'Los Ruiz Añejo', 'Mariachi Blanco', 'Mariachi Oro Especial', 'Olmeca Blanco', and 'Olmeca Añejo', all from Tequila Orendain de Jalisco (Distillery #31). Seagram's also handles the American distribution of the fine tequila 'Patrón'.

IMPORTER #24
Kentucky Distillers, Inc.

Kentucky Distillers imports 'Tres Alegres Compadres' from La Cofradia (Distillery #19).

IMPORTER #25
Laird and Co.

Laird imports the tequila label 'Zapata' from Tequila Orendain de Jalisco (Distillery #31).

IMPORTER #26
Le Vecke Corporation

Le Vecke imports the labels 'Acapulco' and 'La Paz' from Tequila Eucario González (Distillery #29).

IMPORTER #27
McCormick Distilling Co.

McCormick is the importer and bottler of 'Hussong's' tequila, formerly referred to as being 99 percent *agave*, now labelled 100 percent *agave*, made by La Cofradia (Distillery #19). McCormick also imports the labels 'McCormick' and 'Rio Grande' from Tequila El Viejito (Distillery #28), and Tequila Orendain de Jalisco (Distillery #31) and 'McCormick' from Tequila Eucario González (Distillery #29).

IMPORTER #28
M.S. Walker, Inc.

M.S. Walker imports 'Old Mexico' and 'Señorita Margarita' from Tequila Orendain de Jalisco (Distillery #31).

IMPORTER #29
Majestic Distilling Company, Inc.

Majestic imports the label 'Topaz' from Tequila Orendain de Jalisco (Distillery #31).

IMPORTER #30
Montebello Brands, Inc.

Montebello imports 'Tres Alegres Compadres' tequila under a different label name from La Cofradia (Distillery #19).

IMPORTER #31
Munico International Corp.

Munico is owned by the Niciolayevsky brothers of Houston, Texas, and imports the tequila label 'Distinqt', which is manufactured and bottled by Tequila El Viejito (Distillery #28).

IMPORTER #32
Paramount Distillers, Inc.

Paramount imports the labels 'Aquila Tequila', 'Carlos Gold Tequila', 'Carlos White Tequila', 'Coronado White Tequila', 'José Paco', 'La Prima Gold', 'La Prima White', 'Miguel Gold Tequila', and 'Miguel White Tequila', all from La Madrileña (Distillery #20).

IMPORTER #33
Parliament Import Co.

Parliament is now importing 'Tequila Los Valientes', made by Industralizacion y Desarollo, Santo Tomas (Distillery #14).

IMPORTER #34
Potter Distilleries, Inc.

Affiliated with International Potter Distilling Co., this company imports the label 'Potter's' from Tequila Eucario González (Distillery #29).

IMPORTER #35
Premium Imports, Ltd.

Premium imports and distributes 'Conquistador' tequila in the Kentucky and Indiana area as a well tequila for bars. They must be a secondary distributor, since there is no NOM on their labels.

IMPORTER #36
Robert Denton and Co.

Robert Denton and his partner Marilyn Smith are in large part responsible for the current increasing awareness of 100 percent *agave* tequilas in the United States. They began importing 'Chinaco' in 1982 and have persevered in the face of many obstacles. The tequilas they import are now recognized as among the best: 'Chinaco', from Tequilera La Gonzáleña (Distillery #44), and 'El Tesoro de Don Felipe' from Tequila Tapatio (Distillery #39).

IMPORTER #37
Sazerac Company, Inc.

Sazerac is U.S. importer of Herradura Tequila (Distillery #30), one of the largest manufacturers of 100 percent *agave* tequila. They also import the labels 'Tijuana', 'Tina', and 'Torada' from Tequilas del Señor (Distillery #36), and 'Tina' and 'Torada' from Tequila Eucario González (Distillery #29).

IMPORTER #38
St. Maarten Spirits Ltd.

St. Maarten is owned by a partnership of Martin Crowley and John Paul de Joria of the Paul Mitchell hair care products company. They are the brand owners and import the super-premium tequila 'Patrón' manufactured by the distillery Tequila Siete Leguas (Distillery #38). The U.S. distribution rights are held by Joseph E. Seagram and Sons Inc.

IMPORTER #39
Sun Imports, Inc.

This company currently imports the label 'César García' from Tequilas del Señor (Distillery #36).

157

IMPORTER #40
Tequila Imports, Inc.

This company has imported 'Porfidio', which is manufactured by four different distilleries, but Tequila Imports are now involved in a legal battle with the manufacturer. The triple-distilled *blanco* is made by Destiladora Azteca de Jalisco (Distillery #7). The cactus bottle *añejo* is made by Empresa Ejidal Tequilera Amatitán (Distillery #12). The other *blanco* is made by Tequila Cofradia (Distillery #19) and the other *añejo* was made by Tequila El Viejito (Distillery #28).

Tequila Imports is also involved in negotiations to import 'Tequila Alteño', made by Tequila Viuda de Romero (Distillery #41) and possibly a new label, 'Ambarfino' from Agroindustrias Guadalajara (Distillery #2).

IMPORTER #41
Tequila Los Altos Distribution Co.

Tequila Los Altos imports the 100 percent *agave* tequila 'Pueblo Viejo', and the *mixto* 'San Matias', both from Tequila San Matias de Jalisco (Distillery #33).

IMPORTER #42
Tist, Inc.

Tist is importing a premium tequila into the U.S. under the label 'Tequila Lapiz'. Manufactured by Tequileña (Distillery #42) this product is a version of 'Tequila Purasangre' and is imported only as an *añejo*. Tist is also importing 'Xalixco', from the same manufacturer.

IMPORTER #43
United Distilleries North America

United Distilleries possibly imports the tequila 'El Toro' from Tequila Orendain de Jalisco (Distillery #31).

United States Distilled Products Co.

This company imports the labels 'Callende' and José Mendes', both from Tequila El Viejito (Distillery #28).

White Rock Distilleries, Inc.

White Rock imports 'Poland Spring', 'Poland Spring Gold', 'Rockport', 'Shorty's', and 'Sutton Club', all from Destiladora González González (Distillery #9).

William Grant and Sons

Grant and Sons import the labels 'Cancún', 'Del Campo', 'Del Prado', 'Durango', 'El Bandido', 'James Mason', 'Javelina', and 'Northfield', all from Tequila Orendain de Jalisco (Distillery #31).

Other Tequila Companies in Mexico

Aside from the Mexican distilling companies, there are also companies in Mexico that buy tequila from the distilleries to sell under their own names or labels. The legal framework and the conditions of trade in Mexico are different from those in the United States. In Mexico, manufacturers can more easily sell their products directly to the public or the retailer without going through any middleman. But they often do sell to companies that resell the tequila within Mexico under a proprietary name or label. Here are some of these companies, with the labels they currently handle and the distilleries they buy from.

Company	Labels	Distillery
1. Antonio Fernandez y CIA	'Jorongo', 'Hot Jorongo'	Viuda de Romero #41
2. Bodegas Queretano	'Penerenda', 'Peneranda Especial'	Parreñita #32
3. Compania Destiladora	'Henri Vallet', 'Si-Si', 'Tikal'	El Viejito #28
4. Compania Tequilera	'Arenita', 'Virreyes', 'Viva Miguel Villa'	J.J.Reyes C. #16
5. Destileria Porfidio	'Porfidio'	#7, #16, #19
6. Grupo Vampiro	'Vampiro Vampire'	Viuda de Romero #41
7. Las Trancas	'Las Trancas'	El Viejito #28
8. Licore Veracruz	'Dos Coronas'	Tequilas del Señor #36
9. Maya Corporation	'Aztlan', 'Black Hat', 'Caballo Negro', 'Eucario González', 'Santa Cruz'	Euc. González #29
10. Nacional Vinicola	'Santa Rita'	La Cofradia #19
11. Seagram de Mexico	'Coyote', 'Los Ruiz', 'Mariachi', 'Olmeca'	Orendain #31
12. Tequila Cerro Viejo	'El Herradero'	Cascahuin #23
13. Tequila Selectos	'Tres Alegres Compadres', 'Los Cofrades', 'La Cofradia', 'De Los Dorados'	La Cofradia #19
14. Vinicola del Vergel	'Tequila Vergel'	Orendain #31

Key Importers Listed by Country

Finally, I give a list of some of the main international distributors of tequila in countries other than the United States. There are others; these are the ones registered with the *Consejo*.

Company	Labels	Distillery
AUSTRALIA		
1. International Wines and Spirits Ltd	'Mestizo'	Tequilas del Señor #36
2. Inchcape Liquor Mkting Pty Ltd	'Hombre'	El Viejito #28
CANADA		
1. Alberta Distillers	'Tres Alegres Compadres'	La Cofradia #19
2. Dumont Wines and Spirits	'Pacal de Palanque'	Tequilas del Señor #36
3. Highwood Distillers, Ltd.	'Old Mexico'	Eucario González #29
4. Inter. Potter Dist. Corp.	'Potter's'	Eucario González #29
FRANCE		
1. Les Destilleries Dumont Lee	'Tres Alegres Compadres'	La Cofradia #19
2. Les Grand Chais de France	'La Piedrecita'	La Cofradia #19
3. Selection Difution Vente	'Chapala', 'Jalisco', 'Playa Blanca', 'Sombrero Negro'	Tequilas del Señor #36
4. Soc. D'exportation des Grands Vins de Bordeaux Gouin	'Ixtapa'	El Viejito #28
5. Destilleras de Villafranca	'El Palanque', 'Cholula',	El Viejito #28
6. Sardet 3 et Deribaucourt	'Canixta'	Orendain #31
7. Cusenier S.A.	'Yucatan'	Viuda de Romero #41
GERMANY		
1. Anton Riemerschmid Likor	'Silla', 'Espuela'	González González #8
2. Borko Marken Import Co.	'Sierra'	El Viejito #28
3. C. Heinrich Quast GMBH	'Montego'	Orendain #31
4. Dethleffsen GMBH	'R.B. d'Reyes', 'Arriba'	#16, #36
5. Etn P. Bruggman	'Tres Alegres Compadres'	La Cofradia #19
6. Fa. Rodolf Gsonek GMBH	'Sombrero Negro'	Tequilas del Señor #36

161

Company	Labels	Distillery
7. Gsonek GMBH	'Sombrero Negro'	Tequilas del Señor #36
8. Mautner Markhof AG	'Orendain'	Orendain #31

GREECE

Company	Labels	Distillery
1. S. and Constantatos Rousali Bros.	'Acapulco'	Viuda de Romero #41

ITALY

Company	Labels	Distillery
1. Illva Saronno SPA	'Fandango'	Orendain #31

JAPAN

Company	Labels	Distillery
1. Okura and Company	'Mercian'	El Viejito #28
2. Suntory Ltd	'Suntory'	Siete Leguas #38

SPAIN

Company	Labels	Distillery
1. La Vallesana SA	'El Cobrizo'	Orendain #31

UNITED KINGDOM

Company	Labels	Distillery
1. Campbell Meyer and Company	'Gringo's'	Orendain #31

Tasting Notes for the Best Tequilas

Do you need someone else to tell you which pieces of music you should like, or which novels you will most enjoy? No: you can do that yourself. But other people's opinions may help you in various ways. They may put you on the track of music or books worth trying. They may help you to notice aspects of the music or the novels you might otherwise overlook.

This kind of advice can be especially valuable because deep enjoyment of any serious work of art—a symphony, a novel, or a distilled beverage—requires education. By pursuing the sublime and the beautiful, you train your senses and your intellect to appreciate fine things which might not have impressed you at first tasting. The opinion of someone who has only listened to Prince and Michael Jackson on first hearing a Mozart string quartet is quite worthless. Likewise, the verdict of someone who has never tasted wine on taking their first sip of a fine Bordeaux.

But those who have educated themselves in a particular field of artistic creativity do not all agree on everything (though they probably will agree on a lot of things). Connoisseurs of wines, brandies, scotches, or bourbons do not entirely agree on a precise ranking by quality. They cannot reach agreement on which is the best, though they usually do largely agree on which are among the best and which are among the worst.

It's the same with tequila. You can only find out which tequila is best for you, or whether you like several different tequilas best for *different* fine qualities they possess, by gradually educating your palate and nose over a long period. There is no reason to expect that your ultimate conclusions about tequila will be identical to those of Bob Emmons or anybody else.

So you should trust your own nose and your own palate—but trust them to learn and develop over time, so that you will eventually appreciate things you may be unable to appreciate now.

The following tasting notes will help you to know what to look for. I have tasted more tequilas than anyone I know, but I am far from having tasted them all, and quite early on I decided—and here all tequila connoisseurs agree—that only 100 percent *agave* tequilas are likely to be worth the investment. So only those are included here. Some tequilas I have tasted under conditions where I do not feel that I can give a considered judgment—for example, if I'm engaged in a conversation in Spanish about the tequila industry with people I have only just met, and one of them offers me a glass of a tequila I have not previously sampled. For me, a proper tasting requires time, calm, and freedom from distraction. Therefore, I refrain from offering a considered opinion on tequilas I have not tasted under conditions conducive to careful evaluation.

One more cautionary note: Although most 100 percent *agave* tequilas are very consistent by label, this is not always the case. So it may be that the tequila I tasted was not the same as the tequila you tasted, despite the same label.

DISTILLERY #1
Agave Tequilana Prod. y Com., S.A. de C.V.

Currently available only as a *blanco* and a *reposado*, this 100 percent *agave* product is a very pleasant tequila manufactured in the artisanal tradition of the smaller tequila companies. The *blanco* has a very flowery nose when the bottle is first opened, gaining complexity after being in the glass for a few minutes.

164

The tequila reveals the smell of the earth itself with slightly acidic overtones. It fills the mouth well and has a sweetish aftertaste, with a lasting finish. A crisp vegetable flavor reminiscent of celery is present, with a floral undertone, possibly of violets. Altogether a very creditable tequila, though not currently available in the U.S. I have not yet been able to sample the *reposado*.

Additional label names for this company are '1921' and 'Oro Azul'.

DISTILLERY #2
Agroindustria Guadalajara, S.A. de C.V.

This company now has three different 100 percent *agave* tequilas in release: a *blanco* and three-month *reposado* under the '30-30' label, and a six-month *reposado* bottled as 'Jalisciense'. All are very tasty. The 30-30 *blanco* shows good *agave* aroma and taste, with crispness and a fruity flavor, similar to biting into a crisp pear-apple. It makes your mouth water, while filling your palate with a slightly sweet long finish. The nose is full and aromatic, with a slight mustiness reminiscent of mushrooms to add complexity.

The 30-30 *reposado* (three months) begins with a light beige straw color, has a pleasing aroma, with good complexity, smooth floral overtones, a musty earth-like bottom, and just a hint of leathery wood smells. The first sip starts with a tart sweetness, a light alcohol attack, and grows stronger until there is a peppery tingle to the tongue. It maintains its sweetness throughout but grows in complexity after the first taste, filling the mouth with different flavor undertones and good *agave* herbaceousness. There is a long finish and a lasting sweetness that lingers and becomes a smooth aftertaste fading into a quiet glow.

The Jaliscience *reposado* (five months) starts with a faintly darker color than the 30-30 and is less aggressive to the nose, with a light alcohol attack, some wood, and the feel of a meadow following a rainstorm. The first sip is very pleasant, with an *agave* herb taste like the soothing feel of aloe over a sunburn. A definite sweetness followed by a long slide to a nice finish and a very pleasant sweet aftertaste.

None of these tequilas is yet available in the U.S. Plans are being made for their importation, and you may be able to find them in 1997 or later.

Negotiations for importation into the U.S. of a new label, 'Ambarfino', are under way with the company Tequila Imports of Houston, Texas. When it finally begins coming in, it will be available as a *blanco*, a *reposado*, and an *añejo*.

Additional labels of this company are 'Charro de Oro' and the new 'El Amo Aceves'. I was able to acquire a bottle of the 'El Amo Aceves' during my trip in November, 1996. It is a very nice package, the bottle being somewhat square and made of heavy glass, giving it good stability. The tequila itself is an *añejo* of about 16 months.

To the eye, the tequila is a pale gold straw color, very clear and clean. To the nose, there is some light herbaceousness, with a smooth light *agave* nose, and a goodly amount of alcohol. In the mouth, the initial feel is of a sharp alcohol bite with slight herbal bitterness concentrated in the front portion of the mouth. As it spreads, the flavor sweetens slightly and smoothly travels to the palate where it fills the mouth and slowly ebbs to a long sweetish finish. Altogether a fine tequila.

DISTILLERY #3
Agroindustrias Santa Clara de SPR de RL

This company was licensed in the latter half of 1996, and had not started production at the time this book went to print. Two label names that will be used by this company are 'El Nativo' and 'La Cava de los Beas'. The distillery is located just outside the town of Ciudad Guzmán.

DISTILLERY #4
Casa Cuervo, S.A. de C.V.

This distillery, a totally owned subsidiary of Tequila Cuervo, has started making 100 percent *agave* tequilas. In 1995 they produced all *mixto* tequilas, but in the summer of 1996, began producing and exporting a 100 percent *agave* tequila under the name of 'Gran Centenario'. This tequila is imported by Carillon Imports in a bottle identical to that used by tequila 'Dos Reales', another Cuervo *mixto* brand.

I have sampled only the 'Gran Centenario' blanco and found it to be a little different from most blancos. To the eye it has a yellowish quality, not quite white though it does have good clarity and no particulate matter was found. Perhaps this is due to the stated claim that it is stored in wood for a few days (apparently illegal under Mexican law), though not long enough to qualify as a *reposado*.

To the nose there is a strong presence of alcohol, and little *agave* aroma. The first sip reveals a sharp alcohol attack to the sides of the tongue and the palate, some sweetness in the mouth, and a bitter aftertaste that slowly subsides into a slow sweetness, which gradually dies to a slightly tart, sweetish long finish. Overall, this new tequila could use some more refinement, and more *agave* aroma and flavor would not be amiss.

DISTILLERY #5

Compañia Orendain, S.A. de C.V.

This company is the second NOM used by Tequila Orendain de Jalisco and all of its production is at the main plant of 'La Mexicana'. All production using this NOM is the same and is labelled the same as Tequila Orendain de Jalisco (#31).

DISTILLERY #6

Corporación Ansan, S.A. de C.V.

This company was founded in the latter portion of 1996, and the *fábrica* was not completed at the end of that year. A combination of two existing companies, Destiladora de Occidente, and Viuda de Martinez, this plant will presumably be making tequila for both of those labels as well as three new labels, 'Sublime', 'Honorable', and 'Zafarrancho'. None of these products was available for tasting as this book went to press.

DISTILLERY #7

Destiladora Azteca De Jalisco, S.A. de C.V.

The 100 percent *agave* tequilas available from this company are fairly light in the nose with a strong presence of alcohol. The *blanco* is slightly more complex than the *reposado*, with the *reposado* showing the effects of the wood in the lessening of the *agave* aroma and bringing forth the strength of the spirit.

The mouth feel of the *blanco* has a sweetish beginning with little complexity, growing slowly drier and leaving a slightly bitter aftertaste that develops into a long finish, smoothing again to sweetness.

The *reposado* again shows the effect of the wood, with taste starting out even sweeter than the *blanco* and smoothing the harshness of the alcohol with the different level of sweetness, and a slight pepperiness on the tongue. A smooth, long finish dying off to a dry aftertaste and a lingering sweet end. It has a good mouth feel, filling the palate well, and is a fairly smooth tequila.

Both of these tequilas are quite drinkable, but they do not show a great deal of complexity on either the nose or tongue. The company has not yet produced an *añejo*.

DISTILLERY #8

Destiladora de Occidente, S.A. de C.V.

This company makes a 100 percent *agave* tequila named 'Sin Rival', but I have not been able to sample it and it is not currently available in the U.S.

DISTILLERY #9

Destiladora González González, S.A. de C.V.

This distillery makes two 100 percent *agave* tequilas, 'Tequila Mayor', available only in Mexico, and 'Tequila Silla' of which all production is exported to Germany. I have not yet been able to sample either of these tequilas.

168

DISTILLERY #10
Destilados de Agave, S.A. de C.V.

The second brand for Tequila Herradura, this company lends its name to the 'El Jimador' line from that company.

DISTILLERY #11
Elab. y Proc. de Agave y sus Derivados, S.A. de C.V.

This distillery is very small and is exporting its entire output to France under the label 'Revolucionario 501'. The company is now making this product only as a 100 percent *agave* tequila. I tasted it in Mexico at the distillery and found it to have a sweet beginning and harsh aftertaste, with an unidentifiable chemical overtone. My driver, Rudy, also sampled this product and felt that it had a potato-like sting in the flavor; we both found the aftertaste slightly unsettling.

DISTILLERY #12
Empresa Ejidal Tequilera Amatitán, S.A.

This co-operative distillery makes tequila for a number of different labels, including 'La Regional', 'Caballitos Cerrero', and the cactus bottle 'Porfidio', among others.

While I have sampled the cactus bottle Porfidio and found it to be delicious, I have not yet been able to conduct a careful analysis for taste evaluation. None of the other versions is available outside Mexico.

DISTILLERY #13
Fab. de Aguard. de Agave la Mexicana, S.A. de C.V.

This company received authorization to begin making tequila in June of 1996. The distillery had not been finished as of August of 1996, but was expected to begin operations by the end of that year. When the product is finally available, it will be under the label 'El Corral'. Since all companies but one are now licensed to make 100 percent *agave* tequila it seems apparent that this

169

company is joining the growing ranks of the 100 percent *agave* manufacturers.

Industrialización y Dllo. Santo Tomas, S.A. de C.V.

This *cien por ciento de agave* tequila is available only as a *reposado*, due to that portion of the market representing the majority of sales in Mexico. The company is trying to position itself within that leading segment and is apparently succeeding.

The aroma of Los Valientes is sweet to the nose with an overtone of a floral scent (possibly clover?), and maybe cocoa. It is very pleasant but not complex. In color, it is a pale gold, with a hint of red not usually found in the predominantly straw-colored *reposado*s of the other 100 percent *agave* tequilas.

It is smooth on the tongue, with a hint of sweetness while remaining predominantly dry. It fills the mouth well without being overpowering in its alcohol, and it does not have any characteristics that distinguish it. Though not outstanding, it is certainly a good-tasting tequila of medium body and consistency. It should mix with other ingredients or drink straight with equal ability. The flavor lacks the complexity that I have come to expect in a 100 percent *agave* tequila of the highest quality, but this tequila is altogether a pleasant experience.

J. Jesus Partida Melendez

This company was founded in February of 1996, and is currently producing the tequila labelled 'Tres Mujeres'. Sr. Partida named the tequila after his mother and her two sisters, since they were the three women in his life while he was growing to adulthood. The distillery is located down a dirt road next to a pair of roadside stands on the highway between Arenal and Amatitán. This small plant produces 'Tres Mujeres' and 'Miramontes'.

Tequila Tres Mujeres is a light straw color, with a hint of amber to the eye. To the nose, it displays a decent herb aroma but some of the freshness is hidden by the alcohol. The first sip reveals a sharp attack to the center of the tongue, moving out to the sides and back into the throat where it smooths, mellows, and gains sweetness to a long and pleasantly mild finish.

J. Jesus Reyes Cortes, S.A.

This company makes a 100 percent *agave* tequila sold only in Mexico called 'J.R. Jesus Reyes', to differentiate it from another tequila named 'J.R. Jaime Rosales'. This company is also reported to manufacture the triple distilled *blanco* for Porfidio. I have sampled this tequila only in that format.

The Porfidio triple distilled *blanco* is clear and clean, without color, and to the nose is very light in the smell of *agave*, with a strong presence of alcohol. There is very little complexity in the aroma, and the first sip bites the center of the tongue. The tequila starts off with a slight bitterness which grows in intensity to a peak and then slowly becomes sweeter. The initial experience is not particularly mellifluous, but does smooth out after a short period in the mouth. There is a surge of alcohol at the peak, which slowly slides to the mellower taste and out to a long finish with a fairly pleasant aftertaste.

This tequila is a little too light in *agave* flavors for my taste, and could have some aspirations to become a vodka. The triple distillation is the probable cause for the lack of *agave*, and, in my opinion, the third run through the still could profitably be eliminated. It is also a little pricey for a *blanco*, running between $30.00 and $35.00 per 750 ml. bottle when you can find it.

Jorge Salles Cuervo y Sucs. S.A. de C.V.

This company is the only tequila company not licensed to make 100 percent *agave* tequila, and therefore makes only *mixto*. Its labels, 'Tequileño' and 'Tequileño Especial' are available only in Mexico.

La Arandina, S.A. de C.V.

This company produces two 100 percent *agave* tequilas, 'Casca Viejo' and 'Hipodromo', both *reposado*s available only in Mexico. I have not yet had the opportunity to sample these properly.

La Cofradia, S.A. de C.V.

Tequila from this company is currently available in the United States under the McCormick Distilling Company label of 'Hussong's 100 percent *agave*'. The label had for many years stated that the tequila was 99 percent *agave*, which was not a legally-recognized category, since only two classifications then existed, the 51/49 mixture or 100 percent *agave*. This first release as a *cien por ciento* has just come onto the market in the U.S., having been shipped in January, 1996.

The attractive black crockery bottle contains a *reposado* tequila that is a very pale straw color. The nose is clean with definite alcohol and little complexity. The taste is nondescript with a good mouth feel and smoothness. It is predominantly dry, with a sweet sharpness on the initial sampling that quickly recedes, leading to a slow decline until the flavor is gone. The finish does not linger and there is little aftertaste.

La Madrileña, S.A. de C.V.

This company, while licensed to produce 100 percent *agave* tequila, states that it is not presently manufacturing any for sale. While the end-of-year production statistics for 1995 show that they manufactured 26,138 liters during that calendar year, this could be a mistake, or the company may have exported all of that amount.

DISTILLERY #21
Productos Especiales de Tequila, S.A.

In 1996, this company applied for and was granted its license to produce 100 percent *agave* tequila, but none was available at time of going to press.

DISTILLERY #22
Tequila Caballito Cerrero, S.A.

This very small company is not currently manufacturing any tequila in its own plant, but sells about 40,00 liters per year. They do have their own distillery, but are reported to be purchasing most of their current stock from La Regional.

I bought a bottle of this tequila at their outlet in downtown Guadalajara, and upon close examination back in my hotel room could find no indication that it was 100 percent *agave* tequila. After opening the bottle and smelling the tequila, I concluded that it was a *mixto* and gave it away.

DISTILLERY #23
Tequila Cascahuin, S.A.

In 1996, this company applied for and was granted its license to produce 100 percent *agave* tequila, but none was available on going to press. The labels registered to this company are 'Cascahuin' and 'Cabrito'.

DISTILLERY #24
Tequila Catador Alteño, S.A. de C.V.

This very small company makes only 100 percent *agave* tequila, producing 81,900 liters in 1995 under the 'Tequila Catador' label. This tequila is not normally available outside the state of Jalisco. I was able to purchase a bottle on my trip to the distillery in November 1996, and sampled it after my return to California.

To the eye, the tequila is a very pale straw in color, with a slight chatoyance, clean and clear, with a definite bead on the side of the glass. To the nose, it has the aroma of tequila with some *agave* herbaceousness, and a medium alcohol aroma. The first sip is smooth and not overly sharp, but grows in intensity until there is a medium alcohol attack. There is a definite sweetness with a slight sharpness at the edges of the tongue, which slowly ebbs through a very long finish to a glowing aftertaste. The delightful complexity slowly grows as the tequila is kept in the mouth. A surprisingly good spirit, with one of the longest finishes that I have yet experienced in a tequila.

DISTILLERY #25

Tequila Cazadores, S.A. de C.V.

There is some question about whether or not this tequila is 100 percent *agave*. The original list of 100 percent *agave* license holders that I received did not include Tequila Cazadores, but the production listing for year end 1995 shows them making only 100 percent *agave* tequila. There are other questions too. The administrative manager of the company, in October of 1995, personally gave me production figures of 4,000,404 liters through the end of September. The production figures of *La Cámara* through the end of the year showed 2,640,897 liters, a small discrepancy that could reach a difference of 2,000,000 liters, if the first figure were extrapolated to the end of the year.

This company produces only the one type of tequila, a *reposado* with 70 days in the wood, which is one of the biggest-selling tequilas in Mexico. Cazadores and Herradura are neck-and-neck for the lead, and at the time of writing, Cazadores was ahead.

In the nose, this tequila shows some complexity but somewhat over-ridden by the aroma of alcohol. The taste begins with a sharp dryness and a gradual easing to a mellower sweetness. The mouth feel seems concentrated about the lips and the tip of the tongue and doesn't seem to have much effect on the palate. This tequila drinks or mixes well and has no negative taste tones, although it also has few outstanding features.

DISTILLERY #26
Tequila Centinela, S.A. de C.V.

This 100 percent *agave* tequila, an excellent product, is currently available in the U.S. The U.S. market has 'Centinela' in many areas, and the company's second brand, 'Cabrito' can also be found in some places. Tequila Centinela is manufactured in four differing age categories, *blanco*, *reposado*, one-year *añejo*, and three-year *añejo*. The *blanco* is fruity to the nose with some alcohol presence and is herbaceous. The taste is sweet and clean, with a crispness midway through, easing to a slow finish that lingers and fades. It fills the mouth well and strikes the palate cleanly with a sting that mellows into warmth down the throat and into the stomach.

I have not sampled the *reposado*, but the one-year *añejo* is a light straw color and has a good clean nose with little complexity, some herbaceousness and smooth alcohol aromas. In the mouth, it is slightly sweet with a clean attack on the palate and slow warmth. The finish is long and becomes sweeter and more complex as it fades into quietude.

The three-year *añejo* is a slightly darker color than the one-year, and has a clean, slight complexity to the nose that can be overshadowed by the alcohol. In the mouth, the initial taste is of alcohol slowly growing sweeter and more complex, with a vanilla overtone and sharpness to the palate that transforms to a smooth, warm, sweetness fading to a relaxed sigh.

These are very well-made and pleasant drinking tequilas that should be sampled and considered before you decide which tequila is your favorite.

DISTILLERY #27
Tequila Cuervo La Rojeña, S.A. de C.V.

Tequila Cuervo now makes two tequilas said to be 100 percent *agave*, 'Cuervo Tradicional' and 'Cuervo Reserva de la Familia'.

Tradicional is a very light colored *reposado* with strong alcohol and some complexity to the nose. It has a definite overtone of chocolate with another unknown aroma. In the mouth it has a sharp alcohol attack with some sweetness and a light herbaceous tingle on the tongue, with a bittersweet bite fading to a lingering finish.

Reserva de la Familia is an *añejo* with a much darker color, and does show the effects of the wood. It has apparently been aged in new, heavy char barrels in an attempt to obtain as much color as is achievable within the time limitation of a normal *añejo*. To the nose it has some complexity, but reminds me of a well-made bourbon, with the barrels showing their effect in the aromas. The complexity also shows through with a chocolate overtone to the nose. A strong sense of alcohol is present in the first sip, with some *agave* flavor, but this is modified by the strong flavor of the wood that is present in the spirit. All in all, the product seems to be okay, but (as mentioned in Chapter 5) lacking in the distinctive *agave* qualities that have traditionally typified a true tequila. I don't know that it is worth the $70.00 a bottle current price tag.

DISTILLERY #28
Tequila El Viejito, S.A. de C.V.

This distillery makes and bottles many different labels of 100 percent *agave* tequilas. Besides their own label of 'El Viejito', they also manufacture 'Las Trancas', 'J.R. Jaime Rosales', 'Distinqt', 'Sierra' for the German market, and were making the 'Porfidio' *blanco* (not the triple distilled).

I have sampled, under adequate tasting conditions, only three of the products of this company. The first is the 'Distinqt' *blanco*. It has little initial complexity when poured into the glass, though the aroma of *agave* is present, and the alcohol does not assault your sense of smell. With continued exposure to the air, other scents seem to develop, and there is a fresh herbaceous feel similar to a raw potato. The taste is smooth and dry with an indefinable initial taste which is not overpowering in its alcoholic sting. This tequila has a good mouth feel with a medium finish and a smooth, slightly sweet aftertaste.

The second tequila made by this company that I have sampled is the 'Las Trancas' *reposado*. The color is a very pale, not quite colorless beige. The nose is sweet with an overtone of caramel and light alcohol. As it warms after exposure to the air, it also seems to grow in complexity, adding other faint aromas over time. In the mouth it begins with a sweetish start which slowly becomes dry and fades to a very faint hint of sweetness after a medium finish. It drinks very smoothly and does not show any harsh alcohol bite.

Third is the 'El Viejito' *añejo*. To the eye, it is a very light straw colored liquid, clean and almost clear. To the nose, it has a very light *agave* aroma, a small presence of alcohol, and is fairly pleasant. The first sip brings a light alcohol burn around the lips with a stronger alcohol presence at the back of the tongue that slowly seeps into the palate and sinus area. The flavor starts out dry and slowly expands into sweetness, with a sharp attack that slowly ebbs and dies with a very long finish and a smooth pleasant aftertaste.

Another tequila made by this company is 'Aguila' 100 percent *agave*. Packaged in a pretty, cobalt-blue bottle, it is promoted throughout the U.S. by Guadalajara Imports, of St. Louis. Available only as an *añejo*, to the eye this tequila is clear and clean, almost colorless, with a very slight pinkish-beige tint in the liquid. To the nose, it has good *agave* aromas, with light alcohol burn. In the mouth it is smooth and mild, with little bite, and displays complexity with a full mouth feel and good flavors. At the first sip, it slowly attacks the tongue, spreads throughout the mouth and fills the palate. There is good herbaceousness, with some floral overtones, and a long finish and pleasant aftertaste. This tequila drinks well and is an enjoyable experience.

The *blanco* and *reposado* tequilas, along with the Aguila añejo, could sneak up on you as to their alcohol content, since they do not show a strong assault of alcohol to the senses. The El Viejito *añejo* is different, with a more definite alcohol presence in the mouth and a much sharper attack. It is also drier at the beginning and does not display as much *agave* sweetness throughout as do the other three tequilas.

DISTILLERY #29
Tequila Eucario Gonzalez, S.A. de C.V.

This company exports through a number of different companies under many labels, which include 'Albertson's',

'McCormick's', 'Tina', and many others (see the label list, Appendix A, or check the distilleries in Chapter 5). I have not sampled any of the tequilas made by this company.

Tequila Herradura, S.A. de C.V.

Tequila Herradura is one of the distilleries that has always made only 100 percent *agave* tequila. It currently produces tequila under two labels, 'Herradura', which is exported all over the world, and 'El Jimador', which became available in the U.S. in 1996.

Tequila Herradura is available in four types, *blanco*, *reposado*, *añejo* and *muy añejo*.

The *blanco* is clean and clear with a dry complexity to the nose with floral overtones, good herbaceousness, and smooth alcohol. The first sip gives a nip of alcohol to the center of the tongue that spreads throughout the mouth and lightly stings the palate. It begins with a dry, very light bitterness that slowly transforms to a slightly tart sweetness. There is a very long finish and a clean pleasant aftertaste.

The *reposado* is a pale silvery beige in color, almost an ash blond, and has a sweet, slightly herbaceous aroma to the nose. The initial sip gives a crisp tartness to the tongue that quickly eases to a smooth mellowness and a lingering lightly sweet finish that has vanilla and wood flavors.

The *añejo* is a definite golden color with a sweet aroma reminiscent of the smell of a fine leather, again with vanilla highlights and a sense of fruit. A definite sweetness warms the lips and tongue with the first sip, and an elusive slightly nutty (almond?) flavor seems to be included. The initial flavor modifies to a tart dryness, slowly sweetens to a mellow glow over the tongue, and permeates the palate. The tasting of these tequilas was very rewarding.

The latest of products from Tequila Herrradura is currently the most expensive tequila in the world, Herradura Selección Suprema, retailing at around $300 per bottle.

This tequila is an *añejo* with four years in the wood and is called *muy añejo*. To the eye it is a light honey color, with gold highlights and a very slight chatoyance. To the nose, it is sweet with a definite aroma of vanilla and a citrus fruit overtone, along with the wood and a slight hint of leather. The first sip has the sting of alcohol to the lips and tongue, spreading to fill the mouth, and is almost chewy in its consistency. The flavor is sweet throughout the time in the mouth but does vary according to the alcohol attack. There is a long, smooth, sweet finish, and a lasting sweet aftertaste. A very pleasant experience, though the price of this tequila will obviously deter many people from trying it.

DISTILLERY #31
Tequila Orendain de Jalisco, S.A. de C.V.

The only 100 percent *agave* tequila made by this company is a *reposado* labelled 'Ollitas'. It is currently available only in Mexico. To the nose there is a dry nutty aroma reminiscent of walnuts, with a light burn of alcohol. The initial taste reveals a sharp smoothness, declining into warmth and slowly sweetening as it fades in a long finish. It fills the mouth well and has a slightly herbaceous aftertaste.

DISTILLERY #32
Tequila Parreñita, S.A. de C.V.

Few of the tequilas made by this company are currently available in the U.S., though a new label, 'Misión Imperial', reportedly from this company, is now being imported into the southern U.S. They have also begun making the tequila J.R. Jaime Rosales for their current importer. I have not been able to sample any of their products.

DISTILLERY #33
Tequila San Matias de Jalisco, S.A. de C.V.

This company does export a 100 percent *agave* product, labelled 'Pueblo Viejo', as a *reposado*. It is sometimes available in the U.S., imported by the company Tequila Los Altos in Northern California. The color is pale to very pale, and the initial aroma is light and clean with a faint aroma of fruit and little complexity. The first sip reveals a burst of alcohol with a dry attack that slowly sweetens and mellows to an aftertaste which gradually dies. It provides a full mouth, but the first sip can be breathtaking in its sharpness. After one has become used to the spirit, it caresses the palate.

DISTILLERY #34
Tequila Santa Fe, S.A. de C.V.

The main 100 percent *agave* product from this company founded in 1992 is a *reposado* labelled '1,000 Agaves'. It was decidedly a pleasant surprise.

While I was buying a number of bottles of tequila at a liquor store in Guadalajara, the clerk threw in a 200 ml. bottle of Tequila Santa Fe as a gift. From this gesture, I suspected that maybe he didn't think much of this tequila, and when the proper time arrived, sampled it with some trepidation. Much to my astonishment, it was an unusually rewarding experience.

The color is so light that you must check against a white sheet of paper to see any color at all. The nose is smooth and slightly sweet, with a definite aroma of vegetation and a light crisp nuttiness. The first sip brings a warmth to the lips and tongue with a dry, long slide to a mellow sweetness and a long finish. There is an indescribable vegetable flavor that seems to be somewhere between carrot and celery, with a light taste of the wood. The finish is long and dry and leaves a pleasant bitterness in the aftertaste.

When this company was founded, it planned to export this product to the U.S., but was blocked from using its preferred label of 'Santa Fe' by another U.S. importer who had registered and trademarked the name. They may try again, perhaps with a different label. This tequila has excellent qualities and should be well received in the U.S. marketplace.

180

DISTILLERY #35
Tequila Sauza, S.A. de C.V.

Tequila Sauza makes only one tequila which claims to be a 100 percent *agave* tequila. It is called 'Hornitos' and has a green label. 'Hornitos' is a *reposado*, well received around the world, with Sauza being the third largest producer of 100 percent *agave* tequila, at 2,171,829 liters. They trail only Cazadores and Herradura in this portion of the market and Hornitos is probably the only 100 percent *agave* product easily available in every area of the world.

The color is a pale, almost clear beige, and the nose shows a good mixture of *agave* and alcohol aromas without the alcohol's being too strong. A slight floral scent is present with some sweetness. The initial taste is pleasant, though a little sharp, fills the mouth well and lightly stings the palate with alcohol. The flavor strikes with a slight tartness that fades to a memory of smoothness and a lingering hint of sugar. The spirit drinks easily but does not overpower in its complexity. It should be well received at any party, or by any group except the most discriminating connoisseurs.

DISTILLERY #36
Tequilas del Señor, S.A. de C.V.

This distillery produces as many different labels for export and domestic consumption as any company in Mexico. They make only one *cien por ciento de agave* product at present, and it is available in Mexico only by subscription, direct from the distillery. It is labelled 'Herencias del Señor' in Mexico and importation into the United States was being initiated when this book went to press. The importer may be Importer #39, Sun Imports of North Carolina and Tequilas del Señor would then be available under their own label of 'Authentico'. Importer #13, Frank-Lin Distillers Products of San Jose is also interested in this product and would import it under the label of 'Rio de Plata'.

I was able to sample both the *reposado* and the *añejo* versions of this tequila. To the eye, the *reposado* is a light amber color without red overtones. To the nose, there is a sufficiency of alcohol and some complexity with the aroma of oak making its presence felt. In the mouth, there is a noticeable smoothness, with a slight muskiness in the back of the throat. There is a hint of herbs that bites and slowly ebbs to an overall sweetness and a lingering aftertaste with a hint of smoke.

The *añejo* is almost imperceptibly darker in color and slightly more oaky to the nose, with the aroma of alcohol being less than in the *reposado*. The first sip brings a very smooth, sweetish herbaceousness, and a cloying flavor that I cannot identify. Interestingly, the suggestion of smoke that I detected in the *reposado* is not present here, though there is an over-riding feel of maturity and a smooth marrying of the diverse elements into an indefinable oneness. Both of these tequilas are fine and will be well worth sampling when they become more readily available.

A *blanco* version is still in the stage of development by trial and error. Such things take time. In order to approach the proper flavor, the company has already found that it has had to reduce the temperature and increase the cooking time in the autoclaves from hours to days.

DISTILLERY #37
Tequila Sierra Brava, S.A. de C.V.

This company has not yet completed its *fábrica*, though it has been granted its licenses to operate and to produce 100 percent *agave* tequila.

DISTILLERY #38
Tequila Siete Leguas, S.A. de C.V.

This is the company that makes the boutique 100 percent *agave* tequila 'Patrón', on which these tasting notes are based. 'Patrón' has a *blanco* and an *añejo*, but no *reposado* on the market.

The *blanco* is clear and clean in color, as it should be, and has a pleasant herb aroma with the nasal sting of alcohol vapors. A mild vegetable taste follows the first sip, with smooth alcohol and a dry tartness which mellows to a neutral state of sweetness. A lingering aftertaste like the crispness of *jicama* or celery root follows and drifts slowly into calm and quietude.

The *añejo* is closest to the color called champagne beige and has a slight chatoyance in its refractive qualities. The nose reveals an even smoother aroma than the *blanco* with less alcohol and seems slightly sweeter. The first sip calls forth a taste of the earth itself, with a mushroom mustiness and a light acidity leading to a sweetening in the palate. The alcohol attack is also slightly less than the *blanco* and gives a pleasant bite followed by a sharp bitterness which again mellows to a calm state.

These tequilas are among the best. Currently they are the largest selling and best-known of the super-premiums. Many people like the bottles for vases. If you are conducting a tasting for friends or relatives, you should consider this glamorous yet deeply rewarding tequila as a strong candidate for inclusion.

DISTILLERY #39
Tequila Tapatio, S.A. de C.V.

This is the most traditional of all of the distilleries, making only 100 percent *agave* tequila. They still prefer to do most of the work by hand and use very small batch fermentation methods, leaving the *agave* fibers in the juice through the first distillation. They manufacture the tequila 'El Tesoro de Don Felipe', as well as their own 'Tapatio' brand. The tasting samples were 'El Tesoro' *blanco*, *reposado*, and *muy añejo*.

The *blanco* almost sparkles, and the *agave* aroma is very bright and slightly sweet to the nose with good complexity. The first taste fills the mouth with a dry smooth acridity which eases to a warm glow over the tongue and palate. A slight earthiness with a herb flavor that is almost chewy in its consistency and reminiscent of green snap beans on a summer afternoon.

The *reposado* was first released for sale in May of 1996. In color it is a very nice light champagne beige, with some pearlescence and just a hint of green. To the nose, it is slightly sweet and evoked memories of chewing on the stem of a blade of sweet grass when I was a youngster. It has a smooth light vallinin aroma and good *agave*, with little alcohol burn to the nose. The first sip brings an initial null state that expands inside the mouth, slowly moving over the tongue until it reaches the back of the mouth where it explodes with flavors over the palate and up into the sinus. The initial tartness mellows into a smoothness that gradually sweetens to the end. It has a very long finish, with the flavors fading evenly until they are gone. The aftertaste is pleasant and faintly sweet with a tingle at the back of the throat.

The *añejo* is a very light champagne beige color that seems to glow from inside the liquid. To the nose, it first brings the feel of a grassy meadow with wildflowers scattered through the plain and the smell of freshly dug ground. It is lightly sweet from the wood, like the smell of a newly sawn log, and still maintains floral overtones. In the mouth, this spirit conjures the feel of the earth, with very light acidity and little alcohol taste, though there is a light burn to the palate to remind you that the alcohol is present. There are so many different flavors intermingling that it is difficult to sort them out, as they marry and become one in their complexity.

All of these are excellent tequilas against which all others should be compared. They are among the best for this class of spirits and are likely to remain so for some time to come. I recommend that you include this tequila in your liquor cabinet, for when you wish to summon up the flavors of 'Old Mexico'.

DISTILLERY #40

Tequila Tres Magueyes, S.A. de C.V.

This company was founded by don Julio González Estrada in 1942, and he still takes an active part in the operation, though a portion of the corporation has been sold to new partners from Mexico City. Prior to 1996, this company exported only bulk tequila and while they manufactured 100 percent *agave* tequila, none was exported. In late 1995, a distribution agreement was reached with the French company Rémy-Martin, with world-wide availability to be achieved during 1996.

I have sampled both the one- and three-year *añejos* and found them to be exquisite, but at the time this occurred, was not in a situation that would allow me to properly evaluate either. The only version that I was able to bring back to the U.S. and properly assess was the 'Don Julio' *reposado*.

184

This tequila is a pearl champagne beige, very light and clear. To the nose there is a mellow sweetness with floral overtones, light oak, and a grassy feel. In the mouth there is a definite attack to the center of the tongue extending back to the palate. There is a discernable sweetness with a very long, drier finish, and a pleasant herb aftertaste that slowly dissipates.

This tequila should be included among those that you should look out for if you plan to sample and compare all of the tequilas of highest repute.

DISTILLERY #41
Tequila Viuda de Romero, S.A. de C.V.

This company has long made fine tequilas. The company name is nearly 100 years old. Their current 100 percent *agave* product is imported into the U.S. under the label 'Real Hacienda' and is available in some areas, though unfortunately I have been unable to locate it in Northern California, and have not yet tasted it under proper conditions.

This company also makes a fine 100 percent *agave* product labelled 'Alteño', so far available only in Mexico. On my last trip to Mexico in November of 1996, I purchased a bottle and brought it back to the U.S. for evaluation.

To the eye, there is a pale golden coloration to what is almost a clear liquid. To the nose, there is a dry flowery-nutty aroma, somewhat redolent of almonds, with light alcohol burn and little *agave* feel. In the mouth, there is a slight bitterness, with a definite tingle to the entire surface area of the tongue. The initial bitterness slowly fades to sweetness still with the nutty overtone. There is a long finish and a smooth sweet aftertaste that lingers for some time.

DISTILLERY #42
Tequileña, S.A. de C.V.

This company makes both 100 percent *agave* and *mixto* tequilas. They are not currently exporting their 100 percent *agave* tequila, 'Pura Sangre', though rumors state that the label 'Lapis' is the same tequila and is soon to be imported. 'Lapis' may soon be available in the western portion of the United States, but only as a version of the 'Pura Sangre' *añejo*.

'Pura Sangre' is available in Mexico in the three standard groups: *blanco*, *reposado*, and *añejo*.

The *blanco* was sampled at 43 percent alcohol and found to be clear and clean to the eye. The aroma has a definite herb feel with the scent of alcohol less than would be expected, and yields a dry aromatic overtone reminiscent of fresh broccoli. A sharp assault of alcohol greets the first sip, with a dry follow-up that slowly becomes sweeter and leads to a long finish and a pleasantly mellow aftertaste. It permeates the palate and fills the mouth well.

The *reposado* is a pale pearly champagne beige in color. To the nose, its 38 percent alcohol is barely detectable, and it delivers a smooth mellow aroma with floral and very light oak scents. The initial taste is smooth, with a sweetish attack which slowly dries to a null state with a long finish and pleasant aftertaste of asparagus.

The *añejo* is a pale gold in color with more red than the *reposado*, and the nose has good *agave*. The first impression in the mouth is a fullness that is almost chewy, with a smooth taste of an ineffable peppery vegetable flavor. There is an initial sweetness on the tip of the tongue which slowly fades to a mellow dryness as it fills the mouth and clings to the palate in a lingering finish. The aftertaste is pleasant, but has a bite that slowly smoothes out and dives into a slow glowing ending.

This tequila will surprise many people who try it for the first time. It is almost unrecognized even in Mexico, but I expect it to make inroads into the other more established brands over time. You should pick up this tequila whenever you get the opportunity.

A recent development for this company is the label 'Lapiz', which was widely available in the U.S. at the end of 1996. Very attractively packaged in a cobalt-blue triangular pyramid-shaped bottle, this tequila is available only as an *añejo*. To the eye, it is a light yellowish beige, with no red, and very clean. To the nose, it has a delicate aroma with little alcohol burn, a light vanilla overtone and a smooth delicate sweetness, with light floral accents. To the taste, there is a smooth nutty initial attack with very light herbaceousness, and crisp alcohol which permeates the entire mouth. Starting at the center of the tongue, the bite slowly spreads to the back of the mouth and enters the palate with a good sweet flavor which maintains itself throughout a very long finish ebbing to a satisfying aftertaste. This is a good representative of a 100 percent *agave* tequila.

DISTILLERY #43
Tequilera Corralejo, S.A. de C.V.

This company, located in the village of Pénjamo, Guanajuato, opened for production in July of 1996. It has applied for registration for one label, 'Pico de Gallo', though five names were mentioned in a press release in Mexico. I have not been able to sample any tequila made by this company, and understand that most of their production will be exported to Spain.

DISTILLERY #44
Tequilera La Gonzáleña, S.A. de C.V.

This company makes the tequila labelled 'Chinaco' and considered to be one of the best tequilas available, but the company is a little bit of a mystery. It is one of only two tequila distilleries located outside of the state of Jalisco and can be difficult to find. The distillery was closed for a few years following the hijacking of a truckload of their product going through the U.S. on its way to the bottler. This loss hurt the company financially, but production has now restarted and is flowing freely.

I was supplied with tasting samples of all three types of 'Chinaco' by the import company and was able to try the *blanco*, *reposado*, and *añejo*.

The *blanco* is clear and clean in color, and shows a good bead in the glass (what the Mexicans call the soul or spirit of the tequila). The nose is bright and clean with good *agave* and has complexity with a mild alcohol assault to the nasal passages The first sip is dry, then the spirit slowly warms to sweetness, and fills the mouth with chewy vegetable flavors, reminiscent of sweet peas and grass. The finish is long and sweet, and slowly dies to a very nice aftertaste that defies description.

The *reposado* is a very light amber without red, and has some oak in the nose. The *agave* aroma is not less, but slightly more complex, than the *blanco* and lacks a certain tang. The first sip is very smooth and slowly warms to release its complexity. There is little alcohol sting and a swifter transformation from the initial dryness to the long sweet finish than the *blanco*. The lingering flavor slowly fades to a wonderfully light aftertaste that conjures up the scent of lilacs. This is a rewarding tequila.

The *añejo* is a deeper golden color than the *reposado* with just a hint of red. To the nose, it is almost flowery but with an inherent dryness and little alcohol attack, evoking a summer afternoon lying in a flower-strewn meadow. The first sip brings a slight shock of alcohol and dryness to the lips and center of the tongue, slowly filling the mouth and warming to sweetness and complexity on the palate. The long, slow finish ebbs to a neutral state and leaves an aftertaste that is unusual yet pleasant.

As a group, these three tequilas rank among the best available in the U.S. or around the world at the present time. Any of them would be a welcome addition to any private liquor cabinet or high-class serving establishment.

DISTILLERY #45

Tequilera Newton e Hijos, S.A. de C.V.

This company makes both *mixto* and 100 percent *agave* tequila, both currently available only in Mexico. In one of the *licoreras* (liquor stores) in Guadalajara, I found a one-liter bottle of the *mixto blanco*, with a price of N$ 6.00, when the exchange rate was about N$6.50 pesos to the US dollar. This means that this tequila was able to show a profit for both the manufacturer and the retailer at less than one dollar per liter. I have not yet tasted or surveyed any of this company's tequila, but I am suspicious of anything so inexpensive.

This company received its license to make 100 percent *agave* tequila in July of 1996, and has added some new labels. They now make 'Los Corrales', 'El destilador', and 'Puente Viejo'.

DISTILLERY #46
Tequilera Rustica de Arandas, S.A. de C.V.

This company began operations in July of 1996, and the distillery is located on the road to Jesus Maria, behind a large villa with a wide lawn and playground equipment in the front of the property. Label names for the company are 'El Charro', 'Hacienda de Tepa', 'Tres Caballos', 'Tres Reyes', and 'Tepa'. I have not yet tasted any of the tequila made by this company, and it is not yet available outside Mexico.

Tasting Notes for Premium *Mezcales*

I have recently sampled some new and highly-regarded versions of premium *mezcales* that might also be of interest to the reader.

The first is a blend of *mezcales* from different *palenques* that has been redistilled to smooth the final effect. This product is called 'Encantado' ('enchanted'); the brand name is owned by the importer, Carl Doumani of Napa, California, who also owns Stag's Leap Winery.

This product is completely different from tequila, for all of its common antecedents. Made only as a *blanco*, it is as clear and clean as water, with no hint of color. To the nose, there is a definite complexity which combines *agave*, smoke, and a flower-like herbaceousness. The first sip begins with a cool tingle to the front of the tongue, spreading sweetness as it moves back along the inside of the mouth, and slowly brings the strength of the alcohol out when it reaches the palate and explodes into a cool smoke, filling the mouth. The finish is long and slightly tart, with a complex, very long finish that slowly fades to a pleasant, smoky aftertaste.

There is also another company importing premium *mezcales* into the U.S., though their approach is different from Encantado. This company is named Del Maguey, and it imports the output of individual *palenques*. I have seen and sampled four of their offerings and found them to vary from *palenque* to *palenque*, which is only to be expected. Of the four, one ('San Luis del Rio') was very good. Another one ('Chichicapa') was not unpleasant, with a strong overtone of lemon concentrate, but the flavor of the *mezcal* was difficult to determine, because of the lemon covering the delicacy of the spirit itself. The other two ('Minero' and 'Santo Domingo') were definitely not to my taste.

How to Organize a
Tequila Tasting

If you're thinking of tasting tequila, the first thing you'll need, of course, is the tequila. Before you start planning a tasting (or if you intend to pursue your tequila education on your own) I suggest that you first go to the largest liquor store close to your home and see what they have. Armed with the information in this book, make a careful note of what's on the shelf.

Remember that if the label does not say '100 percent *agave*' or *'Cien por ciento de agave'*, or if the tequila was not bottled in Mexico, then it is a *mixto*. Don't be confused by mendacious phrases like 'distilled from the pure juice of the *agave*'. If the wording does not include '100 percent', what you have is a *mixto*. While the best *mixtos* are better than some 100 percent *agave* tequilas, and may perhaps be worth tasting if you are a beginner, you can regard them as part of your primary education. Indeed, as a beginning student of tequila, you may set yourself the assignment of being able to instantly distinguish a *mixto* from a 100 percent *agave* by taste and smell alone.

Bear in mind that, for any given brand, while the *añejo* will normally be more expensive than the *reposado*, which will in turn be more expensive than the *blanco*, this does not necessarily reflect a difference in desirability. *Blanco*, *reposado*, and *añejo* are different, but you may end up, like me, preferring the *blanco*, or, like most Mexicans, the *reposado*.

You might then try a few other stores. You may be surprised at finding which store has the widest range of good tequilas. At these stores, get into conversation with the staff, especially the order clerk, explain that you are looking for tequilas, and find out if they are planning to add new brands to their stock. If there's a particular tequila you would like to try, recommend that they acquire it.

You might try to get a recent copy of the beverage industry newspaper in your state or local area. Most liquor stores should have an old copy or two that they might let you have. You might contact some of the liquor wholesalers and distributors to find a retail outlet that carries the particular label you are looking for. If you still cannot find the tequila that you want, you may have to contact the importer direct to find out where you can purchase the spirit in question. These importers are listed in Appendix D, with their addresses and telephone numbers. Just remember that these companies do not normally deal directly with the public, and will not be able to sell you any of their product. Neither will the wholesaler; you must purchase the spirits from a liquor retailer.

Another approach would be to visit the good Mexican restaurants in your area. Some of these will have a fine range of tequilas; others will not. You may find that the restaurateur or some of the staff are knowledgeable about tequila and where to buy it.

If all of this fails to get you what you want, you will have to start booking your flight to Guadalajara.

I am continually being asked which tequila I consider to be my favorite, or which one is the very best. While there's no doubt that some tequilas are objectively far superior to others (and you can ascertain my views on many of them from Chapter 7), I do not answer questions about a unique 'best tequila', because there are so many subtle differences among tequilas that the best ones can appeal for different reasons. Some are a little sweeter, some have more *agave* flavor, others have an excellent nose, but the final taste of each is different. Where there are so many alternatives and so many subtle nuances, individual preferences are bound to vary, and I would simply ask everyone to investigate for themselves.

My suggestion is to sample as many as you can of the different brands that you can find and can afford to purchase. The overwhelming majority of the 100 percent *agave* brands are listed in this book, though many are not easily available outside Mexico, or even outside Jalisco.

Glassware

Your tequila tasting can involve just you and two or three friends, or it can be a more elaborate affair requiring more planning. Either way, you have to be adequately provided with glassware. You cannot, of course, taste tequila properly from plastic or paper vessels.

Some tasters recommend a white wine glass, but I prefer a cognac glass. Some stores carry them, and they may be found occasionally at a commercial restaurant or bar supply house. A cognac glass is a fairly small-stemmed glass, about six inches tall, with the container portion of the glass resembling a tulip, the bottom part being a little larger than the opening at the top. This slightly bulbous shape allows you to warm the liquor with your hand similar to the way you might do with a snifter. These glasses are usually about five ounces in capacity, and allow your nose to smell the aroma of the spirit without being overpowered by the alcohol present in the liquor. A six-ounce slender wine glass is also adequate.

A snifter is another possibility. A snifter is like a cognac glass except that the shape is more bulbous: the contrast between the narrow opening and the lower bowl of the glass is more extreme. But some tasters find that a snifter concentrates the alcohol vapors to the point that they become stronger than the actual aroma of the other participating smells present in the glass.

You will need a separate glass for each tequila, plus a water glass for cleansing your palate after each sampling (this water should be distilled water or bottled spring water). So if your tasting comprises six people and five tequilas, you will want 30 tasting glasses and six water glasses. If this is not feasible, you will have to thoroughly wash and rinse your glasses at some point in the tasting. This has the drawback that the water used for rinsing, especially its chlorine content if it is tap water, may affect the flavor of the subsequent tequilas, though not as much as would a cloth used for drying the glasses. In any event, you certainly don't want to add one tequila to a glass which retains some detectable traces of a different tequila.

In Mexico, tequila is drunk from glasses ranging from the two-ounce shooter glasses, to two ounce snifters, to full-size brandy snifters. For your tasting, you don't have to be perfectionistic about the precise design of the glassware—this is not as important as its clean condition. Glasses standing in a cupboard collect dust and impart a stale smell and taste to the liquor. Your glasses should be washed in hot water, with detergent, then thoroughly rinsed in copious hot or warm water, and allowed to dry naturally before the tasting.

A cocktail straw might also be included with each glass, to allow minute amounts of each tequila to be sampled. By placing one end of the straw in the tequila, and your finger over the other end, you can sample the tequila a few drops at a time. Some tasters do this to reduce their alcohol consumption during the tasting to the minimum, but some beginners find it helps them to focus their attention on the distinctive flavor peculiarities of each tequila. If you employ this method, you should naturally still observe the appearance and the aroma of the tequila first.

The most dedicated tasting purists will not swallow any tequila; they will use a spittoon. But except on special occasions for connoisseurs, you will do that only alone and in private. If you want to get some idea of the rarefied heights of tasting, you can do this by reading *Proof,* a gripping thriller by Dick Francis, though it does not mention tequila.

Most people will see a tasting as partly a social occasion, enhanced by the beneficial influence of a modest intake of alcohol. Most people will also prefer to consume small amounts of food in between tequilas, perhaps cheese and crackers or some Mexican snacks, though this may somewhat distort the judgment of one's tastebuds. Many people like their tequila with lime, or with lime and salt. There is nothing wrong with that, but for a tasting, it will cloud one's impressions of the tequilas.

Although you want your guests to relax and enjoy themselves, you should not allow the tasting to degenerate into a *purely* social occasion. You don't want the guests to break up into groups conducting their own separate conversations, for instance. This is not something frivolous, or something you can take care of while your mind is on something else: this is *tequila*. You want everyone present to concentrate their minds on the tequila, and there are things you can do to encourage this. Always send out written or e-mailed invitations, preferably written, with a brief explanation of what you are trying to achieve at this particular tasting. Conduct the proceedings in an orderly fashion, so that everyone is sampling the same tequila at the same time, and then everyone participates in the discussion on each tequila. Be careful to get each person's opinion every time—if they don't volunteer it, ask them. You should also begin each tasting with a brief presentation—it need only last for two or three minutes. For example, you could have a large map of Mexico, or of Jalisco, and point out where each of the distilleries represented is located.

How To Taste Tequila

There is a proper way to taste tequila, and if your guests are inexperienced, you should explain this procedure at the outset, reminding them if necessary as the tasting proceeds.

First, you hold the glass up to the light and examine the appearance of the tequila for clarity, color, or unusual characteristics.

Second is the aroma or 'nose'. The sense of smell is an inclusive part of taste and is normally considered its most important single component, but the aroma also has independent importance, before the tequila hits your tastebuds.

Third, you sip the tequila gently and closely observe the taste. No useful purpose is served by ostentatiously sloshing it around in the mouth. Concentrate as the flavor fills your mouth and nostrils. Swallow the tequila and observe the effect. Does the tequila flavor fill the whole mouth or only seem to affect parts of it? How sweet or dry is it? Is the flavor complex? (Generally, the more complex, the better.) Is the complete *agave* flavor present, or has it become broken down or covered up? It may take a bit of practice before you can easily distinguish qualities intrinsic to the tequila from accidents of the way the tequila happens to hit your mouth.

Finally, there is the finish or aftertaste. This can differ considerably from the initial taste, and can be long or short. A long, complex finish is to be preferred. A 'long' finish would last several seconds.

At each stage—appearance, nose, initial taste, and finish—the individual tasters should write down their impressions. Making the effort to describe the experience in words helps to train one's senses to discriminate more subtly, and is therefore a valuable exercise, even if at first it seems uninformative or comical. A written record is also important because humans are amazingly susceptible to becoming confused about their experiences, so they will often mix up their recent memories of smells and tastes. On the fourth tequila, a taster can easily start muddling the memories of the first and second.

So each participant should have pen or pencil and paper immediately available, to take notes that are as accurate as they can make them. The written records may be mere scribbled notes, as long as the writer can interpret them.

If you sample more than five or six tequilas at one tasting, your evaluations may begin to suffer as your nose and tastebuds progressively lose some sensitivity. Aside from that, if you are trying to compare different flavors and aromas, it simply becomes more difficult to keep them all straight in your head, even with written notes, if you sample too many at one sitting. And, of course, even tiny amounts of alcohol will *slightly* impair one's judgment. So you should either confine your researches to from four to six tequilas at one tasting, or discount the reliability of the later samplings.

After writing down the impressions, it's usual for the assembled tasters to discuss them, and compare their different impressions. The tasters will naturally say what they like and don't like, but they should be encouraged to say more than that, to describe the sensations. Is the nose flowery? If so, specifically what flowers do you think of? Is the taste full and complex? Is it smooth or does it have a rough quality? Is the distinctive tequila flavor overwhelmed by the wood—roughly speaking, does it remind you of a bourbon? Is the finish long and satisfying?

Try to expand your senses to take in the totality of the experience. While it is difficult to separate different aromas from the combined totality of smell, and designate each as a known smell, apparently some people can do this, though I have had difficulty finding more than two or three esoteric aromas in any particular spirit. The taste, mouth feel, and impact to the palate is much easier to define and to me this, in combination with the overall sensation of the spirit, is a very good guide to the quality of the tequila or any other beverage in the glass.

The final determination of which tequilas you prefer is up to you. Please don't take anyone else's word for what you should enjoy drinking. All tequilas are different, some a little sweeter, some a little drier, and you may decide that you like several different tequilas for different fine qualities, without feeling obliged to select an outright 'favorite'.

Planning Your Tasting

A tasting can be a few friends at your home, or it can be planned on a larger scale. One advantage of a larger scale is that, by splitting the cost among, say, from ten to twenty participants, you can afford to include some of the more expensive tequilas.

An alternative to holding such a party at your home might be to contact your favorite cocktail lounge or Mexican restaurant in your area. They may very well be as interested as you and might be willing to supply all of the necessary equipment for such an endeavor. They might even consider setting up a regular program, and could probably give you a much better price than you might expect on such an event, particularly if it were to take place early on a week night. You should be careful not to approach them unless you are sure of a minimum number of people you can get to attend, so you might want to hold a few informal tastings first, and then raise the issue of going to a lounge with your tasting group.

If it seems feasible, you should plan a long series of tastings. A tasting one night a week for many weeks is a possibility. As a finale, it would be nice to take the scoring procedures or notes from all of the different tastings of your participating guests and hold a comparison tasting of the top five or six tequilas that your group has evaluated. The final results may surprise you. While the *añejos* will probably make a strong showing, the *blancos* might win over some of your guests. A properly made *blanco* shows the fullest effect of the *agave* and is arguably the most aromatic and delicious of all tequilas.

Another aspect of such a final tasting is that of pitting the best against the best. Most tastings conducted by lounges where they get one of the suppliers involved will, for obvious reasons, compare only inferior tequilas to that supplier's own brand.

Make your tasting a rewarding experience and make sure that attractive food is available between tasting rounds. Mexican food and tequila have evolved together, and a little salsa with tortilla chips can clean the palate very well. Since you are initiating and planning the event, you also have some responsibility to ensure that no one who has recently swallowed several tequilas takes the wheel of a car.

It usually adds both fun and seriousness to the tasting to make it blind. This means that only you, as the organizer, or some deputized person, knows which tequilas are being tasted at the time. The other participants have to give their opinions without knowing whether the bottle cost $40 or $400. This can, of course, lead to some amusing results, and it can also lead individuals to reconsider what they believe are their strong preferences.

By contrast—and this works best only with small groups—you can compile different authorities' tasting notes, and read them out for a particular tequila as you sample it. *The Book of Tequila* is to date the only book to provide extensive tasting notes on numerous different tequilas, but it will no doubt attract imitators, and gourmet magazines will occasionally feature tequila tasting notes, so when the experts disagree, you can debate which of them is right.

In planning your tasting, you should have a clear idea of what you want your guests to learn, and structure the tasting accordingly—*especially* if your guests are inexperienced. The goal of deciding which is best among four or five tequilas is possible, but may be too lacking in focus. You may, for instance, want to compare only different *reposados,* or you may want to compare a *blanco* with a *reposado* or *añejo* of the same, or a different, brand. The more inexperienced your guests, the more you want highly contrasting tequilas. If your tasting is going to comprise different ages of tequilas (that is, if it's not going to be all blancos, all *reposados,* or all *añejos*), then you generally want to begin with the younger ones and move up in age. In fact, it's probably a good idea to begin every tasting with a *blanco* or two, since this will give you most of the pure *agave* flavor, and help you to keep the subsequent samplings in context. It is pointless to include any *mixtos* in a serious tasting, except as the occasional surprise item to keep your tasters on their toes.

Choosing the Tequilas for Your Tasting

How you design the tastings in terms of actual brands is largely up to you. You may have a theory you want to test, or you may have just picked up a normally-unavailable tequila and therefore want to include it in your next tasting. Similarly, if any member of your tasting group has found a tequila they really rave about, or has been to Jalisco and come back with some unusual tequilas, you would include these. One idea would be to use Chapter 5 of this book to identify the distilleries which use the most old-fashioned methods and those which are the most mechanized, then alternate these two kinds to see whether your guests notice the thematic contrast.

However, here are a few suggestions employing the easily-available labels. In each case I have listed six labels, which is the maximum; you may want to pick just four or five from these six:

Tequila Tasting No. 1

1. Patrón *blanco*
2. Distinqt *blanco*
3. El Tesoro *blanco*
4. Centinela *reposado*
5. Herradura *reposado*
6. Chinaco *reposado*

The above is a good, solid survey of high-quality tequilas. At some point you will want to compare all *blancos*, all *reposados*, or all *añejos* in one tasting. You may want to start with the *reposados*, since these are the most easily available and the most popular in Mexico. They may also become the most popular in the U.S. as 'gold' tequilas disappear from the market. Some good tequilas are available only as *reposados*.

Tequila Tasting No. 2

1. Cuervo Tradicional *reposado*
2. Cazadores *reposado*
3. Chinaco *reposado*
4. Sauza Hornitos *reposado*
5. Centinela *reposado*
6. Hussong's *reposado*

You'll most likely find that, the more 100 percent *agave* tequila you drink, the better you'll like *blanco*. When you reach that stage, you'll be ready for the following walk with the gods:

Tequila Tasting No. 3

1. El Tesoro *blanco*
2. Patrón *blanco*
3. Centinela *blanco*
4. Herradura *blanco*
5. Gran Centenario *blanco*
6. Chinaco *blanco*

At some point you'll no doubt want to make a comparison of *añejos,* though the prices may make you procrastinate about this. Never forget that some *mixtos* have exactly the same brand names and types (*blanco, reposado,* or *añejo*) as their 100 percent *agave* counterparts, so be careful to acquire only 100 percent *agave* tequilas:

Tequila Tasting No. 4

1. Aguila *añejo*
2. Lapiz *añejo*
3. Chinaco *añejo*
4. Herradura Selección Suprema *añejo*
5. Patrón *añejo*
6. Centinela Tres Años *añejo*

Other Tasting Ideas

There are now enough good *mezcales* available to organize a *mezcal* tasting, but probably not yet enough to arrange a series of different tastings with different *mezcales*. For complete beginners, you could include a *mezcal* as a surprise item in a series of tequilas.

A slightly different idea, not truly a 'tasting' in the gourmet sense, but still a lot of fun, could be a margarita tasting, or margarita party, using the tequilas that your tastings have determined are the best of each type, and the different orange liqueurs available. In this circumstance, it would be best to use all of the same ingredients except for the one you are testing. Use the same tequila if you are trying to determine which orange liqueur is best, and use the same recipe and liqueur if you are looking for the tequila that makes the best margarita. The differences in taste between really superb margaritas and those that most Americans are used to can be quite astounding. Just remember that the outcome depends on the quality of all the ingredients used. Always use freshly squeezed juices, a 100 percent *agave* tequila, clean ice made from distilled or spring water, and a good-quality orange liqueur (see also the remarks in Chapters 9 and 10).

You could also try a margarita party as something with a broader appeal to get people interested in tequila. Make absolutely clear in advance that these are going to be super-duper gourmet margaritas, different to anything your guests have tasted. Then when the guests agree with you, and ask for the secret of this amazing superiority, point out that the margaritas use only 100 percent *agave* tequilas. After that, you can usually leave it to the individual guests to discover for themselves that fine tequila is so good it can even be drunk without the added orange flavoring.

¡Viva La Margarita !

Without doubt, the single most important factor in the recognition, acceptance, and popularity of tequila outside Mexico has been the continually growing following for the cocktail known as the margarita.

Before the rise of the margarita, the most consumed and most celebrated cocktail was the martini—remember James Bond with his "shaken, not stirred"? But as early as the 1960s, we began to witness the displacement of the martini by the margarita. Many women who had resisted drinking martinis took to margaritas quite readily. As the margarita gained in popularity throughout the 1970s, the martini slowly waned.

The Jimmy Buffet song 'Margaritaville' helped to awaken interest in the margarita and in tequila itself. The lyrics evoke the mood of a Mexican resort town—it could be Acapulco, Ensenada, Cancún, or Puerto Vallarta. The visual images that the song conjures up made people curious about the drink itself. People who heard the song started asking for a margarita, just to see what it was like. Evidently, many of them liked what they tasted.

Nobody was more aware of the rise of the margarita than the tequila makers and their distributors. In 1995 a major lawsuit was filed by a large tequila manufacturer and importer against two other liquor companies who had used the word 'margarita' in the name of a pre-mixed alcoholic product which contained no tequila. The entire tequila industry closely watched the progress of this case, which was settled in early 1996 in favor of the tequila manufacturers. It is now definitely illegal to sell 'margaritas' which do not contain tequila. From the consumers' standpoint, this is not a great restriction, since tequila is not an expensive liquor, and it mixes well with almost any fruit juice.

Many people claim to have invented the margarita, or know who invented it. There are numerous competing legends, a few of which we will now look at. But wherever or whenever it was first concocted, this cocktail now drives the tequila market in the U.S. and is now making conquests all over the world.

So Who Invented the Margarita?

It's usually agreed that the discovery of the margarita occurred between the mid-1930s and the late 1940s. The location varies from Ensenada, Ciudad Juárez, Puebla, or Tijuana (all in Mexico) to La Jolla, Palm Springs, San Diego, or Los Angeles (all in California), or even to other places in New Mexico or Texas.

The ingredients of this cocktail are very simple: tequila, lime or lemon juice, orange liqueur, and ice. Usually, it is served in a 'bird bath' margarita glass, and salt is applied to the rim of the glass, though that is optional. The proportions vary, as do the other ingredients, with any of the many brands of tequila serving as the base and the available liqueurs including Cointreau, Grand Marnier, Triple Sec, Curaçao, or any other liqueur whose base is oranges. The lime or lemon juice proportions vary widely according to which recipe you choose.

I will now relate a few of the many stories about the origin of this cocktail. I apologize to all those who have been confidently recounting one of these stories under the impression that it's the gospel truth about the margarita, and who will now be disconcerted to find that it is one of several competing legends.

Of all of the persons with a claim to be considered the inventor of the margarita, probably the most widely recognized is that of Mrs. Margaret Sames, of San Antonio, Texas. I have seen this story on one of the newsmagazine weekly TV presentations, and read of it in many newspapers, magazines, and liquor industry publications.

The story goes as follows. In December of 1948, Mrs. Sames and her husband Bill were entertaining a group of friends at their cliffside villa in Acapulco. She had a wide circle of friends which included Nicky Hilton of the Hilton hotel chain, and the owner of the Tail o' the Cock restaurant in Los Angeles, a man named Shelton A. McHenry, who were all staying over during the Christmas season. Wanting to serve something special to her friends, Mrs. Sames took her favorite liqueur, Cointreau, added tequila and lime juice and topped the champagne glasses with just a little salt on the rim, as in a traditional tequila shooter. Everyone raved about the unique taste and the way the various ingredients complemented each other.

This new drink kept the party going for two weeks, and during the second week, Bill Sames said that she couldn't keep calling her concoction, 'the drink', and brought home two beautiful glasses with the name 'Margarita' etched on them, which is how the drink got its name. 'Margarita', of course, is both a girl's name, the Spanish equivalent of 'Margaret', and the Spanish word for 'daisy'.

Probably the second most accredited story is that of Carlos 'Danny' Hererra, who with his wife ran a restaurant and hotel in the late 1930s, called 'Rancho La Gloria', located on the road between Tijuana and Rosarita Beach, close to the Caliente race-track. Among the crowd of actors, Phil Harris, Alice Faye, and others, was a young movie starlet named Marjorie King, who could not, we are told, drink any alcohol except tequila (all the others made her sick).

The story tells that Marjorie, who was called 'Margarita' in Mexico, didn't wish to appear unladylike by drinking straight tequilas, so Danny began fixing her a cocktail with tequila, fresh lime juice, and Cointreau (it seems that, fortunately, Cointreau didn't make her sick either). Naturally, he named the drink after her. Others saw what she was drinking and ordered the same. Within a very short time the recipe for the drink had spread north

205

across the border and was sweeping through the Southern California cocktail lounges. When the liquor distributors found out about this new cocktail, they launched nationwide promotions, and the margarita was on its way.

Then there's the theory that the Tail o' the Cock Restaurant on La Cienega Boulevard in Los Angeles is where the drink was invented. There are several stories giving priority for the invention to this establishment, and here are two of them.

The first starts with the granting of the exclusive U.S. distribution rights for José Cuervo tequila to Young's Market Company of Los Angeles, and the desire of its president, Vernon Underwood, to increase the marketability of this new acquisition. He went to his friend Shelton A. McHenry, owner of the Tail o' the Cock, and, with the help of the head bartender, Johnny Durlesser, they came up with a mixture of tequila, lime juice, and Curaçao, which Durlesser named after his wife Margaret, hispanicizing her name and thereby Mexicanizing the drink, to 'Margarita'.

The other legend is a variation in which Durlesser duplicated the drink for a woman who had tasted it in Mexico (possibly at a party at the Sames villa) and introduced the recipe to his other bartenders and servers. Underwood became curious as to why this restaurant was now ordering five cases of tequila a week, when all of the other establishments in the area were using only two bottles per month. He checked it out and very soon launched an advertising campaign using the slogan, 'Margarita—it's more than a girl's name'.

Next is the tale that the inventor was one Francisco 'Pancho' Morales, the bartender at Tommy's Place on Juárez Avenue in Ciudad Juárez, across the border from Fort Sill, Texas. On the 4th of July, 1942, when the place was crowded with hard-drinking soldiers from the base, a beautiful woman ordered a 'magnolia', an established cocktail made with gin, lemon juice, cream, and grenadine. Having forgotten how to make a magnolia, Pancho winged it, using tequila, the ever-present limes, and Cointreau instead of the gin and grenadine. Fortunately the woman liked the drink and Pancho, confusing his flowers, named it 'Margarita'. Because Pancho was a teacher in the Juárez bartenders' school, the drink was soon well-known all over the state of Chihuahua.

Another story is that of the manager of the Crespo Hotel in the city of Puebla, in Puebla state, Danny Negrete, who invented the cocktail in 1936 for his girlfriend, named—you've guessed it—Margarita. She always took a little salt with every spirit she drank, so Danny decided to make it a little easier for her by putting the salt on the rim of the glass. He used the most common ingredients to hand, tequila and lime juice, added Cointreau for a little sweetness, mixed it in a cocktail shaker and strained it into the salted glass. Margarita, of course, loved it.

Many sources claim that the drink was a variation that grew out of other cocktails. One often mentioned is the similarity to a once-popular drink called the sidecar, in which two ounces of cognac, half an ounce of lemon juice, and a quarter-ounce of Cointreau are shaken with cracked ice and strained into a glass rimmed with sugar. This drink was supposed to have originated in Paris, in 1931, at Harry's New York bar, named for a young American millionaire playboy who drove around Paris from bar to bar in the sidecar of a friend's motorcycle. The margarita is said to have evolved by stages from this concoction.

Then there's the unknown bartender who invented it in Palm Springs just after the Second World War, when the fast crowd was hanging out in this area and the men began drinking tequila in the traditional Mexican way. The margarita was an offshoot designed for the ladies, combining the ingredients used in the normal shooters for the men, but placing them in a cocktail glass. The lime juice can be quite sour, so our nameless bartender added a little orange liqueur to sweeten it, shook it over ice to mix it well, and put the salt on the rim, to keep it separate from the liquid so that its taste was more effective.

Spreading the Word

There are certainly dozens, and there may be hundreds of these stories. Many of the legends come from people who claim to have personally invented the margarita, or from those who know on the best authority that they have the true story.

When I first began looking into this, I hoped that I might be able to pin down the one true story. But now, I doubt that. Perhaps the drink was discovered in many places independently, by many different people. Such things have happened before, where different people make the same discovery without contact or knowledge of anyone else's efforts. Witness the telephone: Alexander Graham Bell reached the patent office only four hours before another inventor with a similar device.

If that seems unlikely, we should recall something from Chapter 3: the mixing of '*mezcal* wine' with fruit juice goes back for centuries in Mexican history, and has been a staple of the fighting men on both sides of Mexico's many internal troubles since 1810. The addition of salt to the rim of the glass is traditional, both with straight tequila, tequila and lime, or with any mixture of tequila and fruit juice. Adding salt to drinks is fairly common in cultures with a hot climate and heavy manual labor, for under these circumstances the body can easily begin to suffer from salt loss. It is not such a big step to add orange liqueur as well as citrus fruit juice. There are many variants of the margarita recipe today (see Chapter 10 for a couple of them). So whoever 'invented' the margarita only made a slight modification in something that was traditionally Mexican, and yielded something slightly new which was then further modified by others, and is still being modified today.

Amid all the legends, however, one thing is certain. A substantial public demand for margaritas began in Southern California. It probably did become one of the most called-for drinks at the Tail o' the Cock restaurant before the rest of the U.S. had learned of this new cocktail. It may have crossed over the border from Mexico sometime during the late 1940s, but by 1950 it was the hit of the L.A. cocktail scene.

Rather sadly, this wonderful cocktail has suffered since it has become so popular. The premixing of the drink in large, mechanical, ice cream freezers, with artificial ingredients, and the most inexpensive *mixto* that a bar can buy, is an ignoble travesty of this superb cocktail, and damages the image of tequila. Most people have never tasted a true rendition of a real margarita. To be sure, there are restaurants that offer excellent margaritas, properly made with fine ingredients, but so far these establishments are a few honorable but isolated pioneers. The sno-cone type of margarita has become, unfortunately, the norm, and is the way that most Americans are introduced to margaritas and to tequila.

The main points are to use 100 percent *agave* tequila and shake the mixture with ice, straining it into a salted glass. Don't add cocktail foam and don't use anything premixed. Preferably don't use a blender, but if you do, be very careful not to include too much ice. In the choice of tequila, experiment with *blanco, reposado,* and *añejo.* The results will be decidedly different.

A few restaurants are trying to spread the word about tequila and margaritas. At Tommy's Mexican Restaurant on Geary Street in San Francisco, Julio Bermejo, the owner's son, spreads the gospel of 100 percent *agave* tequilas and makes among the best margaritas I have tasted, using only the best ingredients. Another spot is the Frontera Grill on North Clark Street in Chicago. They support the 100 percent *agave* tequilas very well and also carry the best *mezcals.* The El Torito chain of restaurants also makes a policy of carrying 100 percent *agave* tequilas, and you can get a good margarita there.

Recipes for some versions of the margarita appear in the next chapter. There is considerable variation, and you should feel free to experiment. In Mexico, a common additional ingredient is a liqueur called 'Damiana', the concentrated essence of a wildflower from the back country of Baja California. Mexicans will commonly use an orange liqueur, made in Mexico, called 'Controy', instead of the more expensive Cointreau. U.S. bars, of course, mostly use Triple Sec, Curaçao, or any other orange-based liqueur as a cheap substitute for Cointreau.

10

Some
Tequila Recipes

(O)ne of the many wonderful properties of the *agave* flavor is that it can accompany and heighten other flavors, whether fruity or savory, without losing its unmistakable presence. Good 100 percent *agave* tequila is therefore an excellent ingredient in recipes both for drinks and dishes.

Let's begin with a question I am asked almost every day: how should one drink tequila itself—straight, with lime alone, or with lime and salt?

It is perfectly respectable to add lime or salt to tequila. In fact, it's OK to experiment with all kinds of juices—some tequila drinkers do prefer lemon to lime, for instance. Drinking citrus juice with *mezcal* wine is a centuries-old tradition, so you should feel no hesitation in combining these juices with either tequila or *mezcal*, if that is what you prefer.

I suggest, however, that you make sure that you really do prefer it. At first, you may experience the lime and salt as a welcome contrast to the *agave* flavor. But there is some masking of the interesting components of the *agave*. You may find that, as you become familiar with the *agave*, you gradually come to prefer the tequila by itself, especially if it's an excellent tequila. So if you do like citrus with your tequila, I suggest that, every now and then, you begin your drink of tequila by sipping a small amount on its own. You should also know that Mexican limes are distinctly sweeter than limes commonly available in U.S. supermarkets.

Now we move on to that most famous of all concoctions employing tequila, the margarita. I present the best version of the standard or conventional margarita and then the 'original' recipe of Mrs. Margaret Sames.

Margarita Recipes

The traditional margarita is made from tequila, an orange liqueur such as Triple Sec or Cointreau, lime or lemon juice, and ice. The rim of the glass may be salted, but try it without salt one time to see how you like it. A margarita, like any good cocktail, has to be freshly made.

The Traditional Margarita

1 ounce 100 percent *agave* tequila
1 ounce orange liqueur
1 ounce lime or lemon juice
1 c ice

Place all the ingredients in a blender, and blend until the ice is more than half melted, pour into wide-mouthed glass, with an already-salted rim.

The experience of many people with margaritas has been confined to having these drinks served frozen or very slushy. The cold can mask the flavors of fine tequilas, try them when the ice has just melted and they are beginning to warm a little.

You should experiment with different orange liqueurs. Some of the orange liqueurs available in the United States are: Citronge, a liqueur imported from Mexico by St. Maarten's; Cointreau, a French import which is reputedly the original orange liqueur in margaritas; Grand Marnier, another respected French liqueur; Mandarin Napoléon, a liqueur based on brandy, made with tangerines; Cuarenta y Tres, a liqueur from Spain; Curaçao; and Triple Sec. Controy is widely used in Mexico but not widely available in the U.S.

Although these are all orange liqueurs, each is distinctly different in taste. Triple Sec is widely used in bars because it is cheap, and many people find that they prefer Cointreau. However, some people do prefer the less assertive taste of Triple Sec, in a margarita, to the bold, biting presence of the Cointreau. (To be strictly technical, Triple Sec is a generic term, and some of these liqueurs are brands of Triple Sec. But here I follow ordinary usage. No one normally refers to Cointreau as a Triple Sec, and any liqueur with the words 'Triple Sec' prominent on the label is sure to have a much thinner flavor than Cointreau.)

The Sames Margarita

3 ounces 100 percent *agave* tequila
1 ounce Cointreau
1 ounce lime juice
1 c small ice cubes

Place all of the ingredients into a cocktail shaker and shake for 30 seconds, then strain into a glass with a lightly salted rim.

This recipe for the Sames margarita is the 'original' recipe reputedly devised by Mrs. 'Margarita' Sames, as described in Chapter 9. With that much tequila in the drink, it's no wonder that their Christmas party lasted for two weeks, though since the tequila was 100 percent *agave*, they would not have been troubled by hangovers.

Both the Sames and the traditional margarita were originally made in a cocktail shaker and the ingredients were strained into a glass that could either be salted or unsalted. As the margarita became the most popular cocktail, it came to be made as a frozen mixture, with an inferior taste. Many people can be put off by the sometimes harsh flavors of the limes which we in the U.S. will normally find in our stores. If you get limes that seem too sour, try substituting fresh lemon juice. If fresh lemons or reconstituted lemon juice are not available, Rose's sweetened lime juice or syrup in place of the fresh lime juice may do. But citrus flavors are best when freshly squeezed.

213

Other Cocktails

The Brave Bull

1 ounce 100 percent *agave* tequila
1 ounce Kahlúa
1 squeeze of lime
ice

The Brave Bull is now usually made with Kahlúa though it was first made with Crème de Cacao. For something a little different try a good coffee liqueur, such as Tía María. Some people add this combination to hot, fresh-brewed coffee for a morning pick-me-up.

Perro de Sal

1 ounce 100 percent *agave* tequila
4 ounces Ruby Red grapefruit juice
1 squeeze of lime
ice

This variation on the 'Salty Dog' makes a very nice change from the somewhat flavorless vodka normally used, and the slight sweetness of the red grapefruit adds a lot.

Grito de Dolores

6 ounces V8 juice
2 ounces orange juice
1 ounce lime juice
½ ounce Worcestershire sauce
5–10 drops of jalapeño hot sauce
¼ t garlic or garlic salt
salt and pepper to taste

1½ ounces 100 percent *agave* tequila, in a separate glass

In Mexico, *sangrita* is ever-present, whenever and wherever tequila is served, which means every restaurant and bar in the country. Some Americans may not like the spicy heat in the average *sangrita*, since some versions are nothing more than *chile*, with some orange or lime juice.

You can mix the tequila in with the other ingredients, to produce a much more interesting relative of a Bloody Mary. But my recommendation is that you sip the tequila straight, and use the *sangrita* mixture as a chaser. That way you can get the full flavor of both drinks. If you mix them together, there is a risk the *sangrita* will obscure some of the nuances of a fine quality tequila.

Malinche

6 ounces peach/passionfruit juice
2 ounces unsweetened pineapple juice
2 ounces Rose's sweetened lime juice
1 ounce *blanco* 100 percent *agave* tequila

This new variation on very traditional themes takes advantage of the varieties and blends of juices now on the market. The peach-passionfruit juice mixture is available from Kern's, and the addition of the unsweetened pineapple juice and sweetened lime juice melds well with the other flavors. I like to put the juices in the blender, just to froth and aerate them for a second or two. Then pack an 8–12 ounce glass full of ice, add the tequila and fill the rest of the glass with the frothy juice. It used to be thought that 'Malinche' (pronounced 'Malin-chay') was the name of the mistress and interpreter of Hernán Cortés. Historians now believe it was an Indian name for Cortés himself.

Tequila Toddy

1½ ounces 100 percent *agave* tequila
½ ounce sugar
twist of lemon
4 ounces hot water

Combine the ingredients and then serve in a heat-proof glass or cup

The hot water in the toddy brings out the full flavors of the tequila. Just be sure that you really like the tequila that you use to make this drink, for it will also bring out some quite subdued flavors and aromas, including any unpleasant ones.

The Bandolera is yet another of those fruit juice combinations which go so well with tequila.

Bandolera

1½ ounces 100 percent *agave* tequila
¾ ounce fresh lime juice
3 ounces fresh orange juice
¾ ounce orange liqueur
crushed ice

Fill a 12-ounce glass with ice and add all the ingredients, then stir well.

For another outdoor drink, take a punch bowl, expand the ingredients in the Bandolera, add pineapple juice and place a small block of ice inside the bowl with the ingredients. Float lime wheels on top of the liquid.

Another variation of a cooling drink for a summertime party; take a large watermelon (30–40 lbs), pack it firmly in ice so that it cannot move, cut a medium-sized hole in the top and remove 90 percent of the flesh, being sure to get all of the seeds, but leave a good amount of juice in the shell, add the Malinche mixture previously listed, until there is just enough room to add 1 bottle of 100 percent *agave blanco* tequila, and place a dipper to serve inside or alongside the watermelon. *Salud!*

Desserts and Baking

Tequila goes well with many of the flavors used in fruit desserts. Both of these recipes were made with sugar-free Jell-O, and no cooking is required, which keeps the alcohol in the pie. The taste of the tequila comes through well—some who volunteered as guinea pigs on my taste tests thought a little *too* well. If you feel that way, slightly reduce the quantity of tequila until you hit on the optimal amount.

These pies require no baking, and except for the sugar used in the whipped cream were made as sugar-free desserts by using Jell-O sugar free gelatin (As discussed later in this section, try using fructose rather than cane sugar in these recipes).

Tequila-Orange Pie

1 box orange gelatin
2 7-ounce cans mandarin orange segments
2 c whipped cream
4 ounces 100 percent *agave* tequila

Tekiwi-Lime Pie

1 box lime gelatin
3 medium kiwi fruits
2 c whipped cream
4 ounces 100 percent *agave* tequila

Dissolve the gelatin in 4 ounces of boiling water, and after cooling for a couple of minutes, add the tequila. Mix in the whipped cream, until it is all blended together. For the orange pie, using a pre-prepared crust (I used a Keebler's shortbread pie shell), put a layer of orange segments on the bottom of the pan, almost touching. Pour the filling into the shell, watching that you don't overfill, and place in the refrigerator to cool and set. After about an hour, when the filling has soft set, put another layer of orange segments on the top and a dollop of whipped cream in the center, return to the refrigerator until firmly set. If you want to use a little less tequila, simply increase the amount of boiling water by 1 ounce for every ounce of Tequila you decrease.

For the Tekiwi-Lime version, you can't put down a layer of kiwi on the bottom of the shell because the gelatin won't set. Simply make the filling the same way, and using center slices of kiwi, cover the top of the pie with the kiwi, again placing a dollop of whipped cream in the center.

For the whipped cream, I used a pint of heavy whipping cream and ½ cup of sugar, whipping the cream until stiff. You might try cutting the amount of sugar to ¼ cup,

217

since some of my guinea pigs said it was too sweet. Another tip is to use fructose rather than cane or beet sugar, or an artificial sweetener for a totally sugar-free pie. While the gelatin is setting, the whipped cream rises to the top of the pie thus creating a topping that is flavored and colored the same as the rest of the pie filling and adds a layering effect to the finished product.

Tequila Lemon Chiffon Cake

2¼ c cake flour
1½ c fructose
1 T baking powder
1 t salt
½ c cold water
2 ounces 100 percent *agave reposado*
1/2 c vegetable oil
2 t vanilla
2 t grated lemon peel
7 large egg yolks
8 egg whites
½ t cream of tartar

Tequila Lemon Glaze

⅓ c Butter
1½ c fructose
1½ t 100 percent *agave reposado*
  tequila
½ t grated lemon peel
4 T lemon juice

Place the egg whites and cream of tartar in a large bowl and set aside. Combine all of the other ingredients in a large bowl and beat until smooth. Beat the egg whites and cream of tartar until stiff. Gradually add the egg yolk mixture to the egg whites, folding with a rubber spatula until blended. Pour into an angel food cake tube pan, 10 × 4 inches. Bake in a 375-degree oven on the lowest rack level for about 75 minutes or until the top springs back when touched lightly. Turn the pan upside down on a heat-proof bottle or funnel immediately so that cake will not compress. Cool for 2 hours.

For the lemon glaze; over low heat, melt the butter in a small saucepan, add the fructose, lemon peel and lemon juice, and stir until it is a thick syrup. Remove from heat and let cool for 5 minutes, add the tequila and stir until well blended. Refrigerate glaze for 15–20 minutes or until it becomes a smooth syrup and then apply to top of cake, lightly spreading with a spatula and letting it slowly slide down the sides and center hole. Makes 12 to 16 servings.

Tequila-Buttermilk Corn Bread

1½ c corn meal, any color	½ c all-purpose flour
1½ c buttermilk	¼ c shortening or vegetable oil
2 t baking powder	½ t baking soda
1 t sugar (fructose)	1 t salt
2 large eggs	2 ounces 100 percent *agave* tequila
1 t lime juice	

Heat oven to 450 degrees, grease bottom and sides of standard 9" × 1½" round or 8" × 8" × 2" square baking pan. Mix all of the ingredients together in a medium mixing bowl and beat strongly until not quite smooth. Pour batter into pan and bake until golden brown (about 25 minutes).

For a sweeter bread, add 3 tablespoons fructose or 2 oz. honey. For a spicier bread, add ½ c finely chopped chives or green onion tops, with a little *chile*, if desired.

Appetizers and Entrées

Tequila Salsa Dip

1 large tomato
1 small green bell pepper
1 T chopped garlic
½ c sliced green onions
2 T chopped fresh cilantro
1 T finely chopped jalapeños
3 T lime juice
½ t salt
1 lb cream cheese
2 ounces 100 percent *agave* tequila
1½ T jalapeño hot sauce (if necessary)

Seed and remove the veins from the jalapeños, Place all of the fresh ingredients in a food processor and process until a lumpy salsa. Place in large mixing bowl and add Cream Cheese and Tequila. Blend by hand until cheese begins to smooth. Blend further with mixer until completely combined. Add 'Bufalo' jalapeño sauce to taste.

Tequila Marinade-Barbecue Sauce

1 6-ounce can tomato paste
12 ounces unsweetened pineapple juice
1 medium onion, finely chopped
¼ lb stick of butter
1 t freshly ground pepper
1 t salt
1 T crushed garlic
2 ounces 100 percent *agave* tequila
2 T fresh lemon juice
1 t fresh lime juice
2 T Worcestershire sauce
2 T soy sauce
12 small orange-green chiles, seeded and deveined, finely chopped

Put the pineapple juice into a two-quart saucepan and bring to boil. Reduce heat and slowly simmer until reduced by half and of a medium syrup consistency. Place onions, garlic and jalapeños in a blender or food processor with lemon and lime juice; puree until smooth. Add tomato paste, butter, salt, and pepper to pineapple juice and continue simmering until smooth. Add onion-garlic-*chile* mixture to   simmering pot and stir until absorbed completely. Remove from heat and add Worcestershire and soy sauces, continuing to stir until fully blended. Allow to   cool, add tequila, and continue stirring until fully blended. Makes about one quart.

Tequila Béarnaise Sauce

HOLLANDAISE SAUCE	BÉARNAISE INGREDIENTS
3 egg yolks	1 t black peppercorns
3 t water	2 T white wine vinegar
1 c unsalted, clarified butter	1 oz 100 percent *agave* tequila
Salt	2 shallots, chopped
pinch of cayenne pepper	3 T dried tarragon
1 t strained fresh lemon juice	1 T fresh chopped tarragon
	1 T fresh chopped parsley

In a thick-bottomed, small, non-reactive saucepan prepare Hollandaise by combining egg yolks, water, and salt. Whisk for a moment and cook over very low heat, whisking rapidly and continuously until mixture is thick enough that whisk marks can be seen while stirring. Be careful that mixture does not become too hot or eggs will curdle. When mixture is of medium thickness, remove from heat and continue stirring for about 1 minute. With pan off heat, slowly add 1 tablespoon butter at a time, while continuing to whisk. After mixture has absorbed 3 tablespoons, slowly dribble the remaining butter into the pan and continue stirring. Add lemon juice, salt and pepper, and if necessary season to taste. Set aside for a minute.

Place vinegar, cracked peppercorns, shallots, and dried tarragon in another small saucepan, and bring to a boil. Reduce contents until barely moist, remove from heat and add tequila, stirring briefly. Take hollandaise mixture and add fresh chopped tarragon, parsley and whisk in reduction. Stir until smooth.

Serve immediately over meat, fish, chicken or poached eggs.

The following five food recipes using tequila were kindly provided by Marilyn Smith, partner in Robert Denton and Company.

Avocado Delight

2 c sour cream
1–2 T El Tesoro Silver
⅔ cup mayonnaise
1 t garlic powder
2 ripe avocados (pared and pitted)
1 t onion powder
1 t salt
½ c minced dill or 2 T dill weed

Combine sour cream, mayonnaise, avocados, and lemon juice together in a blender. turn blender on and off for 1 minute intervals until ingredients are perfectly smooth. Add dill, tequila, onion powder, garlic powder, salt and pepper. Puree until ingredients are smooth. Makes about 4 cups and can be used as either a sauce or a dip.

El Tesoro Chicken

6 half breasts, boneless and skinless
2 T butter
½ t salt
¼ t white pepper
2 T minced onions
1 clove of minced garlic
¼ c El Tesoro Silver
1 c heavy cream
¼ t dried tarragon leaves

In a large skillet, brown the chicken in butter. Cover the pan and cook chicken until tender (10–15 minutes), then sprinkle with salt and pepper. Remove chicken to heated platter and keep warm. Soften the onion and garlic in the pan drippings, and mix in the tequila, tarragon, and cream. Simmer, uncovered, until sauce is reduced and slightly thickened. Pour sauce over chicken and serve over rice with fresh parsley garnish. Serves 4–6.

Camarones al Tequila (Tequila Shrimp)

1 lb raw shrimp
5 T butter
½ c El Tesoro Silver
4 T all-purpose flour
⅛ t cayenne pepper
1 c milk or light cream
¼ c dry white wine

Melt 1 tablespoon of butter in a pan, add shrimps and sauté. Warm ¼ cup of the tequila in a smaller pan, add to the shrimps and set aflame. (Note: When flaming tequila, be very careful by being prepared to remove pan from stove if flames get too high).

In a separate pan, prepare a thick sauce by melting the remaining butter, remove from heat and add flour, salt, and cayenne pepper. Stir in the milk, the remaining tequila, and the wine. Return the pan to heat and cook until the sauce comes to a boil and thickens—stirring constantly. Reduce heat to a simmer, add shrimp, and continue simmering until shrimps are thoroughly warmed and serve. Serves 4–6.

Baked Red Snapper with Tequila

4–6 medium tomatoes
4-6 yellow onions, Medium
1 whole red snapper, bass, or pike (thoroughly cleaned)
5 t lemon juice
½ t salt
2 t oregano, or ½ t powdered oregano
2 c dry white wine
½ c Chinaco Silver tequila

Preheat oven to 350 degrees F. Skin and thinly slice the onions and tomatoes and arrange half on the bottom of a roasting pan. Wash the fish in a solution of water and 1 T lemon juice. Dry the fish and rub the remainder of the lemon juice over it. Place the fish on top of the bed of onions and tomatoes in the pan. Cover the fish with the rest of the onions and tomatoes in the pan, and pour in the tequila and white wine. Bake for 35 minutes.

Very carefully remove fish from pan and place on a serving platter, adjust the seasoning of the remaining onion-tomato mixture to taste and arrange along one side of fish. Serves 4–6, depending on the size of the fish.

Piña al Fuego

8 slices pineapple
¾ c brown sugar
4 ounces Chinaco *reposado* or *añejo* tequila
1 quart vanilla ice cream

Coat the pineapple slices with the sugar and place in a sauté pan to heat. Add the rest of the brown sugar and allow them to cook until golden brown on both sides. Pour tequila over pineapple slices and ignite. Allow liquid to boil for three minutes. Serve over vanilla ice cream. Serves 2–4.

The following recipes have been contributed by Martin Crowley of St. Maarten Spirits, the importer and owner of the brand name, 'Patrón'.

Patrón Chicken Marinade

1 chicken, cut into pieces	6 ounces fresh lemon juice
2 ounces Patrón *añejo* tequila	6 bay leaves
2 cans chicken broth	1 t crushed garlic

Combine ingredients other than chicken, then pour over chicken. Marinate overnight in the refrigerator, grill at your convenience.

These following recipes were presented to make one complete dish, but may also be used separately or in combination with other recipes.

Patrón Barbecue Shrimp with Mixed Green Salad and Lime Tequila Vinaigrette Dressing

TEQUILA VINAIGRETTE DRESSING

1 red bell pepper	1 yellow bell pepper
½ yellow onion	2 t crushed garlic
1 bunch cilantro	1 t black pepper
2 c olive oil	1 c peanut oil
4 t kosher salt	1 c maple syrup
2 ounces Patrón *añejo* tequila	1 c red wine vinegar
juice of 2 limes	1 c fresh orange juice

Finely chop the peppers and onion, and coarsely chop the cilantro. Combine all ingredients in a stainless steel bowl and whisk until thoroughly combined, cover and refrigerate until used. Makes about 1 quart dressing.

BARBECUE FLOUR SPICE

1¼ white flour	¾ c sugar
½ c kosher salt	¼ c black pepper
¼ c white pepper	1 T cinnamon
1 c paprika	¼ c garlic powder
1 T ginger powder	

Combine dry ingredients in a small bowl and mix until completely blended.

TEQUILA MARINATED RED ONIONS

1 thinly sliced red onion   juice of ½ lime
1 t kosher salt   1 t maple syrup
3 ounces Patrón *añejo* tequila

Combine ingredients and allow onions to marinate for 1 hour prior to use.

SALAD INGREDIENTS

4 large shrimp per person
½ c barbecue powder
½ c olive oil
1 pkg. fresh salad greens

Coat the shrimp with barbecue powder by mixing in small bowl until thoroughly covered. Put 1 ounce of the olive oil in a medium-sized sautéing pan, and turn heat to high for three minutes. Place shrimp in pan and cook until lightly browned. Place salad greens on individual plates, evenly pour on two ounces of Lime-tequila Vinaigrette dressing, top with shrimp, and add marinated red onions.

While preparing and testing these recipes, a singular fact became apparent to me. If you are planning on using tequila as a flavoring agent in recipes, it may be best, when adding a sweetener, to employ fructose, since this is the same type of sugar as that of the *agave*. If a cane sugar derivative is added, a slight bitterness can become apparent in the final dish.

It's my theory that if any liquor is used as a flavoring agent in a recipe, even wine and beer, and a sweetening agent is also used, the sweetener should be of chemically the same type of sugar as that used to manufacture the spirit in question, or chemically as similar as possible. At least, this idea should be tested.

For example, when using wine, brandy, or tequila, some form of the sugar fructose should be used. If we're dealing with wine or brandy, grape sugars would be preferable, or an unsweetened form of grape juice which can be reduced, thereby increasing the sweetness. When using a beer or whiskey product, like scotch, bourbon, or corn whiskey, the form of sugar should be maltose, or possibly corn syrup. Only a dish that uses the spirit rum should be sweetened with cane sugar, or possibly molasses.

This principle also suggests to me that if distilleries must produce *mixto*, they might achieve better results by adding only a type of sugar compatible with *agave*—grape sugar, for instance, might produce better results than cane sugar. However, that could be academic, as the days of *mixto* may be numbered. In general, using sugars consistent with the types of sugars naturally present in the fermentable base product would be a procedure worth trying in the manufacture of all types of alcoholic beverages.

11

How I Learned About Tequila

$\mathbb{P}$rior to the early 1980s, good tequila—100 percent *agave* tequila—was almost unknown in the United States, except for the occasional American who might have personally discovered it on a visit to Mexico. The only exception was Herradura, for which we have to thank Bing Crosby and Phil Harris. For over 30 years, Herradura was the only 100 percent *agave* tequila widely and regularly available in the U.S.

I had occasionally tasted tequila over the years, and I was very much aware of the 'margarita revolution' of the 1960s, 1970s, and 1980s. But it wasn't until 1990 that I first tasted Herradura. I was surprised and impressed by the full, haunting flavor of this '100 percent *agave*' tequila—though at the time I had no idea what this phrase meant.

Nor did I then know that Chinaco had been available in the U.S. as early as 1983, later followed by Patrón and El Tesoro. Once alerted by Herradura, however, I discovered these more recent arrivals, and became aware that here was a new world of extraordinary richness and complexity, comparable to, but possibly surpassing, the fine cognacs.

I asked around in hotels and restaurants, and enquired about tequila in libraries and bookstores. I was amazed at the absence of detailed and reliable information on the subject.

Then I heard that a few far-sighted restaurateurs were going to great lengths to acquire the best tequilas, though at the time this was based on little more than word of mouth, since most people in the tequila industry were oblivious to the potential demand for higher-priced, higher-quality tequilas, and most of the best tequilas were still virtually unobtainable north of the border. The 'voluntary' ban on TV ads for spirits contributed to the slow rate of diffusion of information. Nowhere was there an authoritative source of information on good tequila. Some companies even had the audacity to advertise their *mixtos* in ways that featured authenticity, superior quality, and a sense of history; so widespread was the ignorance that these ads were not greeted with howls of laughter.

The examples of single-malt scotch and small-batch bourbon indicated a possible direction for tequila, but at the same time there was a great boom in the consumption of *mixto*, mainly as an ingredient in very poor-quality margaritas. This seemed to offer the easiest way to expand sales of tequila in the U.S. The everyday margaritas were becoming so remote from anything resembling tequila that they began to be sold without any tequila component, even *mixto*. But the tequila companies took legal action and put a stop to the tequila-less margarita.

Eventually, I decided that I had to write the book no one else had written, and that, despite my then rudimentary Spanish, I would have to go to Jalisco and talk to anyone I could find who could tell me about tequila.

First Trip to Jalisco

My strongest impression on arrival in Jalisco was the disparity between the poverty of the countryside and the comparative affluence of the cities. But in both town and country I saw a great sense of energy and willingness to work.

In the cities, there are always people trying to sell anything they can from the street corners—every stop light seems to have its vendors trying to sell candy or chewing gum. There are many street entertainers—jugglers, musicians, acrobats—at the major intersections, and music is never far away. There was a piano player in the hotel restaurant for the breakfast crowd. The push-carts of food vendors are everywhere, and every block seems to have a food service establishment of some type, either a stall serving fast food or a sit-down restaurant.

In the countryside, outside the main population center of Guadalajara, there seems to be a restaurant around every bend in the road, and each village has a small establishment serving food every two or three hundreds yards or so. The buildings themselves are different in the countryside. The favorite building material seems to be brick, and there are walls around almost all homes and business establishments.

I already knew that the majority of homes in Latin America were built along different lines from those in the U.S., but I didn't at first understand how this simple aspect of the physical environment affected the outlook of the people. The central court-yard style of house, with no outward-looking windows, is highly discreet, exposing only that which the owner wishes the rest of the world to see. It encourages introversion and reticence, or per-haps it reflects these innate characteristics. The people who live in these dwellings can often be very private and controlled in their personal lives, with their families being protected as much as pos-sible from the outside world. But if you can gain their friendship and trust, they are among the most considerate people anywhere. No doubt Mexico's history and political system have also con-tributed to the pervasive reticence.

When I first arrived in Jalisco, I wasted more than a week try-ing to contact some of the companies that I had been unable to contact prior to leaving on the trip. Many tequila companies had told me: 'Call us when you get here, and we will set up an appointment for your visit, and show you our facilities.' Once I arrived, however, very few of the people that I wished to contact seemed to be available. It seemed that everybody just happened to be out of town when I arrived. I was to become very familiar with this pattern of reticence and, in a few cases, paranoia. Here, how-ever, I will mention a few of the notable exceptions.

My first successful visit was to Rio de Plata, the distillery of Tequilas del Señor. This distillery is a small plant that takes up about a city block in one of the industrial areas of Guadalajara. I was shown through the plant, allowed to take pictures, and granted an interview with the owner, Sr. Manuel Garcia, and his international marketing manager, Mr. Hendrik Nollen.

I learned a lot about Rio de Plata's history and tasted some of their products. Besides tequila, they make many other alcoholic beverages, including various types of liqueurs. They had recently begun making a new premium 100 percent *agave* tequila called 'Herencias del Señor'. I sampled some and was favorably impressed, finding it to be very pleasant and smooth to the palate. Their marketing techniques struck me as odd, however. They were selling this product on a limited basis by subscription only. Persons had to join a mail order club and the company would periodically ship them a bottle or two. This allowed them to build up their stocks without being inundated with demands from retail stores.

When I needed a ride to my second distillery, Hacienda San José del Refugio, the manufacturing center for Herradura, in the village of Amatitán, I met Sr. Rodolfo 'Rudy' Vasquez Magaña, a Guadalajara taxi-driver who would be my driver for this and all my subsequent visits. I was introduced to Rudy by a bellman at my hotel, and later discovered that a sizeable cut from my first fee to Rudy (which I had thought a bit on the high side) had gone to the bellman.

In Amatitán, we turned down a dirt road and drove alongside a brick wall until we reached a large green metal gate. From the outside, the property resembles an old western fort, with a wall that looks about twenty feet high and two hundred yards long. After the guard opens and you drive through the large gate, you find yourself inside the walls, in a cobblestone parking area of about two acres. You approach another gate, in which there are three guards in a gate-house, and are finally admitted, on foot, to the actual manufacturing and office area.

When we arrived, I was informed that the person appointed to show me around was tied up elsewhere. I began to think, 'This is the same old Mexican distillery runaround', but this proved not to be the case. I was given a very efficient personal tour by a knowledgeable young woman with excellent English, and later heard from Herradura, who apologized, answered all my remaining questions and provided me with a meeting with the owner, Sr. Guillermo Romo de la Peña.

The buildings inside the hacienda are exquisite, and have an almost new look about them, though many have been standing for over 125 years. I learned that for a residence or compound to be called an 'hacienda' there must also be a church or chapel included somewhere. I did not go inside the family residence, and presume that the chapel is located there.

The manufacturing facilities themselves are very neat and clean, with most of the equipment made of gleaming stainless steel. There is a powerful impression of efficiency and painstaking attention to detail. The entire compound probably exceeds five hectares.

As I was to find at other Mexican businesses, my impression was that most of the work takes place early in the day. The lunch break in Jalisco begins at 2:00 P.M., and normally lasts for two hours. During the lunch period, everything stops. The businesses close and lock their doors, and everybody goes home or to their favorite restaurant for the main meal of the day.

I was driven to the village of Arandas by Sr. José Luis Sánchez Rojas, better known as 'Pepe', to tour the 'Centinela' distillery. This ride was my first introduction to the Mexican phenomenon called *baches* (potholes). Though none was actually large enough to swallow the car, they did seem sufficient to jar your intestines loose. I have described my visit to Centinela in Chapter 5. The people were friendly, and obviously enjoyed teasing the *norteamericano* who wanted to know all about tequila.

I was later shown around by Martin Grassl, a young entrepreneur of German antecedents, founder and owner of Destileria Porfidio. Sr. Grassl has a Mexican wife and speaks at least five languages well. He has an extensive knowledge of the region and its distilleries. He began with the idea that there would be an expanding export market for fine tequila, then began to buy 100 percent *agave* tequila to resell under his own label, and then founded Porfidio.

231

Martin took me to one of the older distilleries in the village of Tequila, called 'La Martineña'. It was built in the late 1800s and has been in more or less continuous use since then. We went to liquor outlets in Guadalajara where Martin expounded from his vast knowledge of the Mexican retail trade. We also toured the suburbs, primarily in the vicinity of Tlaquepaque, a well known center for arts and crafts. I wanted to look at the facilities that make bottles for Porfidio, both glass and ceramics. We checked at a glass factory that makes the cactus bottles, and stopped at two companies that make ceramic bottles. One of these was a company that had made some ceramic containers in which tequila had been shipped to Japan. Upon arrival, the bottles were all found to be empty, the tequila having leaked out during shipment due to improper glazing. A lawsuit was looming.

Outside of this facility was a very prominent hill. I was informed that archaeologists had investigated this little mountain and had concluded it was really an ancient pyramid, covered over through the centuries. Whether this was just another legend for a gullible tourist I have not yet been able to ascertain.

The main shopping plaza of Tlaquepaque is interesting but obviously designed mainly for tourists. A large number of companies in the area, run by woodcarvers, metalworkers, jewelers, and artists, make many kinds of decorative art. I saw everything from inexpensive jewelry to very expensive woodcarvings, including beautiful, full-sized carousel horses.

At Destiladora González González in Guadalajara I was greeted by Sr. Miguel Cedeño, who was helpful in explaining what methods were used to manufacture tequila. He has a master's degree in microbiology, and was very enlightening about the way in which the yeast, microbes, and bacteria contribute to the fermentation and the flavor development of tequila.

I also visited the offices of Tequila El Viejito and interviewed the owner, Sr. Antonio Nuñez Hurtado. This company makes many of the 100 percent *agave* tequilas imported into the United States under different labels.

At this time I still could not ascertain just how many tequila distilleries there were. I had a frustrating time trying to talk to someone in authority at *La Cámara*. I eventually did get from their office a membership list, which turned out to be fairly accurate and complete, though not entirely so.

I had an instructive conversation with Sr. Eduardo González, one of the sons of don Julio González Estrada, the founder of Tequila Tres Magueyes. The company had for many years produced only *mixto* for sale, but don Julio (Eduardo's father and founder of the company) had always made a few barrels of 100 percent *agave* tequila for his own and his family's private use. He would, on occasion, have friends visit and tour his distillery and would give them a bottle of his own private stock. It was so well received that the guests began requesting the opportunity to purchase it, and don Julio began manufacturing it for sale.

The next day I was picked up by Tres Magueyes driver Raul Romero for the trip to the distillery, where I was introduced to Don Carlos González Estrada, the brother of Don Julio. He is a very large and handsome older man with white mustachios, who has served as a model for some of the company advertising. The distillery manager, Sr. Marco Antonio Cedano Nuñez, is very knowledgeable about tequila and very open about his company. He explained a great deal that I didn't know about the manufacturing techniques and the methods used in the total process of making tequila. I became convinced that this company was on the right track, and I still think so.

After the tour of the distillery, Raul drove me back to Guadalajara, with a side trip to visit a friend of Raul's who owned a restaurant located on the shore of Lake Chapala, the largest lake in Mexico, a country deficient in internal bodies of water. The lake is very shallow, and during the dry season may shrink drastically, but when the rains return, fills up to capacity again. There is a large 'colony' of U.S. citizens living in the area of the lake, and the restaurant, owned by a former U.S. resident, gets a lot of business from them.

Further Trips

After returning to the United States, I realized that although I had now learned a lot, I was merely scratching the surface. I quickly returned to Jalisco for more investigations.

I visited the distillery of Tequila Tapatio, a company that I had heard much about from their importer, Robert Denton. After a teeth-rattling drive over roads that were the worst yet, I arrived at the offices of Tequila Tapatio. This building is located about 100 yards from the offices of Centinela. Carlos Camarena, the son of don Felipe Camarena, greeted me and answered many questions; then we went to the *agave* fields, so that I could witness the harvesting and take pictures of the *jimadores* at work, or in this instance, *el jimador,* since there was only one man cutting, with another helping with the loading of the harvested *cabezas* into the waiting pickup. While the harvesting was going on, Carlos was explaining how to tell when each *agave* was ready to be harvested. He pointed out the signs, the rust-colored spots at the bases of the silvery blue leaves, the places where the flower spike had been cut, the shrinking as the plant drew its energy out from the leaves and concentrated it into the growth at the center, what would become the *piña*.

When we left the fields and drove to the distillery, we came to a very large red brick building under construction. The reception area was filled with *piñas,* and a young man with a broadax was cutting them into halves and quarters, readying them for the ovens. While many of the larger companies had recently remodelled and expanded, their manufacturing plants usually installed autoclaves, but not Tapatio. They were planning four new ovens of 60 metric tons capacity each, and were planning to build three new *tahonas* for the crushing and juicing of the *agave.* As far as I could determine, Tapatio is the only company that still uses *all* of the old ways.

In another section of the plant, a man was down inside a large circular pit, lined with stones, using a wooden shovel to load *agave* fiber into large wooden buckets. As each was filled, one of three other men would take the bucket, place it on top of his head and carry it to a small (3,000 liter) wooden fermentation tank— one of about 25—climb a short ladder, and hand it to another man who was inside the tank. The fiber would be re-mixed with the *agave* juice, and a yeast mixture would be added by carrying a smaller bucket, of about three gallons, from a tank that had already been partially fermented. This strain of yeast was developed and first used by the founder of the company, the current don Felipe's father, in the 1940s.

After the juice is fully fermented, taking about a week under normal conditions, the fermented juice, now called *mosto*, is carried in buckets to the first run still. This still is made of copper, of 1,500 liters capacity, and signs of the leftover fiber are all around. After the first distillation, the still must be emptied by hand and readied for the next batch of *mosto*. The second run still is also made of copper but is only 750 liters in size. Its job is to take the first run spirits (now called *ordinario*), and concentrate the alcohol further until it reaches the desired proof, usually between 76 and 84 proof or 38 to 42 percent alcohol by volume.

I found the methods used by Tapatio to be absolutely fascinating, and felt as if I were looking through a window on the past, seeing the way that tequila had been made over a century ago.

Rudy then drove me to the Cazadorés plant, an imposing new *fábrica* which was a complete contrast to Tapatio. The capabilities exhibited by this new plant were definitely modern. With 52 30,000-liter stainless steel fermentation tanks full of juice, this plant, when operating at full capacity, can produce over 12,000,000 liters of tequila a year.

I visited *El Consejo Regulador del Tequila* and received much helpful information. Although I didn't realize it immediately, I had begun to research tequila at just the point where the climate was becoming more favorable than it had been, thanks largely to the good work of the *Consejo*, a regulatory and public relations body for the industry. Under its director, Ramon González Figueroa, *El Consejo* has done excellent work in increasing awareness of the quality of 100 percent *agave* tequilas.

I had an informative visit to El Llano, the distillery which makes Tequila Arette (see Chapter 5). The most memorable sight on that visit was the old *tahona* that was still installed, although it hadn't been used for years. The street on which El Llano is located also has the distilleries for Tequila Cuervo's La Rojena, La Perserverancia of Tequila Sauza, and La Martineña, a distillery then involved in a legal dispute over possession of the plant. One street over, on Calle Tabasco, are two other distilleries, La Areñita of Productos Especiales de Tequila, and La Mexicana of Tequila Orendain de Jalisco.

On the return trip from Tequila, I visited La Regional of the company Empresa Ejidal Tequilera Amatitán in the village of Amatitán. Rudy and I spent some time looking for the distillery La Fortuna, owned by the new company, Elaboradora y Procesadora de *Agave* y sus Derivados. The plant had formerly belonged to the now defunct company, Destiladora de Arenal, but the ownership had been restructured, moving some of the partners out and acquiring new investors and a new strategy. When we did find it, the plant was probably the smallest that I have seen, even smaller than Tequila Tapatio before the expansion.

In the Highland *agave* fields near the village of Capilla de Guadalupe, I again witnessed a *jimador* in action. The harvester, Juan Perez, was obviously experienced and very smooth with his cutting action. He harvested three large *agaves* in about 15 minutes.

As well as visiting distilleries, I kept a lookout for new bottles of tequila. I was fortunate to find as many different brands as I did, since many of the rarer tequilas could be obtained only by going to the company offices to buy them direct. Many of the smaller firms, or those that had their tequila made by a distillery they did not own, were not widely available even in Guadalajara. Among the tequilas which were difficult to find were 'Tequila Caballitos Cerrero' made by La Regional, 'Tequila Catador' made by Catador Alteño, and all of the brands made by Tequila Parreñita. Parreñita may however start to export tequila to the U.S. very soon, under the label of 'Misión Imperial'.

The Right Way to Make Tequila

After my first few visits to Jalisco, I formed some basic conclusions which I have not seen the need to revise. We should be clear that the reason *mixto* is cheaper to produce than 100 percent *agave* tequila is not that the sugar used for fermentation is less expensive. (I checked on the relative prices just before this book went to press, and it just so happened that on this occasion *agave* was actually cheaper than non-*agave* sugars.) The difference in cost arises from the more time-consuming processes which need to be carried out in making 100 percent *agave* tequila.

I came to understand that, because of this difference in the manufacturing processes, it can be problematic to make 100 percent *agave* and *mixto* simultaneously in the same distillery. It's not impossible: some companies producing *mixto* do indeed manage to product excellent 100 percent *agave* tequila. But it does create problems. Nearly all of the ways in which *mixto* production can be accelerated will noticeably damage the flavor of 100 percent *agave*.

The direct steam injection of the autoclaves causes the bitter-honey to be washed from the cuticles of the *pencas*, and this must be removed or it will have a deleterious effect on the final taste of the tequila. The high temperature which enables rapid cooking can cause some of the flavor-giving congeners to be lost.

No one yet knows which of the chemical components of the *agave* give it the elusive flavors that turn it into tequila. We do know that some methods make very fine tequilas while others do not. It appears that the mysterious chemical components are very sensitive to heat. During the fermentation process, the must should be allowed to take its time, and not become overheated. The addition of chemical accelerators or yeast nutrients to the *mosto* may create too much heat, destroying some of the delicate flavor-enhancers.

Each stage in the manufacturing process should be handled with great care. As in the manufacture of the finest wines, attention to detail is important. Only pot stills should be used to make tequila. For some reason, column stills or rectification units do not manage the transfer of the flavor congeners to the final product as well as do the traditional pot stills.

Whatever the factors that affect the final flavors of the tequila, it is clear that when traditional methods are employed, the tequila has more *agave* flavors, more complexity, and fewer discordant tones competing with the central *agave* flavor.

These traditional methods should always be used in the manufacture of 100 percent *agave* tequila. If *mixtos* survive the impending changes, they may be relegated to the manufacture of pre-mixed margaritas and other prefabricated cocktails. If any *mixto* does continue to be manufactured, then I predict that distilleries will become strictly segregated, with 100 percent *agave* made in some and adulterated tequilas in others. The distillers of the future will not wish to make *mixto* in the same facility as 100 percent *agave* tequila.

The Future
of Tequila

Consumption of alcoholic beverages is chronically declining in the United States. Tequila is one of the few exceptions; tequila consumption shows a long-term increase. While total U.S. alcoholic beverage sales declined 23 percent during 1985–95 (a decline of 30 percent if related to population on a per capita basis), tequila has generally increased at around 2–3 percent per year.

There have been some bumps. Tequila consumption declined sharply in 1994, for instance, both in Mexico and the U.S., but the decline was largely reversed by an increase in 1995, and as this book went to press, it seemed that 1996 would also show a healthy increase. The major part of recent increases has been in 100 percent *agave* tequila.

Causes of the Decline in Alcohol Consumption

There are many causes of the decline in alcohol consumption, including the unrelenting assault by religious and other mindless anti-alcohol groups. However, I believe the underlying causes of the decline derive from social changes.

If we look at trends in the consumption of alcohol, we see that there has been a tremendous drop in the 'on-sale' part of the market, partly offset by an increase in the 'off-sale' segment. In other words, Americans are drinking less in restaurants, cocktail lounges, taverns, and bars, and comparatively more at home. As a result, the 'off-sale' part of the industry (sales through establishments licensed to sell liquor for consumption off the premises) is now the dominant part.

There seem to be four main reasons for this development. The first three arise negatively, from forces which deter people from going out for a drink.

The first cause is the various changes in the laws and regulations, tightened controls, and increased enforcement efforts, with regard to alcohol-related activities, but especially to drunk driving violations. In many states, the legal limit for your blood alcohol if you're in charge of a vehicle is 0.07 percent. Any chances of getting off through pleas of hardship or extenuating circumstances have been steadily whittled away.

In California, an arrest for drunk driving has been calculated, on average, to cost the offender between $15,000 and $20,000. This figure combines the court costs, increases in insurance fees, time lost from work, possible jail sentences (mandatory for second-time offenders), attorneys' fees, and fines.

Most people don't think that enjoying the effects of a couple of drinks is worth a high risk of being out by $20,000. And a couple of drinks is just what 0.07 percent blood alcohol means: any combination of beer, wine, or spirits that equals two ounces of 40 percent alcohol, consumed over a period of one hour, will bring your blood alcohol to about 0.1 percent.

The second cause is the decline in the desire to meet new people in bars, especially with a view to sex. The fear of contracting a sexually-transmitted disease has become so prevalent as to discourage the old 'singles bar' type of lifestyle.

Third, there is the increased fear of violence in our society, stimulated by a constant media blitz about drive-by shootings and other risky events in public places. Even though the crime rate has been declining, people are still adjusting to the earlier increase in violence, and they feel safer at home.

The fourth cause, however, is a positive one. There simply are far more and better entertainment prospects at home than there used to be, even a decade or two ago. There is the VCR and the neighborhood video rental store. Just as bars and lounges have declined, so have movie theaters. Then there is cable and satellite TV, with scores of specialized channels and ever-increasing screen sizes. Together with the VCR, the result is to bring something even better than a movie theater into the home at a very reasonable price. The rise of the DSS (Digital Satellite System or 'Direct TV') will further reinforce the stay-at-home trend, with 175 channels, including 20 movie channels, and 15 sports channels with all professional sports games and most college games available.

When you add to this the personal computer, used by 40 percent of homes and rising every day, an appliance which provides education, entertainment, and business aids, plus access to the Internet and the World Wide Web, you can see why fewer people are going to want to spend their evenings drinking in a bar. On the Web, you can 'converse' with people of closely similar interests anywhere in the world, not merely with the poor guy who happens along to your local tavern.

These developments are the culmination of a trend that has been under way for centuries: modern technology has made the home potentially a comfortable and pleasant place to be for the mass of people. A hundred years ago, for most people, the local tavern was far more comfortable and entertaining than their home could ever be.

The problems that now exist in the liquor industry show no signs of abating. The decline of alcohol sales has caused the virtual demise of the 'lounge act' or 'bar band'. Live entertainment can be very expensive. A full-time, five- or six-piece group, working five or six nights a week, will regularly cost over $3,000, and the better the group, the more expensive it will be. With incomes falling because of declining drinks purchases, bar managers have found entertainment the easiest place to make cuts, which in turn may reduce the attractiveness of the bar. In Las Vegas, it used to be commonplace for a good quality group to be able to earn up to

$10,000 per week, but such rates are now a thing of the past. The hotel and restaurant businesses have also been hit, because they derived part of their business from close proximity to drinking-and-entertainment establishments.

For the last fifty years, the liquor sales portion of the hotel business has been a major source of revenue, sometimes carrying the hotel through times of poor overall sales. I'm aware of a number of hotels in the western U.S. whose lounge earnings during the month of December could exceed a million dollars. But more recently, most of the new hotels have excluded the cocktail lounge from the construction blueprints. Ten years ago, hotels wanted to own and control the restaurants and lounges in their hotels. Today, the hotel companies will be more likely to lease the restaurant and lounge part of the business to an outside company. Labor costs have risen, and so have liability costs, with the courts' new attitude that if you serve someone alcohol you can be held liable for what they do after they leave your establishment.

A Boon and a Blessing

So present trends will intensify, and some traditional outlets for alcoholic drinks will find themselves increasingly hard-pressed. But it would be a mistake to suppose that these trends imply that alcohol will cease to be of interest to a lot of people. People have been drinking alcoholic beverages for thousands of years. Alcohol is a boon and a blessing to humankind: it is an aid to enjoyment, relaxation, socializing, and merriment. It can stimulate creative new ideas. True, alcohol can kill you if you abuse it, but the same is true of knives, stairs, tall buildings, medicines, or football.

Although prolonged consumption of large amounts of alcohol can harm your health, prolonged consumption of modest amounts can be a health benefit. This has been recognized by civilized societies throughout history, and is endorsed by the Bible ("Take a little wine for your stomach's sake." 1 Timothy, 5:23), but now it is gaining support from an ever-increasing series of scientific research studies. When these scientific findings were first publicized, it was often implied that the health benefits came only from red wine, but, admirable as fine red wine is, that spin is misleading. It appears that any kind of alcoholic drink, in the right amounts, will yield the health benefits. Aside from alcohol's medicinal virtues, it is beyond serious dispute that temperate consumption of alcohol can delightfully enrich and enhance the emotional *quality* of life.

There is a risk of individuals, through weakness of will, becoming alcoholics. But any freedom inevitably brings with it the chance of going wrong and doing harm. And it can easily be observed that cultures which encourage modest alcohol consumption regularly, with food, from an early age, produce far less alcoholism or drunkenness than cultures which depict alcohol as something so dangerous it had best be avoided altogether.

The Pursuit of Quality

Wherever some alcoholic beverage has shown an increase in consumption in recent years, it has most often been because of a preference for the better-quality, more authentic product, even if it is higher priced.

The most striking example is the rise of the single-malt scotches, alongside the drastic decline of blended scotches. The same is true in the bourbon market, where blends have almost completely disappeared, and within the 'single malt' bourbons (though that term is not used of bourbon, it would apply to all the most familiar bourbons), there has arisen an expanding market for 'single barrel' labels, and a definite interest in bourbon made by labor-intensive, old-fashioned methods. In both cases, single-malt scotches and single-barrel bourbons, these premium drinks are more challenging and have more character than the cheaper, more generic brands.

A somewhat similar pattern is detectable in wines. As Americans have consumed more wine, they have also gradually sought out better, more expensive wines, with the *grand crus* of France being in good demand and the more upscale wines of California also showing a healthy growth in sales.

U.S.-made brandies are showing definite advances in quality,

243

with a number of new distilleries making alembic spirits very much in the style of the better cognacs of France. The explosion of interest in good, old-fashioned beer indicates a similar tendency, with the proliferation of many micro-breweries and their offshoots, the high-quality brew-pubs.

The huge declines in alcohol consumption are mainly concentrated in that portion of the market that used to be the backbone of the liquor industry: inexpensively manufactured spirits primarily used for mixing with other ingredients—the cocktail lounge or bar well spirits, liquors commonly termed 'well brands'.

Although tequila was put on the U.S. map in the form of *mixto*, as a cheap ingredient in a fashionable cocktail, the growth now is chiefly in the higher-quality segment of the tequila market, the 100 percent *agave* tequilas. Ever since the adulteration of tequila to create *mixto* was begun in the 1930s, every type of shortcut and cost-cutting simplification that humans could devise to make tequila cheaper has been implemented, and with every step the quality of the tequila has deteriorated. Many distilleries were reluctantly compelled to produce *mixto* to remain in business, and many companies did disappear during those trying years.

A reversal is now under way. Newer distilleries are opening, and some are employing the old-fashioned, painstaking methods, while some older companies are moving back into production of 100 percent *agave* tequila. Everyone who closely watches the tequila industry now believes that there will be a tremendous growth of 100 percent *agave* tequila. Even *mixto* is being improved by raising the required proportion of *agave*, but this, of course, will reduce the price differential between *mixto* and 100 percent *agave*, causing consumers to ask: 'Why not pay a little more for the real thing?' The only controversial point here is whether *mixto* can survive at all.

Alcohol and Education

The liquor industry has not done a very good job of educating people about alcohol. They have evidently been too intimidated to mention the health benefits of alcohol in their advertising. They have dutifully spent millions of dollars on telling people not to drink too much and not to drink when about to drive, but this is not true education, which would include emphasis on the health, social, psychological, and cultural benefits of alcohol, and the differences between various kinds and qualities of beverages.

Rarely do liquor suppliers send out their representatives to hold seminars, and when they do, attendance is usually limited to invited guests from within the beverage industry. The wait-staff in restaurants, the servers in taverns, bartenders and cocktail waitresses are the students at such training sessions. Occasionally, the manager of an upscale country club might allow his or her assistant to attend, but rarely is the public welcomed.

Education, then, should combine three aspects now usually separated: first, the benefits of alcohol consumption; second, the risks of alcohol consumption and the advisability of moderation; and third, an appreciation of the different kinds of alcoholic drinks, so that the consumer can distinguish high quality from poor quality. Moderation and a fine appreciation of liquor go together, for those whose tastes are educated enough to savor a fine alcoholic drink will rarely get drunk.

The best ways to perform these educational tasks will no doubt emerge over time. Many of the new brew-pubs specialize in differing flavors of beers within their types and offer 'short' or small glasses of beer for the sampling of these differing flavors. Wineries have much the same educational tool available to them with their tasting rooms. These methods allow the public access to the flavors of the wines that are produced by these companies prior to purchasing any bottles.

One stratagem for salvaging something of the bar and lounge sector of the industry is specialization as to type of alcoholic beverages. There are already a number of establishments scattered across the country that have adopted this format and been successful. One restaurant and lounge in Northern California has over 100 different varieties of single-malt scotch. Another is currently carrying 35 labels of vodka. In New York City, there is a lounge named 'Bubbles' that specializes in champagnes. And a Mexican restaurant in San Francisco (Tommy's) is steadily promoting public knowledge of the better tequilas and carries almost all of the currently imported 100 percent *agave* brands.

It should also be expected that any restaurant which serves ethnic foods will have available the drinks that would normally be served in their country of origin. In an Italian restaurant, the customer should be able to order from a good selection of Italian wines and liqueurs, not just Chianti. Greek restaurants should have on hand different brands of *ouzos* and the resinated wines of that country. And what would a Japanese restaurant be without sake and good Japanese beers? A fine *shochu* would also not be amiss. Mexican restaurants should of course always stock the best tequilas, *mezcals,* and Mexican beers.

These are just a few suggestions about the way the industry might develop its educational and marketing role. I cannot begin to guess all the methods which will in fact be implemented. However, the industry must also come to terms with the reality that people have become generally more home-centered, and less inclined to a night out.

People will not become hermits. The VCR and the Web are not complete substitutes for warm interaction in the flesh. People will therefore want to entertain at home. Here you can offer your friends good drinks and good company. Sitting in your favorite chair, in a warm and well-equipped home, on a cold, snowy, or rainy winter's night, with a glass of your favorite beverage, or perhaps with some rare and fine drink that you are about to sample for the first time, you can enjoy an evening of relaxation, conviviality, and stimulating discussion with your family and friends.

This perhaps represents the future positioning of alcoholic drinks. Among these drinks, one of the noblest and proudest will be traditionally-manufactured 100 percent *agave* tequila, the true spirit of Mexico.

Appendix A

Tequila Labels

1,000 Agaves. Tequila Santa Fe (Distillery #34)

1910. La Cofradia (#19)

1921. Agave Tequilana (#1)

30-30. Agroindustrias Guadalajara (#2)

7 Leguas. Siete Leguas (#38)

Acapulco. [Le Vecke] Eucario González (#29), Viuda de Romero (#41)

Aguila. [Guadalajara Imports] El Viejito (#28)

Alteño. Tequila Viuda de Romero (#41)

Ana R. Viuda de Cuervo. Tequilas del Señor (#36)

Antaño. Siete Leguas (#38)

Aniversario. Orendain (#31)

Arenal. Parreñita (#32)

Arette. Azteca de Jalisco (#7)

Aristocrat. [Heaven Hill Distilleries] Orendain (#32)

Arriba. Tequilas del Señor (#36)

Authentico. Tequilas del Señor (#36)

Azabache. [Agaves Finos] Parreñita (#32)

Azteca. [David Sherman] González González (#9)

Aztlan. Eucario González (#29)

Bam-Bam. Eucario González (#29)
Bambarria. Tequilas del Señor (#36)
Bardon d'Arignac. Tequilas del Señor (#36)
Barranca de Viudas. Catador Alteño (#24)
Barrancas. Catador Alteño (#24)
Barranqueño. Tequila Cuervo (#27)
Beamero. [Jim Beam Brands] La Madrileña (#20) and San Matias (#33)
Bicentenario. [Heublein] Tequila Cuervo (#27)
Black Death. [Cabo Distributing] Eucario González (#29)
Black Hat. [Cabo Distributing] Eucario González (#29)
Bowman's. [Smith-Bowman and Amerex] La Madrileña (#20)

Caballito Cerrero. Tequila Caballito Cerrero (#22)
Caballo Moro. Parreñita (#32)
Caballo Negro. Eucario González (#29)
Cabrito. Centinela (#26)
Cacama. González González (#9)
Calende. [U.S. Distilled Products] El Viejito (#28)
Caliente. La Gonzáleña (#44)
Camarena. La Arandina (#18)
Camino Real. [Bacardi] Cascahuin (#23)
Cancún. [Wm Grant and Sons] Orendain (#31)
Canixta. [Sardet et Deribaucort] Orendain (#31)
Caporales. El Viejito (#28)
Carlos. La Madrileña (#20)
Casa Gallardo. [David Sherman] González González (#9)
Cascahuin. Cascahuin (#23)
Casca Viejo. La Arandina (#18)
Casta. Tequileña (#42)
Casteneda. [Distillery Stock USA] La Madrileña (#20)
Catador. Catador Alteño (#24)
Cava de Don Augustin. La Arandina (#18)
Cava de los Beas. Agroindustrias Santa Clara (#3)
Cava de Villano. [Tequilas Selectos] La Cofradia (#19)
Cazadores. Cazadores (#25)

Centenario. [Heublein] Tequila Cuervo (#27)

Centenario La Rojeña. [Heublein] Tequila Cuervo (#27)

Centennial. [David Sherman] González González (#9)

Centinela. [El Dorado Imports] Centinela (#26)

Centinela Imperial. [El Dorado Imports] Centinela (#26)

Cesar García. Tequilas del Señor (#36)

Chamucos. Tequileña (#42)

Chapala. [Selection Difution Vente] Tequilas del Señor (#36)

Charro de Oro. Agroindustrias Guadalajara (#2)

Chinaco. La Gonzáleña (#44)

Cholula. [Destilleras de Villafranca] El Viejito (#28)

Colorin. Eucario González (#29)

Conmemorativo. [Domecq Imports] Tequila Sauza (#35)

Coronado. [Paramount] La Madrileña (#20)

Coronel. La Cofradia (#19)

Coyote. [Seagram de México] Orendain (#31)

Cuernavaca. Eucario González (#29)

Cuernito. Cascahuin (#23)

Cuervo. [Heublein] Tequila Cuervo (#27)

Cuervo 1800. [Heublein] Tequila Cuervo (#27)

Cuervo Centenario Extra. [Heublein] Tequila Cuervo (#27)

Cuervo Especial. [Heublein] Tequila Cuervo (#27)

Cuervo Rojo. [Heublein] Tequila Cuervo (#27)

Cuervo Tradicional. [Heublein] Tequila Cuervo (#27)

Dalia. Eucario González (#29)

D'Antaño. Siete Leguas (#38)

Del Campo. [Wm Grant and Sons] Orendain (#31)

Del Mayor. González González (#9)

De los Dorados. La Cofradia (#19)

Del Prado. [Wm Grant and Sons] Orendain (#31)

Diligencias. Tequilas del Señor (#36)

Distiller's Pride. [Heaven Hill] Orendain (#31)

Distinqt. [Munico International] El Viejito (#28)

D.J. Ramirez. Viuda de Romero (#41)

D.J. Ramirez Historico. Viuda de Romero (#41)

Don Benito. Fábrica de Aguard. (#13)

Don Camilo. La Cofradia (#19)

Don Federico. Eucario González (#29)
Don Juan. Agave Tequilana (#1)
Don Julio. Tres Magueyes (#40)
Don Margarito. Eucario González (#29)
Don Paco. La Gonzáleña (#44)
Don Pancho. La Madrileña (#20)
Don Quixote. El Viejito (#28)
Don Serapio. Tequilas del Señor (#36)
Don Tacho. Parreñita (#32)
Dos Amigos. La Arandina (#18)
Dos Coronas. [Licores Vera Cruz] Tequilas del Señor (#36)
Dos Reales. [Heublein] Tequila Cuervo (#27)
Durango. [Wm Grant and Sons] Orendain (#31)

El Bandido. [Wm Grant and Sons] Orendain (#31)
El Charro. Tequilera Rustica (#46)
El Cid. [David Sherman] González González (#9)
El Cobrizo. [La Vallesana] Orendain (#32)
El Corral. Fábrica de Aguard. (#13)
El Destilador. Tequilera Newton (#45)
El Gran Viejo. Azteca de Jalisco (#7)
El Grito. La Cofradia (#19)
El Herradero. [Tequila Cerro Viejo] Tequila Cascahuin (#23)
El Jimador. Herradura (#30)
El Palanque. [Dist. de Villafranca] El Viejito (#28)
El Tequileño. Jorge Salles Cuervo (#17)
El Tequileño Especial. Jorge Salles Cuervo (#17)
El Tesoro de Don Felipe. Tapatio (#39)
El Toro. [U.S. Distilled Products] Orendain (#31)
El Viejito. El Viejito (#28)
Especial Newton. Tequilera Newton (#45)
Espuela. [Anton Riemerschmid] González González (#9)
Eucario González. Eucario González (#29)
Extra. [Domecq Imports] Tequila Sauza (#35)

Fandango. [Illya Saronno] Orendain (#31)
Fierro. [Casa Madero] Tequilera Newton (#45)
Fonda Blanco. [David Sherman] González González (#9)

Fortin de Loco. Santo Tomas (#14)

Galardon. [Domecq Imports] Tequila Sauza (#35)
Gallo Giro. [Domecq Imports] Tequila Sauza (#35)
Garcia. Tequilas del Señor (#36)
Garibaldi. Viuda de Romero (#41)
Gascon. Eucario González (#29)
Gavilan. [David Sherman] González González (#9)
Giro. [Domecq Imports] Tequila Sauza (#35)
Gran Centenario. Casa Cuervo (#4)
Grand Linar. Tequilas del Señor (#36)
Gringo's. [Campbell Meyer] Orendain (#31)

Hacienda. [David Sherman] González González (#9)
Hacienda de Tepa. Tequilera Rustica (#46)
Hechiceros. Elab. y Proc. de Agave (#11)
Henri Vallet. [CIA Destiladora] El Viejito (#28)
Herencia de Plata. Tequilas del Señor (#36)
Herencia del Señor. Tequilas del Señor (#36)
Herradura. [Sazerac] Herradura (#30)
Herradura Selección Suprema. Herradura (#30)
Hipodromo. La Arandina (#18)
Hombre. [Inchcape Liquor] El Viejito (#28)
Honorable. Corporación Ansan (#6)
Hornitos. [Heublein] Tequila Sauza (#35)
Hot Jorongo. [Antonio Fernandez] Viuda de Romero (#41)
Huerta Vieja. Tequilas del Señor (#36)
Hussong's. La Cofradia (#19), El Viejito (#28)

Inmemorial Viuda de Romero. Viuda de Romero (#41)
Ixtapa. [Société d'Exportation] El Viejito (#28)

Jalisciencc. Agroindustrias Guadalajara (#2)
Jalisco. [Selection Difution Vente] Tequilas del Señor (#36)
James Mason. [Wm Grant and Sons] Orendain (#31)
Jarana. La Madrileña (#20)
Javelina. [Wm Grant and Sons] Orendain (#31)
Jesús Reyes. J. Jesús Reyes Cortes (#16)

Jimador. Herradura (#30)

Jorge Ruiz. La Escondida (#32)

Jorongo. [Antonio Fernandez] Viuda de Romero (#41)

José Cortez. Tequilas del Señor (#36)

José Cuervo. [Heublein] Tequila Cuervo (#27)

José Gaspar. Tequilas del Señor (#36)

José Mendes. [U.S. Distilled Products] El Viejito (#28)

José Paco. [Paramount] La Madrileña (#20)

J.R. Jaime Rosales. [Franzia Imports] Parreñita (#32)

Juárez. [Frank Lin] González González (#9), Eucario González (#29)

La Areñita. [Compania Tequilera] J. Jesus Reyes Cortes (#16)

La Cofradia. La Cofradia (#19)

La Prima. [Paramount] La Madrileña (#20)

La Parreñita. Parreñita (#32)

La Piedrecita. Tequilas del Señor (#36)

La Paz. [Le Vecke] Eucario González (#29), San Matias (#33)

Lapiz. Tequileña (#42)

La Rojeña. [Heublein] Tequila Cuervo (#27)

Las Flores. Eucario González (#29)

Las Trancas. El Viejito (#28), Tequileña (#42)

Ley. [Nacional Vinicola] Tequilas del Señor (#36)

Limitado. Eucario González (#29)

Los Cinco Soles. El Viejito (#28)

Los Cofrades. La Cofradia (#19)

Los Corrales. Tequilera Newton (#45)

Los Juanes. González González (#9)

Los Ruiz. [Seagram de México] Orendain (#31)

Los Valientes. [Parliament Import] Santo Tomas (#14)

Margalime. Tequilas del Señor (#36)

Mariachi. [Seagram de México] Orendain (#31)

Matador. [Jose Cuervo International] Tequila Cuervo (#27)

Maxim's de Paris. González González (#9)

Mayor. González González (#9)

McCormick. [McCormick] El Viejito (#28), Eucario González (#29), Orendain (#31)

Mercian. [Okura] El Viejito (#28)

Mestizo. [International Wines and Spirits] Tequilas del Señor (#36)

Mexicali. San Matias de Jalisco (#33)

Mexican Gold. [Jenkins Spirits] Orendain (#31)

Mexican Silver. [Jenkins Spirits] Orendain (#31)

Miguel. [Paramount] La Madrileña (#20)

Miramontes. J. Jesús Partida Melendez (#15)

Misión Imperial. Parreñita (#32)

Mi Viejo. El Viejito (#28)

Monarch. [Hood River] Orendain (#31)

Montego. [C. Heinrich Quast] Orendain (#31)

Montezuma. [Barton Brands] González González (#9), La Madrileña (#20)

Newton. Newton e Hijos (#45)

Northfield. [Wm Grant and Sons] Orendain (#31)

Ohrner Co. HJC. Newton e Hijos (#45)

Ojo de Agua. San Matias de Jalisco (#33)

Old Mexico. [Highwood Distillers] Eucario González (#29)

Olé. San Matias De Jalisco (#33)

Ollitas. Orendain (#31)

Olmeca. [Seagram de México] Orendain (#31)

Orendain. Orendain (#31)

Oro Azul. Agave Tequilana (#1)

Oro Viejo. Tequilas del Señor (#36)

Pacal de Palanque. [Dumont] Tequilas del Señor (#36)

Parreñita. Parreñita (#32)

Patrón. [St. Maarten] Siete Leguas (#38)

Penca Azul. Parreñita (#32)

Peneranda. [Bodegas Queretano] Parreñita (#32)

Peneranda Especial. [Bodegas Queretano] Parreñita (#32)

Pepe Lopez. [Brown-Forman] San Matias de Jalisco (#33)

Pico de Gallo. Tequilera Corralejo (#43)

Playa Blanca. [Selection Difution Vente] Tequilas del Señor (#36)

Poland Spring. [White Rock] González González (#9)

253

Poncho Rojo. [Bacardi] Cascahuin (#23)
Porfidio. [Todhunter Imports] Azteca de Jalisco (#7), J. Jesús
    Reyes Cortes (#16)
Portales. Eucario González (#29)
Posadas. Eucario González (#29)
Potter's. [International Potter] La Madrileña (#20), Eucario
    González (#29)
Pueblo Viejo. San Matias de Jalisco (#33)
Puente Viejo. Newton e Hijos (#45)
Puerta Grande. Parreñita (#32)
Pura Sangre. Tequileña (#42)

Quito. Tequilas del Señor (#36)

Ralph's. Eucario González (#29)
RB D'Reyes. J. Jesús Reyes Cortes (#16)
RB Rey. J. Jesús Reyes Cortes (#16)
Real Hacienda. Viuda de Romero (#41)
Regional. Empresa Ejidal (#12)
Reserva de la Casa. Tequila Tres Magueyes (#40)
Reserva de la Familia. Tequila Cuervo (#27)
Reserva del Señor. Tequilas del Señor (#36)
Revolución. Tequila Santa Fe (#34)
Revolucionario 501. Elab. y Proc. de Agave (#11)
Rio Baja. [David Sherman] González González (#9)
Rio de Plata. [Frank-Lin] Tequilas del Señor (#36)
Rio Grande. [McCormick] El Viejito (#28), Orendain (#31)
Rio Lerma. Eucario González (#29)
Riserva Privada. González González (#9)
Rockport. [White Rock] González González (#9)

Salvador's. La Cofradia (#19)
San Matias. San Matias de Jalisco (#33)
Santa Cruz y Dis. Eucario González (#29)
Santa Fe. Tequila Santa Fe (#34)
Santa Rita. La Cofradia (#19)
Sarape. El Viejito (#28)
Sauza. Tequila Sauza (#35)

254

Sauza Blanco. El Viejito (#28)
Save-On. Eucario González (#29)
Shorty's. [White Rock] González González (#9)
Skaggs Alpha-Beta. Eucario González (#29)
Sierra. [Borko Marken] El Viejito (#28)
Sierra Mezcalita. Eucario González (#29)
Sierra Mazmalita. San Matias de Jalisco (#33)
Siete Leguas. Siete Leguas (#38)
Silla. González González (#9)
Sin Rival. Destiladora de Occidente (#8)
Si-Si. [Compania Tequilera] El Viejito (#28)
Six-Gun. Tequilas del Señor (#36)
Sombrero Negro. Tequilas del Señor (#36)
Suave Herradura. [Sazerac] Herradura (#30)
Suave Patria. Tequileña (#42)
Sublime. Corporción Ansan (#6)
Sutton Club. [White Rock] González González (#9)

Tempo. [Jim Beam Brands] La Madrileña (#20)
Tenoch. La Cofradia (#19)
Tepa. Tequilera Rustica (#46)
Tepeyac. La Cofradia (#19)
Tico. Tequilas del Señor (#36)
Tierra Viva. Tequilas del Señor (#36)
Tijuana. [Sazerac] El Viejito (#28)
Tikal. [CIA Destiladora] El Viejito (#28)
Tina. [Sazerac] El Viejito (#28)
Tolteca. González González (#9)
Tonatiuh. La Cofradia (#19)
Topaz. [Majestic] Orendain (#31)
Torada. [Sazerac] Tequilas del Señor (#36), El Viejito (#28)
Tres Alegres Compadres. La Cofradia (#19)
Tres Caballos. Tequilera Rustica (#46)
Tres Generaciones. [Domecq Imports] Tequila Sauza (#35)
Tres Magueyes. Tequila Tres Magueyes (#40)
Tres Mujeres. J. Jesús Partida Melendez (#15)
Tres Reyes. Tequilera Rustica (#46)
Tres Rios. El Viejito (#28)

255

Tucan. El Viejito (#28)
Two Fingers. [Hiram Walker] La Madrileña (#20)

Vampiro Vampire. [Grupo Vampiro] Viuda de Romero (#41)
Virreyes. J. Jesús Reyes Cortes (#16)
Viuda de Romero. Viuda de Romero (#41)
Viuda de Sanchez. Tequila Cuervo (#27)
¡Viva Miguel Villa! [Compania Tequilera] J. Jesús Reyes Cortes
    (#16)
¡Viva Zapata! Tequileña (#42)
Von's. El Viejito (#28)

Xalisco. Tequileña (#42)
Xalixco. Tequileña (#42)
Xuárez. El Viejito (#28)

Yucatán. [Cunesier] Viuda de Romero (#41)

Zafarrancho. Corporación Ansan (#6)
Zapata. [Laird and Company] Orendain (#31)
Zapopan. La Cofradia (#19)

Appendix B

NOMs of Tequila
Production Companies

Any genuine, 100 percent *agave* tequila (and any aged tequila) must by Mexican law have a NOM on the label or the bottle. The following list of NOMs, in numerical order, will enable you quickly to ascertain the origin of any bottle produced by any distillery in operation as this book went to press.

#740. Industrialización y Desarrollo de Santo Tomas, S.A. de C.V.

#856. (and #1154) J. Jesús Reyes Cortes, S.A.

#1068. Agroindustrias Guadalajara, S.A. de C.V.

#1079. Agave Tequilana Productores y Comercializadores, S.A. de C.V.

#1102. Tequila Sauza, S.A. de C.V.

#1103. Tequila San Matias de Jalisco, S.A. de C.V.

#1104. Tequila Cuervo, S.A. de C.V.

#1105. Tequila Catador Alteño, S.A. de C.V.

#1107. Tequila El Viejito, S.A. de C.V.

#1108. Jorge Salles Cuervo y Sucesores, S.A. de C.V.

#1109. Destiladora Azteca de Jalisco, S.A. de C.V.

#1110. Tequila Orendain de Jalisco, S.A. de C.V.

#1111. Tequila Viuda de Romero, S.A. de C.V.

#1112. Tequila Santa Fe, S.A. de C.V.

#1113. Tequila Eucario González, S.A. de C.V.

#1114. Tequila Caballito Cerrero

#1115. Tequila Parreñita, S.A. de C.V.

#1117. Destiladora de Occidente, S.A. de C.V.

#1118. Tequila Tres Magueyes, S.A. de C.V.

#1119. Tequila Herradura, S.A. de C.V.

#1120. Tequila Siete Leguas, S.A. de C.V.

#1121. Empresa Ejidal Tequilera Amatitán, S.A.

#1122. Casa Cuervo, S.A. de C.V.

#1123. Tequila Cascahuin, S.A.

#1124. Tequilas del Señor, S.A. de C.V.

#1127. Tequilera la Gonzáleña, S.A. de C.V.

#1128. Tequila Cazadores, S.A. de C.V.

#1131. La Arandina, S.A. de C.V.

#1137. La Cofradia, S.A. de C.V.

#1139. Tequila Tapatio, S.A. de C.V.

#1140. Tequila Centinela, S.A. de C.V.

#1141. Elaboradora y Procesadora de Agave y sus Derivados, S.A. de C.V.

#1142. La Madrileña, S.A. de C.V.

#1143. Destiladora González González, S.A. de C.V.

#1146. Tequileña, S.A. de C.V.

#1154. (and #856) J. Jesús Reyes Cortes, S.A.

#1172. CIA Orendain, S.A. de C.V.

#1173. Tequilera Newton e Hijos, S.A. de C.V.

#1196. Productos Especiales de Tequila,

#1235. Tequilera Rustica de Arandas, S.A. de C.V.

#1258. J. Jesús Partida Melendez.

#1298. Tequila Sierra Brava, S.A. de C.V.

#1333. Fábrica de Aguardiente de Agave la Mexicana, S.A. de C.V.

#1359. Destilados de Agave, S.A. de C.V.

#1360. Corporación Ansan, S.A. de C.V.

#1368. Tequilera Corralejo, S.A. de C.V.

#1384. Agroindustrias Santa Clara de S.P.R. de R.L.

Appendix C

Addresses of Tequila Companies

1. Agave Tequilana. Acacias 122-F, Rinconada del Sol, 45060 Zapopan, Jalisco, Mexico. Fax and phone (523) 647-7144
2. Agroindustrias Guadalajara. Rancho El Herradero #100, Capilla de Guadelupe, 47700 Jalisco, Mexico. Phone (523) 712-1515. Fax (523) 712-1331
3. Agroindustrias Santa Clara. Isla Española #2430, Fracc. Colon S.J., 44920 Guadalajara, Jalisco, Mexico. Phone (523) 811-7238
4. Casa Cuervo. Circunvalación Sur No. 44-A Las Fuentes, 45070 Zapopan, Jalisco, Mexico. Phone (523)634-4477. Fax (523) 634-8893
5. Compañia Orendain. Avenida Vallarta No. 6320, 46400 Zapopan, Jalisco, Mexico. Phone (523)527-1827. Fax (523) 627-1376
6. Corporación Ansan. Mexico Olimpiada 68 S/N La Laja, Zapotlanejo, Jalisco, Mexico. Fax and phone (523) 651-5932
7. Destiladora Azteca de Jalisco. Silverio Nuñez No. 108, 46400 Tequila, Jalisco, Mexico. Phone (523)742-0246. Fax (523) 742-0719

8. Destiladora González González. Puerto Allarta No. 1131, 44330 Guadalajara, Jalisco, Mexico. Phone (523) 637-8484. Fax (523) 651-5397
9. Destiladora de Occidente. Hidalgo No. 829, 44670 Guadalajara, Jalisco, Mexico. Phone (523) 742-0100
10. Destilados de Agave. Comercio 168, Colonia Centro, Guadalajara, Jalisco, Mexico. Phone (523) 614-9657. Fax (523) 613-1698
11. Elab. y Proc. de Agave y sus Derivados. Av. Ferrocarril No. 140, 44350 El Arenal, Jalisco, Mexico. Phone (523) 748-0275
12. Empresa Ejidal Tequilera Amatitán. Cam. a la Barranca de Tecuane, S/N 45380 Amatitán, Jalisco, Mexico. Phone (523) 745-0043
13. Fábrica de Aguardientes de Agave la Mexicana. Rancho Llano Grande Km 2.5 Carr. Arandas-Léon, Arandas, Jalisco, Mexico. Phone (523) 784-6001 and (523) 784-6051
14. Industrialización y Dllo. Santo Tomas. Niños Heroes No. 1976, 55610 Guadalajara, Jalisco, Mexico. Fax and phone (523) 826-4881
15. J. Jesús Partida Melendez. García Barragan No. 52, Arenal, Jalisco, Mexico. Phone (523) 748-0140 or (523) 742-1074
16. J. Jesús Reyes Cortes. Carretera Internacional No. 100, 46400 Tequila, Jalisco, Mexico. No phone
17. Jorge Salles Cuervo y Sucs. Leandro Valle No. 991, 44100 Guadalajara, Jalisco, Mexico. Phone (523) 614-9400
18. La Arandina. Periferico Norte Lateral Sur No. 762, 45130 Zapopan, Jalisco, Mexico. Phone (523) 636-2430. Fax (523) 656-2176
19. La Cofradia. Mariano Barcenas #435, Sector Hidalgo, 44200 Guadalajara, Jalisco, Mexico. Phone (523) 613-6690. Fax (523)613-6641
20. La Madrileña. Arroz. 89, Col. Santa Isabel Industrial, 09820 Mexico D.F. Phone (525) 582-2222. Fax (525) 581-1326
21. Productos Especiales de Tequila. Tabasco No. 36, 46400 Tequila, Jalisco, Mexico. Phone (523) 742-0241. Fax (523) 742-0129
22. Tequila Caballito Cerrero. Simon Bolivar No. 186, 44140 Guadalajara, Jalisco, Mexico. Phone (523) 615-1338 or 4881. Fax (523) 616-0023

23. Tequila Cascahuin. Hospital No. 423, 44280 Guadalajara, Jalisco, Mexico. Fax and phone (523) 614-9958l
24. Tequila Catador Alteño. Rancho Los Ladrillos (Conocido), Jesus Maria, Jalisco, Mexico. Fax and phone (523) 704-0277
25. Tequila Cazadores. Km. 3 Libramiento Sur, 47180 Arandas, Jalisco, Mcxico. Phone (523) 784-5570. Fax (523) 784-5189
26. Tequila Centinela. Francisco Mora No. 8, 47180 Arandas, Jalisco, Mexico. Phone (523) 783-0468. Fax (523) 783-0933
27. Tequila Cuervo La Rojeña. Circunvalación Sur No. 44-A, Las Puentes, 45070 Zapopan, Jalisco, Mexico. Phone (523) 634-4298. Fax (523) 634-8893
28. Tequila El Viejito. Eucalipto No. 2234, 44900 Guadalajara, Jalisco, Mexico. Phone (523)812-9092. Fax (523) 812-9590
29. Tequila Eucario González. P. Himno Nacional No. 5-A, 46400 Tequila, Jalisco, Mexico. Phone (523) 742-0470. Fax (523)742-0483
30. Tequila Herradura. Av. 16 de Septiembre No. 635, 44180 Guadalajara, Jalisco, Mexico. Phone (523)614-0400. Fax (523) 613-1698
31. Tequila Orendain de Jalisco. Av. Vallarta No. 6230, 45010 Zapopan, Jalisco, Mexico. Phone (523)627-1827. Fax (523) 627-1376
32. Tequila Parreñita. Av. Alcalde No. 859, 44100 Guadalajara, Jalisco, Mexico. Fax and phone (523) 613-6078
33. Tequila Santa Fe. Calz. Gebernador Curiel No. 1708, Guadalajara, Jalisco, Mexico. Phonc (523) 811-7589. Fax (523) 811-7903
34. Tequila San Matias de Jalisco. J.J. González Gallo No. 2565, 44890 Guadalajara, Jalisco, Mexico. Phone (523) 635-2046. Fax 635-8780
35. Tequila Sauza. Av. Vallarta No. 3273, 44100 Guadalajara, Jalisco, Mexico. Phone (523) 679-0600. Fax (523) 679-0690
36. Tequilas del Señor. Rio Tuito No. 1193, 44870 Guadalajara, Jalisco, Mexico. Phone (523) 657-7787. Fax (523) 657-2936
37. Tequila Sierra Brava. No address or telephone numbers were available at the time of this printing
38 Tequila Siete Leguas. Av. Independencia No. 360, 47750 Atotonilco el Alto, Jalisco, Mexico. Phone (523) 917-0996. Fax (523) 917-1891

39. Tequila Tapatio. Alvatro Obregón No. 35, 47180 Arandas, Jalisco, Mexico. Phone (523) 783-0425. Fax (523) 783-1666

40. Tequila Tres Magueyes. Av. La Paz 2180, 44140 Guadalajara, Jalisco, Mexico. Phone (523) 630-3034. Fax (523) 615-2161

41. Tequila Viuda de Romero. Jose Maria Morelos No. 285, 46400 Tequila, Jalisco, Mexico. Phone (523) 742-0006. Fax (523) 742-0215

42. Tequileña. Bruselas No. 285, 44600 Guadalajara, Jalisco, Mexico. Phone (523) 826-8070. Fax (523) 827-0249

43. Tequilera Corralejo. Hacienda Corralejo, Estación Corralejo, Pénjamo, Guanajuato, Mexico. Phone (524) 977-0203. Fax (524) 877-0334

44. Tequilera Gonzáleña. González, Taumalipas, Mexico. For information, call (U.S.) (810) 229-0600.

45. Tequilera Newton e Hijos. Ruperto Salas No. 168, Col. Benito Juárez, 45190 Guadalajara, Jalisco, Mexico. Fax and Phone (523) 660-2945

46. Tequilera Rustica de Arandas. Norberto Gomez No. 408, Fracc. el Sol, 20030 Aguascalientes, Mexico. Fax and Phone (524) 916-1046

And now two other useful addresses:

47. El Consejo Regulador del Tequila. Mexicaltzingo No. 2208, Planta Baja, Col Moderno, C.P. 44150 Guadalajara, Jalisco, Mexico. Phone (523) 616-9982 or 4673. Fax (523) 616-9975

48. La Cámara Regional de la Industria Tequilera. Calz. Lazaro Cardenas 3289, 5th floor, 45000 Guadalajara, Jalisco, Mexico. Phone (523) 121-5021. Fax (523) 647-2031

Addresses of U.S. Tequila Importers

Barton Brands Ltd. 55 East Monroe Street, Chicago, IL 60603. Phone (312) 346-9200. Fax (312) 855-1220

Black Prince Distillery. 691 Clifton Avenue, Clifton, NJ 07015. Phone (201) 365-2050. Fax (201) 365-0746

Brown-Forman Beverage Company. P.O. Box 1080, Louisville, KY 40201. Phone (502) 585-1100. Fax (502)774-6980

Cabo Distributing Company. 9657 East Rush Street, South El Monte, CA 91733. Phone (818)575-8090. Fax (818) 350-3880

Carillon Imports. 500 Glenpoint Centre, West Teaneck, NJ 07666. Phone (201) 836-7799

Chatham Imports Inc. 257 Park Avenue, 7th Floor, New York, NY 10010. Phone (212) 473-1100. Fax (212) 473-2956

Consolidated Distilled Products Inc. 3247 South Kedzie Avenue, Chicago, IL 60623.

David Sherman Corp. 5050 Kemper Avenue, St. Louis, MO 63139. Phone (314) 772-2626. Fax (314) 772-6015

Distillery Stock USA Ltd. 58-58 Laurel Hill Blvd. Woodside, NY 11377. Phone (718) 651-9800. Fax (718) 651-7806

Domecq Imports Company. 143 Sound Beach Avenue, Old Greenwich, CT 06870. Phone (203) 637-6500. Fax (203) 637-6595

El Dorado Importers. 761 Parker Avenue, Santa Rosa, NM 88435. Phone (505) 472-3379. Fax (505) 986-6060

Florida Distillers Company. 530 Dakota Avenue, Lake Alfred, FL 33859. Phone (941) 956-1116. Fax (941) 956-1181

Frank-Lin Distillers Products Ltd. 675 North King Road, P.O. Box 610877, San Jose, CA 95161-0877. Phone (408) 259-8900. Fax (408) 258-9527

Guadalajara Imports. 18104 Park Avenue, St. Louis, MO 63104. Phone (314) 776-5060. Fax (314) 776-5117

Heaven Hill Distilleries Inc. P.O. Box 729, Bardstown, KY 40004; Phone (502) 348-3921. Fax (502) 348-0162

Heublein Inc. 16 Munson Road, Farmington, CT 06034. P.O. Box 5083, Hartford, CT 06102. Phone (860) 702-4000. Fax (602) 677-7257

Hiram Walker and Sons, Inc. 3000 Town Center, Suite 3200, Southfield, MI 48075l. Phone (810) 948-6500. Fax (810) 048-8921

Hood River Distilleries Inc. 770 Riverside Drive, Hood River, OR 97031. Phone (541) 386-1588. Fax (541) 386-2520

Illva Saronno Corp. 1952 Route 22 East, Bound Brook, NJ 08805

Jenkins Spirits Corp. Ltd. 21 Perimeter Road, Londonderry, NH 03053. Phone (603) 623-3231. Fax (603) 623-6645

Jim Beam Brands Company. 510 Lake Cook Road, Deerfield, IL 60015. Phone (847) 948-8888. Fax (847) 948-0395

Joseph E. Seagram and Sons, Inc. P.O. Box 7, Lawrenceburg, IN 47025. Phone (812) 537-8557.

Kentucky Distillers Inc. 201 Church Street, P.O. Box 67, Stanley, KY 42375. Phone (502) 764-1131.

Laird and Co. 1 Laird Road, Scobeyville, NJ 07724. Phone (201) 542-0312

Le Vecke Corp. 1491 Santa Fe Drive, Tustin, CA 92680. Phone (714) 259-8600

McCormick Distilling Company. 1 McCormick Lane, Weston, MO 64098. Phone (816) 640-2276. Fax (816) 640-2402

M.S. Walker Inc. 20 Third Avenue, Somerville, MA 02413. Phone (617) 776-6700. Fax (617) 776-5808

Majestic Distilling Company Inc. P.O. Box 7372, Baltimore, MD 21277. Phone (410) 242-0200. Fax (410) 247-7831

Montebello Brands, Inc. Bank Street and Central Avenue, Baltimore, MD 21202. Phone (410) 282-8800. Fax (410) 282-8809

Munico International Corp. 1 West Loop South, Suite 701, Houston, TX 77027.

Paramount Distillers Inc. 3116 Berea Rd, Cleveland, OH 4111. Phone (216) 671-6300. Fax (216) 671-2299

Parliament Import Company. 3303 Atlantic Avenue, Atlantic City, NJ 08401. Phone (800) 472-7542

Potter Distilleries, Inc. 18700 N.E. San Rafael, Portland, OR 97230

Robert Denton and Company. 2724 Auburn Road, Auburn Hills, MI 48326. Phone (248) 299-0600. Fax (248) 229-3836

Sazerac Company, Inc. 803 Jefferson Highway, New Orleans, LA 70121. Phone (504) 841-3436

St. Maarten Spirits, Ltd. 3625 W. Harmon, Las Vegas, NV 89103. Phone (702) 262-9446

Sun Imports, Inc. 1365 Westgate Center Drive, Suite E, Winston-Salem, NC 27103. Phone (910) 659-5653. Fax (910) 659-9427

Tequila Imports. 3401 Louisiana, Suite 235, Houston, TX 77002. Phone (713) 522-4900. Fax (713) 522-4011

Tequila Los Altos Distributing Company. 312 Lang Road, Burlingame, CA 94010. Phone (415) 348-6945. Fax (415) 348-3357

Tist, Inc. 1535 Mockingbird Lane #402, Dallas, TX 75235. Phone (214) 634-8653. Fax (214) 634-8648

United Distilleries North America. 6 Landmark Square, Stamford, CT 06901. Phone (203) 359-7100. Fax (203) 359-7199

United States Distilled Products Company. 1607 South 12th Street, Princeton, MN 55371. Phone (612) 389-4903

William Grant and Sons. 130 Fieldcrest Avenue, Edison, NJ 08837. Phone (908) 225-9000. Fax (908) 225-0950

White Rock Distillers, Inc. 21 Saratoga Street, Lewiston, ME 04240. Phone (207) 783-1433.

Appendix E

Mexican Law Governing Tequila

Mexico has a regulatory system called the NORMA. One of its requirements is the placing of a specific number, called a NOM, on manufactured products. The original purpose was to enable determination of liability for manufacturers. All products made in Mexico carry a NOM somewhere. All bottles of tequila are required to have a NOM, either on the label or as part of the bottle itself, so that the identity of the manufacturer or bottler can be instantly determined.

The following is a translation of some of the less technical requirements of the regulations set up under the NORMA for the manufacture of the product called 'tequila'.

0. INTRODUCTION

The product that is referred to in this Norm is the designated alcoholic drink named TEQUILA.

1. OBJECTIVES

This official Norm establishes the characteristics that must be fulfilled for the designated alcoholic drink to be called TEQUILA.

2. REGIONS OF APPLICATION

The controlled area includes all of the state of Jalisco and certain designated areas in four other states. These areas are:

In the state of Guanajuato, the towns of Abasolo, Ciudad Manuel Doblado, Cueramaro, Huanimaro, Pénjamo, and Purisima del Rincon.

In the state of Michoacán, the towns of Brisenas de Matamoras, Chavinda, Chilchota, Churintzio, Cotija, Ecuandures, Jacona, Jiquilpan, Maravatio, Nuevo Parangaricutiro, Numaran, Pajacuaran, Periban, La Piedad, Regules, Los Reyes, Sahuayo, Tabcitaro, Tangamandapio, Tangancicuaro, Tanhuanato, Tinquizddin, Tocumbo, Venustiano Carranza, Villamar, Vistahermosa, Yurecuaro, Zamora, and Zinaparo.

In the state of Nayarit, the towns of Ahuacatlan de Canas, Ixtlan, Jala, Jalisco, San Pedro Lagunillas, Santa Maria del Oro, and Tepic.

In the state of Tamaulipas, the towns of Aldama, Altamira, Antiguo Morelos, Gomez Farias, González, Llera, Mante, Nuevo Morelos, Ocampo, Tula, and Xicontencatl.

No alcoholic product produced outside these areas may be called 'tequila'.

3. REFERENCES

This section lays down specifications for chemical testing of TEQUILA by the Consejo Regulador and La Cámara.

4. DEFINITIONS

For the purposes of this Norm, the following definitions are established:

4.1. ABOCADO

The procedure used to soften and smooth the flavor of TEQUILA by the addition of one or more flavoring or coloring agents, permitted by the Secretariat of Health and Assistance.

4.2. AGING

A slow transformation that permits the spirit TEQUILA to acquire the organic characteristics desired by using physical processes or natural chemical changes that take place when stored in wooden casks for a period of time.

4.3. TEQUILA

A regional alcoholic drink obtained by distillation or rectification of musts prepared with the extracted sugars from the hearts of the *Agave tequilana weber,* blue variety, which have been previously submitted to alcoholic fermentation with yeasts. It shall be permitted to use 40 percent of other sugars in the preparation of said musts. TEQUILA is a transparent, clear liquid that has the flavor typical of tequila. It is colorless but may have a slight yellowish tinge when matured in oak casks or barrels. When it is unaged but *abocado,* it may have coloration added.

4.4. AGED TEQUILA (TYPE IV)

The product must be submitted to an aging process of at least one year in casks or barrels of oak wood that may not exceed 600 liters is size. Water may be used to adjust the percentage of alcohol to commercial levels. In the case of a mixture of different age groups of tequilas, the age of the youngest component will apply.

4.5. WHITE TEQUILA (TYPE I)

The product obtained in the distillation or rectification of the required musts and adjusted with water to dilute the tequila to the required marketable alcohol level.

4.6. REPOSADO TEQUILA (TYPE III)

A product that must be aged at least two months in oak wood. Water may be added to adjust the level of alcohol to the marketable requirement.

4.7. ABOCADO OR GOLD TEQUILA (TYPE II)

Caramel or other coloring agents may be added to unaged abocado TEQUILA to change the color to a desired level.

5. CLASSIFICATION

5.1. According to the manufacturing specifications, TEQUILA, the object of this Norm is classified as:

5.1.1. 100 percent *agave* TEQUILA is required to originate only from the musts and exclusively contain sugars originating from the *Agave tequilana Weber*, blue variety.

5.1.2. TEQUILA is required to originate from the musts of the *Agave tequilana Weber*, blue variety, but may contain up to 40 percent other sugars.

5.2. According to the characteristics, the tequilas are subject to the requirements mentioned in 4.4, 4.5, 4.6, and 4.7.

6. SPECIFICATIONS

6.1. TEQUILA, the object of this NORM, must comply with the specifications noted in Table 1.

6.2. General requirements.

6.2.1. The aging of *añejo* TEQUILA must be effected in oak barrels, each with a maximum capacity of 600 liters.

6.2.2. For the purposes of diluting to commercial proof, the distiller or rectifier should use distilled or demineralized drinking water.

7. SAMPLING

This section refers to the specifications for taking samples for testing.

8. BARRELS

This section covers other sampling regulations, sealing, and inspection of barrels used for aging.

9. LABELS AND TAGS

9.1. Each container must have a label or permanent impression on which is noted in outstanding, legible forms, the following information:

The name of the product, related to the facts that are pursuant to the classification of the NORM; volume of contents expressed in liters or milliliters; percentage of alcohol by volume or proofage of contents; name and address of the manufacturer or merchant under whose brand the product is sold, the brand name, and the legend, 'Made in Mexico'.

If the product is a shipment in bulk, the previous data will appear on the documents of the commercial transaction.

10. CONTAINERS

Each container of TEQUILA, the object of this NORM, shall be sealed and packaged so that the recipient is guaranteed that its conservation and quality do not change. The capacity should not exceed five liters, and in no case should containers bearing the brand names of other manufacturers be used.

APPENDIX

A.1. The formal requirements for the fulfillment of this Norm.

A.1.1. The manufacturer of 100 percent *agave* tequila must comply with the following requirements:

Said entity must request authorization, in writing, from the Director of Normas to produce 100 percent *agave* tequila.

Said product (100 percent *agave* tequila) must be bottled at the point of origin, where the *agave* plants are grown and the tequila is produced.

If authorization is made for the production of 100 percent *agave* tequila, the manufacturing processes must be accomplished under the permanent inspection rules pursuant to the General Procedures Address. Once authorization is granted, the manufacturer will be allowed to use the words, 'Made from 100 Percent *Agave*', on the containers, labels, wrappers, and invoices, and for advertising and publicity purposes. On any container labels marked '100 percent *agave*' must also be included the legend, 'Produced and bottled under the watchfulness of the Mexican government', independent of Section 9.1.

Appendix F

Tequila Output Statistics

In liters at 55 percent alcohol

Distillery Company	1994	% of Total	1995	% of Total
Tequila Cuervo	20,117,943	36.73	20,416,945	33.17
Tequila Sauza	8,450,733	15.43	10,311,386	16.57
La Madrileña	3,216,971	5.87	4,665,509	7.58
Orendain de Jalisco	3,446,083	6.33	4,565,464	7.42
González González	1,175,854	2.15	3,010,834	4,89
Tequila Cazadores	1,175,854	2.15	2,112,947	3.43
Eucario González	2,020,324	3.69	2,048,181	3.33
Tequila Herradura	2,730,222	4.98	1,877,548	3.05
Tequila El Viejito	1,308,871	2.39	1,702,987	2,87
San Matias de Jalisco	930,568	1.70	1,760,247	2.86
Tequilas del Señor	1,308,871	2.39	1,702,987	2.77
La Cofradia	403,392	0.74	1,329,294	2.16
Tres Magueyes	2,360,303	4.31	1,276,768	2.07
Tequileña	806,129	1.47	1,090,458	1.47
Viuda de Romero	768,706	1.40	782,476	1.27

La Arandina	274,515	0.50	565,487	0.92
Tequila Cascahuin	345,459	0.63	346,017	0.56
Tequila Siete Leguas	235,063	0,43	262,610	0.43
Jorge Salles Cuervo	490,751	0.90	255,194	0.41
Azteca de Jalisco	285,041	0.52	250,801	0.40
Tequila Centinela	75,851	0.14	248,547	0.40
Tequila Newton e Hijos	0	0.00	210,555	0.34
Destiladora de Occidente	0	0.00	203,110	0.33
Tequila Tapatio	138,114	0.24	146,429	0.25
Tequila Parreñita	96,595	0.18	133,466	0.22
Empresa Ejidal	51,286	0.09	83,307	0.14
Tequila Santa Fe	47,063	0.09	52,234	0.08
Agroindustrias Guadalajara	0	0.00	43,031	0.07
Santo Tomas	9,000	0.02	17,216	0.03
Productos Especiales	516,000	0.94	15,049	0.02
Elab. y Proc. de Agave	0	0.00	6,600	0.01
Viuda de Martinez	0	0.00	0	0.00
Satisfactores	0	0.00	0	0.00
J. Jesús Reyes Cortes	12,300	0.02	0	0.00
Total	54,769,748	100.00	61,555,153	100.00

273

Appendix G

Tequila Export Statistics

In liters at 55 percent alcohol

Company	1994	%	1995	%
Tequila Cuervo	16,788,965	43.98	16,788,965	42.08
Tequila Sauza	4,489,404	11.91	4,953,436	12.42
La Madrileña	3,080,273	8.17	4,224,060	10.59
Orendain de Jalisco	2,683,004	7.12	2,909,909	7.29
González González	3,183,424	8.44	2,731,697	6.85
Tequila El Viejito	1,130,653	3.00	1,851,054	4.64
Eucario González	1,701,461	4.51	1,810,321	4.54
Tequilas del Señor	1,273,390	3.38	1,446,723	3.63
Tequila Tres Magueyes	2,406,000	6.38	998,446	2.50
La Cofradia	210,265	0.56	994,663	2.49
Vinicola del Vergel	0	0.00	336,273	0.84
Tequila Siete Leguas	128,073	0.34	203,191	0.51
Destiladora de Occidente	0	0.00	190.949	0.48
Tequila Viuda de Romero	158,173	0.40	158,698	0.40
Tequila Herradura	115,577	0.31	127,734	0.32
La Gonzáleña	0	0.00	28,980	0.07

LYNX Exportado	0	0.00	27,660	0.07
Tequila Tapatio	0	0.00	27,164	0.07
Tequila Cazadores	0	0.00	27,037	0.07
Compania Orendain	33,144	0.09	21,469	0,05
San Matias de Jalisco	7,198	0.02	10.027	0.03
Botunas Arrigunaga	0	0.00	8,325	0.02
Tequila Centinela	2,177	0.01	6,912	0.02
Vinicola de Guadalajara	0	0.00	6,780	0.02
CIA Destiladora	0	0.00	4,050	0.01
Tequila Cascahuin	873	0.00	930	0.00
Destiladora Oaxaquena	0	0.00	801	0.00
Destileria Porfidio	0	0.00	470	0.00
Takata	0	0.00	36	0.00
Yamakawa	0	0.00	27	0.00
Imp. y Exp. Technicos	0	0.00	2	0.00
Comercializadora Exp.	0	0.00	2	0.00
Seagram de México	0	0.00	0	0.00
Productores Especiales	524,017	1.39	0	0.00
Antonio Fernandez y CIA	0	0.00	0	0.00
J. Jesús Reyes Cortes	0	0.00	0	0.00
La Arandina	0	0.00	0	0.00
Azteca de Jalisco	0	0.00	0	0.00
Total	37,176,756	100.00	39,869,800	100.00

Appendix H

Prices of Tequilas in Guadalajara

In New Pesos, November, 1995. The exchange rate was about 6.50 new pesos (N$) to one U.S. dollar.

Siete Leguas	Añejo	750 ml	N$	117.50
	Reposado	750 ml	N$	39.00
	Blanco	750 ml	N$	30.71
Tequila Alteño	Reposado	1,000 ml	N$	42.00
Tequila Arette	Blanco	750 ml	N$	28.57
	Reposado	750 ml	N$	36.23
Tequila Cabrito	Reposado	1,000 ml	N$	40.00
Tequila Casca Viejo	Blanco	1,000 ml	N$	18.00
Tequila Cazadores	Reposado	750 ml	N$	49.00
Tequila Centinela	Añejo 3 year	750 ml	N$	168.05
	Añejo 1 year	750 ml	N$	87,00

	Reposado	750 ml	N$	48.30
	Blanco	750 ml	N$	39.38
Tequila Cuervo	1800	750 ml	N$	100.00
	Blanco	750 ml	N$	22.00
	Tradición al	500 ml	N$	47.51
Centenario	Reposado	750 ml	N$	57.00
	Plata	750 ml	N$	33.75
Tequila Diligencias	Añejo	750 ml	N$	62.70
	Reposado	750 ml	N$	31.00
Tequila Don Julio	Canastilla	750.ml	N$	188.16
	Garrafita	750 ml	N$	83.00
	Limited Production	1,000 ml	N$	141.00
Tequila Dos Amigos	Reposado	750 ml	N$	36.00
Tequila El Jimador	Reposado	700 ml	N$	40.00
Tequila El Tequileño	Reposado	1,000 ml	N$	43.50
	Blanco	1,000 ml	N$	31.00
Tequila El Tesoro	Muy Añejo	750 ml	N$	108.00
	Blanco	750 ml	N$	60.27
Tequila El Viejito	100% Añejo	750 ml	N$	69.99
	100% Reposado	750.ml	N$	58.99
	100% Blanco	750 ml	N$	38.00
	Añejo	750.ml	N$	36.75
	Reposado	750 ml	N$	31.50
	Blanco	1,000 ml	N$	21.00
Tequila Herradura	Añejo	750 ml	N$	115.00
	Reposado	750 ml	N$	54.00
	Blanco	750 ml	N$	41.00

Tequila Hipodromo		1,000 ml	N$	61.00
Tequila Jorongo	Reposado	750 ml	N$	23.10
	Blanco	750 ml	N$	28.35
Tequila Juárez	Añejo	750 ml	N$	21.00
Tequila Las Trancas	Licorera	820 ml	N$	119.70
	Reposado	1,000 ml	N$	31.50
	Blanco	1,000 ml	N$	17.12
Tequila Los Valientes	Reposado	1,000 ml	N$	73.50
Tequila Mayor	Reposado	1,000 ml	N$	57.75
	Blanco	1,000 ml	N$	48.30
Tequila 1,000 Agaves	Reposado	1,000 ml	N$	60.00
Tequila Orendain	Aniversario	750 ml	N$	82.83
	Ollitas	750 ml	N$	33.82
	Extra	1,000 ml	N$	17.00
	Blanco	1,000 ml	N$	15.00
Tequila Porfidio	Añejo (cactus)	750 ml	N$	303.45
	Añejo (two-year)	500 ml	N$	152.25
	Blanco (cactus)	750 ml	N$	262.50
	Blanco (3 distil)	750 ml	N$	258.75
Tequila Pueblo Viejo	Añejo	750 ml	N$	59.64
	Reposado	750 ml	N$	48.00
	Blanco	750 ml	N$	34.00
Tequila Pura Sangre	Añejo	750 ml	N$	97.00
	Reposado	1,000 ml	N$	59.00
	Blanco	1,000 ml	N$	49.00
Tequila Real Hacienda	Añejo	750 ml	N$	31.50
	Reposado	1,000 ml	N$	42.00
	Blanco	1,000 ml	N$	30.45

Tequila Regional	Reserva	750 ml	N$	98.00
	Añejo	750.ml	N$	46.91
	Reposado	750 ml	N$	32.39
	Blanco	750 ml	N$	25.60
Tequila Reserva Del Patrón		750 ml	N$	42.00
Tequila San Matias	Añejo	750 ml	N$	27.83
	Reposado	750 ml	N$	22,24
	Blanco	750 ml	N$	14.43
Tequila Santa Fe	Reposado	1,000 ml	N$	32.00
	Joven	1,000 ml	N$	19.00
Tequila Sauza	Tres Generaciones	750 ml	N$	110.00
	Conmemorativo	750 ml	N$	50.00
	Hornitos 100%	750 ml	N$	39.00
	Extra	750 ml	N$	19.51
	Blanco	750 ml	N$	18.00
Tequila Sombrero Negro		1,000 ml	N$	23.00
Tequila Tapatio	Añejo	1,000 ml	N$	66.50
	Reposado	1,000 ml	N$	61.00
	Blanco	1,000 ml	N$	59.00
Tequila Tres Magueyes	Reserva	1,000 ml	N$	70.00
	Reposado	1,000 ml	N$	34.67
	Blanco	1,000 ml	N$	21.49
Tequila Viuda de Romero	Inmemorial	750 ml	N$	26.25
	Reposado	1,000 ml	N$	13.00
	Joven	1,000 ml	N$	12.00
Tequila Xalixco	Añejo	750 ml	N$	47.39
	Reposado	1,000 ml	N$	25.54

Glossary

ABOCADO. (or *joven abocado*) Also called 'gold'. Unaged tequila, in practice always *mixto*, to which coloring and flavoring agents, predominantly or entirely caramel, have been added.

AGAVE. A genus of succulent plants with several hundred known species, mainly found in southern North America.

AGUAMIEL. 'Honey water', the unfermented sap of the *agave* used for making *pulque.*

ALEMBIC STILL. An old-fashioned or pot still, as opposed to a column still.

AÑEJO. 'Aged', applied to tequila stored in oak for at least one year.

AUTOCLAVE. A large pressure cooker, employed to cook the *agave* in the less traditional distilleries.

BACANORA. A distilled drink, not tequila, made from *agave* juice in Sonora.

BAGASSE. A French word now adopted into most languages, meaning the fibrous pulp left after juice has been extracted from a plant (usually *agave* or sugarcane).

BAGAZO. Bagasse.

BARRICA. Spanish for 'barrel'.

BLANCO. Spanish for 'white'. Clear tequila, unaged and untreated with additives.

BODEGA. Warehouse or storage facility.

CABEZA Spanish for 'head'. The swollen central stem of the *agave*, the part used for making distilled beverages such as tequila.

CAMPESINO Farmer or peasant.

CHATOYANCE. A 'cat's eye' visual effect, observable in gemstones and some drinks.

COA. Specialized tool used for harvesting *agave.*

COMITECA. A regional drink, not tequila, made from distilled *agave* juice.

CRIOLLO. Creole. Mainly, a person of European ancestry but not European birth. Also, a person of predominantly European ancestry.

CONSEJO, EL. The Tequila Regulatory Council, with headquarters in Guadalajara.

FÁBRICA. Factory, the unromantic word most often used for a tequila production plant.

GOLD. This is a legally recognized term for a *joven abocado* tequila. Confusingly, a few companies also employ it for their 100 percent *agave reposados.*

HORNO. Spanish for 'oven'. Remember that 'h' is always silent in Spanish.

JIMADOR. Prounced 'heem-a-dor'. The laborer who harvests the *agave.*

JOVEN ABOCADO. See Abocado. Joven means 'young', here unaged. *Abocado* means 'decanted', here a fancy term signifying that something has been added to smooth the taste and color the appearance of the tequila.

MAGUEY Everyday term in Mexico for an *agave* plant.

MESTIZO. A person of mixed European and Indian ancestry.

MEZCAL. A distilled drink, not tequila, made from *agave* juice in many parts of Mexico, but mostly in Oaxaca. Also: a now largely archaic name for *agave.* Also: a synonym for *mezcal* wine. As Spanish 'z' is pronounced like English 's', *mezcal* is sometimes anglicized to 'mescal'.

MEZCAL WINE. An archaic term for the whole class of distilled drinks made from *agave* juice, including tequila.

MIXTO. An inferior kind of tequila made by fermenting a mixture of *agave* juice with non-*agave* plant sugars.

MOSTO. Spanish for 'must', any unfermented plant product ready for fermentation.

NOM. *Norma Oficial Mexicana.* A number assigned to each tequila company, showing which company made or bottled the tequila.

NORMA. In Mexico, the statutory regulations designating a particular kind of product.

ORDINARIO. The first run distillate of the *agave.*

PENINSULAR. In Mexican history, a person of purely European ancestry, resident in Mexico but born in Iberia; usually a Spanish government appointee.

PIÑA. Spanish for 'pineapple', but also applied to the *agave cabeza,* which looks like an enormous pineapple.

PIPA. Tanker truck, used to transport *mixto* within Mexico and to the U.S.

PILONCILLO. Unrefined dried sugarcane juice.

PLATA. Spanish for 'silver'. Exactly the same kind of tequila as *blanco.*

PULQUE. A fermented, undistilled alcoholic drink made from the *agave.*

RAICILLA. A distilled drink, not tequila, made from *agave* juice.

REPOSADO. Rested'. Tequila stored in oak for at least two months but less than one year.

SECOFI. A Mexican law enforcement agency, which oversees El Consejo and the tequila industry.

SOTOL. A distilled drink, not tequila, made from *agave* juice.

SUPER PREMIUM. An industry term for a tequila positioned as a more expensive, high quality product. A super premium tequila is not necessarily very good, though many of them are.

TABERNA. A tavern; also the old name for a plant making distilled alcoholic drinks. Such a plant would usually have a tavern attached.

TAHONA. A stone wheel and pit arrangement, traditionally used to crush and extract the juice from cooked *agave.*

WORT. An infusion of plant products to be used in making wine or spirits.

Bibliography

Brown, Gordon. 1995. *Classic Spirits of the World: A Comprehensive Guide.* London: Multimedia Books.

Cámara Regional de la Industria Tequilera, La. n.d. El Tequila. Guadalajara: La Cámara Regional de la Industria Tequilera.

Cedeño, Miguel, C. 1995. Tequila Production. *Critical Reviews in Biotechnology* 15(1), 1–11.

Grossman, Harold J. 1983. *Grossman's Guide to Wines, Beers, and Spirits.* 7th edn. New York: Scribner's.

Harris, James F., and Waymack, Mark H. 1992. *Single-Malt Whiskies of Scotland: For the Discriminating Imbiber.* Chicago: Open Court.

Hutson, Lucinda. 1995. *Tequila: Cooking with the Spirit of Mexico.* Berkeley: Ten Speed Press.

Jackson, Michael. 1991. *Michael Jackson's Complete Guide to Single Malt Scotch.* Philadelphia: Running Press.

———. 1993. *The World Guide to Whisky.* Philadelphia: Running Press.

Lipinski, Robert A., and Kathleen A. Lipinski. 1989. *Professional Guide to Alcoholic Beverages.* New York: Van Nostrand.

Lucero, Al. 1994. *Maria's Real Margarita Book.* Berkeley: Ten Speed Press.

Meyer, Michael C., and William L. Sherman. 1991. *The Course of Mexican History.* 4th edn. New York: Oxford University Press.

Muria, Jose Maria. n.d. A Drink Called Tequila. Guadalajara: El Colegio de Jalisco.

———. 1994. Moments of Tequila. *Artes de México* 27 (November-December, an issue of this magazine devoted to tequila, with bilingual text). For enquiries about *Artes de México,* write to Plaza Rio de Janeiro 52, Colonia Roma, C.P. 06700, D.F. Mexico.

Orellano, Margarita de. 1994. A Micro-History of Tequila: The Cuervo Case. *Artes de México* 27 (November-December). See above, Muria 1994.

Walker, Anne, and Larry Walker. 1994. *Tequila: The Book.* San Francisco: Chronicle Books.

Waymack, Mark H., and Harris, James F. 1995. *The Book of Classic American Whiskeys.* Chicago: Open Court.

Zamora, Rogelio Luna. 1991. *La Historia del Tequila, de Sus Regiones y Sus Hombres.* Rev. edn. Mexico D.F.: El Consejo Nacional para la Cultura y las Artes.

Index

287